Praise for Ahdaf Soueif's

Cairo

"[*Cairo*] takes the reader to the front lines of the conflict in the streets with vignettes worthy of a novel. . . . Soueif's ability to render grand events in human terms and put Egypt's current conflict into historical and global context makes *Cairo* a book that demands attention."　—*The Christian Science Monitor*

"Soueif is a political analyst and commentator of the best kind."
—*London Review of Books*

"Offers an invaluable window into the mind-set of a large proportion of the engaged Egyptian population. . . . A testimony to the dramatic cultural shift that has taken place in Egypt and elsewhere in the Arab world in public attitudes toward power."
—*Bookforum*

"Bursts of lyricism, poetry and love illuminate the factual account and political commentary, and it works beautifully."
—*The Independent* (London)

"Heartfelt, courageous, and hopeful. . . . An intimate portrait of an extraordinary city at an extraordinary moment in its history."　—*Evening Standard* (London)

"The author captures beautifully her anguish at Cairo's degradation during the years of dictatorship and Mubarak's calculated sowing of division among the people. . . . With the recent violent eruptions in the country, Soueif's work as an eloquent witness is a work in progress."　　　　　—*Publishers Weekly*

"Soueif offers both an extraordinary eyewitness document and a sense of the historical import of the revolution. . . . A deeply personal, engaged tribute by the far-flung Egyptian novelist and journalist as she returned to witness the revolution in her hometown."　　　　　—*Kirkus Reviews*

"As an active participant and a keenly observant chronicler of the impassioned rebellion, [Soueif's] firsthand account offers insight into the heady days of the original revolution and its tumultuous aftermath. . . . Interweaves affectionate and peaceful memories of Cairo, Egypt, and her family into the fiery narrative. As Egyptian citizens continue to live the revolution, she provides a uniquely personal perspective on both the events of 2011 and the ensuing years."　　　　　—*Booklist*

Ahdaf Soueif

Cairo

Ahdaf Soueif is the author of two novels, *In the Eye of the Sun* and *The Map of Love*, which was shortlisted for the Booker Prize in 1999; a story collection, *I Think of You*; and an essay collection, *Mezzaterra: Notes from the Common Ground*. She lives in Cairo, where she was born.

www.ahdafsoueif.com

ALSO BY AHDAF SOUEIF

The Map of Love

In the Eye of the Sun

I Think of You

Mezzaterra

Cairo

Cairo

MEMOIR OF A CITY TRANSFORMED

Ahdaf Soueif

Anchor Books
A Division of Random House LLC
New York

FIRST ANCHOR BOOKS EDITION, OCTOBER 2014

Copyright © 2012, 2014 by Ahdaf Soueif

All rights reserved. Published in the United States by Anchor Books,
a division of Random House LLC, New York, a Penguin Random House
company. Originally published, in different form, in the United Kingdom
by Bloomsbury Publishing, London, in 2012. Subsequently published in
hardcover in the United States by Pantheon Books, a division of
Random House LLC, New York, in 2013.

The Library of Congress has cataloged the Pantheon edition as follows:
Soueif, Ahdaf.
Cairo : memoir of a city transformed / Ahdaf Soueif.
pages cm
Revised edition of: Cairo : my city, our revolution.
London : Bloomsbury, 2012.
Includes bibliographical references.
1. Cairo (Egypt)—History—21st century. 2. Cairo (Egypt)—
Social conditions—21st century. 3. Egypt—History—Protests, 2011.
4. Egypt—Politics and government—21st century.
5. Egypt—Social conditions—21st century. 6. Soueif, Ahdaf. I. Title.
DT148.S69 2013   962'.16056—dc23   2013003190

Anchor Books Trade Paperback ISBN: 978-0-345-80351-1
eBook ISBN: 978-0-307-90811-7

Book design by Maggie Hinders
Maps by Omar Robert Hamilton

www.anchorbooks.com

Printed in the United States of America
10 9 8 7 6 5 4 3 2 1

For the young people of Egypt;
the shuhada who died for the revolution,
and the shabab who live for it

CONTENTS

A NOTE ON SPELLING ARABIC SOUNDS
IN LATIN CHARACTERS

Writing some of the sounds of Arabic in Latin characters has been an issue since the Middle Ages. Systems of transliteration vary, along with their levels of complexity.

What I've chosen here is to adopt a new system that was, I believe, initiated by Arab bloggers. It's very simple:

1. Where there is a traditional accepted—and unique—spelling in Latin letters for an Arabic sound, I retain it. As in: *gh* for غ —like the French *r*; *kh* for خ—as in the Scottish *loch*.

2. Three sounds are written as numerals:
   The hamza, ء, pronounced as a glottal stop in the middle or at the end of a word, is written as a *2*. So if we were doing this in English, the cockney *butter* would be written *bu2er*. The ain, ع, a soft vibration in the back of the throat, is written *3*. The *heavy h* ح, is written *7*.

   However, where words already have an image and a presence for the reader of English, I've kept them as they are. So *Tahrir* has not become *Ta7reer*, *Ahmad* has not become *A7mad*, *Aida* has not become *3aida*, and so on.

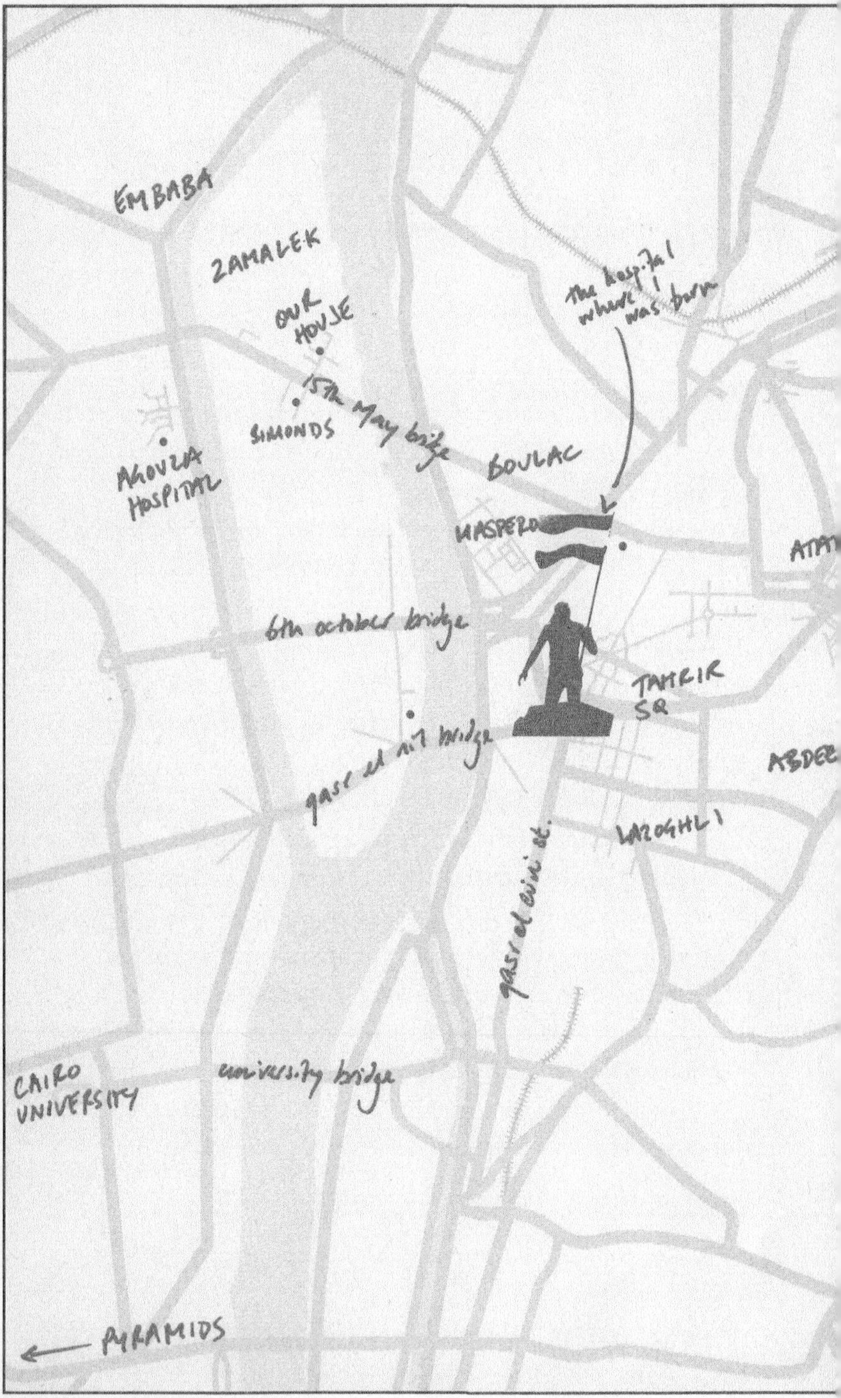

EMBABA

ZAMALEK

OUR HOUSE

the hospital where I was born

15th May bridge

SIMONDS

BOULAC

AGOUZA HOSPITAL

MASPERO

ATT

6th october bridge

TAHRIR SQ

gasr el nil bridge

ABDEL

LAROGHLI

gasr el aini st.

CAIRO UNIVERSITY

university bridge

← PYRAMIDS

ABBASEYYA

COPTIC
HOSPITAL

AIRPORT

N

CEMETERY

CAIRO

1 MILE

1 KILOMETER

PREFACE

Almost twenty years ago I signed a contract to write a book about Cairo; my Cairo. But the years passed, and I could not write it. When I tried, it read like an elegy, and I would not write an elegy for my city.

Then, in February 2011, I was in Tahrir, taking part in the revolution and reporting on it. Alexandra Pringle, my friend and U.K. publisher, called me; this, she said, must be the moment for your Cairo book. I fought the idea. But I feared she was right.

I say "feared" because I wanted more to act the revolution than to write it. And because I was afraid of the responsibility. Jean Genet, in his book that I most admire, *Un captif amoureux*, writes: "I am not an archivist or a historian or anything like it. . . . This is my Palestinian revolution told in my own chosen order." I cannot say the same. This story is told in my own chosen order, but it is very much the story of *our* revolution.

It proved impossible to sit in a corner and write about the revolution. What was happening needed every one of us to be available at all times to do whatever the—let's call it "the revolutionary effort" might need, whether it was marching or standing or talking or mediating or writing or comforting or articulating or . . . So I tried to "revolute" and write at the same time, and I soon realized two things: one, that I could not write what was fast becoming the past without writing the present; and two, that for this book to be as I wanted it to be and believed it should be, an intervention rather than just a record, it needed to take in—and on—as much of this present as possible.

And so I wrote *Cairo: My City, Our Revolution*, which was published in London in January 2012. The "present" that it took in went up to October 2011. And the structure, the storytelling mode, that seemed truest to the story then, showed the period from 12 February to 31 October as an "interruption" to the course of the revolution. It was still possible then to believe that the revolution as we knew it, as we had lived it, would continue, and that we would pick up from where we had left off.

Now, over a year later, we can no longer believe this. What we are living now can no longer be seen as an interruption; we are living the revolution in the course and the form it has had to take. Our revolution does continue, but it has become bigger, harder, more real(istic), and more diverse; it has lost a lot of its innocence and may, perhaps, have to lose even more.

And once again, it was a friend and publisher who made me deal with this change: LuAnn Walther, my U.S. editor. So this, the American edition of my book, takes in this later period: the winter, spring, and summer after October 2011. In preparing it, I was tempted to tidy up the story, to make it more streamlined, to sweep through our Egyptian story from January 2011 to "now" in chronological time. But the story resisted, and something in me resisted. Because the story I've been writing is not just about the events that took place, but about how I, how we, perceived and felt and understood them. And it's also a story about me, my family, and my city—told to a reader, a friend, out of a particular moment, a particular emotion.

And so I have preserved the integrity of my text. I have not rewritten it but have let the past remain unchanged and carried on with it in the only way I could: picking up the story from where I had left it before. The revolution is not an event but a process, a process we're all going through, and this book is going through it with us, fitting itself to the altered forms of the revolution and to the transformations of the city.

And at its heart there are those eighteen golden days, eighteen days that were given to us, when we all pulled together to get rid of the head of the regime that was destroying us and our country and everything we held dear; eighteen days that brought out the best in us and showed us not just what we could do but how we could be. And it was this way of "being," as well as what it achieved, that captured the imagination of the world, that made the Egyptian revolution an inspiration for the people's movements that are crystallizing across the planet. Every Egyptian I know is both proud of this and humbled by it. I know I am.

Cairo, December 2012

Eighteen Days

25 JANUARY—11 FEBRUARY 2011

The river is a still, steely gray, a dull pewter. Small scattered fires burn and fizz in the water. We've pushed out from the shore below the Ramses Hilton and are heading into midstream. My two nieces, Salma and Mariam, are on either side of me in the small motorboat. As we get farther from the shore, our coughing and choking subside. We can draw breath, even though the breath burns. And we can open our eyes—

To see an opaque dusk, heavy with tear gas. Up ahead, Qasr el-Nil Bridge is a mass of people, all in motion, but all in place. We look back at where we were just minutes ago, on 6 October Bridge, and see a Central Security Forces personnel carrier on fire, backing off, four young men chasing it, leaping at it, beating at its windshield. The vehicle is reversing wildly, careering backward east toward Downtown. Behind us, a ball of fire lands in the river, a bright new pool of flame in the water. The sky is gray—so different from the airy twilight you normally get on the river at this time of day. The Opera House looms dark on our right, and we can barely make out the slender height of the Cairo Tower. We don't know it yet, but the lights of Cairo will not come on tonight.

A great shout goes up from Qasr el-Nil. I look at Salma and Mariam. "Yes, let's," they say. I tell the boatman we've changed our minds: we don't want to cross the river to Giza and go home. We want to be dropped off under Qasr el-Nil Bridge.

And that is why we—myself and two beautiful young women—appeared suddenly in the Qasr el-Nil Underpass among the Central Security vehicles racing to get out of town and all the men leaning over the parapet above us with stones in their hands stopped in midthrow and yelled "Run! Run!" and held off with the stones so they wouldn't hit us as we skittered through the screeching vehicles to a spot where we could scramble up the bank and join the people at the mouth of the bridge.

That day the government—the regime that had ruled us for thirty years—had cut off our communications. No mobile service, no Internet for all of Egypt.[1] In a way, looking back, I think this concentrated our minds, our will, our energy: each person was in one place, totally and fully committed to that place, unable to be aware of any other, knowing they had to do everything they could for it and trusting that other people in other places were doing the same.

So we ran through the underpass, scrambled up the bank, and found ourselves within, inside, and part of the masses. When we'd seen the crowd from a distance, it had seemed like one bulk, solid. Close up like this, it was people, individual persons with spaces between them—spaces into which you could fit. We stood on the traffic island in the middle of the road. Behind us was Qasr el-Nil Bridge, in front of us was Tahrir, and we were doing what we Egyptians do best, and what the regime ruling us had tried so hard to destroy: we had come together, as individuals, millions of us, in a great cooperative effort. And this time our project was to save and to reclaim our country. We stood on the island in the middle of the road, and that was the moment I became part of the revolution.

〜〜〜〜

A month before, a week before, three days before, we could not have told you it was going to happen. Yes, there had been calls to use National Police Day on 25 January as an occasion for protests, but there had been so many protests and calls for protests over the years that it hadn't seemed special. Those of us who were in Egypt intended to join, for form's sake and to keep up the spirit of opposition. Those of us who weren't, well, weren't.

Me, I was in India, at the Jaipur Literary Festival. Late on the twenty-fourth, I did an interview with Tehelka TV:

> For a very long time now, our perception is that [Egypt] is not being run in the interests of the Egyptian people. The primary motivation of the people who are governing us is that they should remain in power in order to continue ransacking and looting the country. Now, the main support that they have is, of course, the Western powers—particularly the United States. And the price that they pay in order to be supported is to run policies that favor Israel.
>
> We've been watching what's been happening in Tunisia and we've been very excited by it. You hear: now, will Egypt move? And you hear: Egypt is too big . . . too heavy.
>
> It really does not look as if the government is going to allow a peaceful and democratic change. So . . . what's going to happen? Will we get a situation where people . . . sort of, erupt? And will you get . . . blood on the streets? Will the army come down? Nobody knows. It feels very unstable. And it feels dangerous. And all the activism that happens is in specific areas. And it's all young people and it's all really without a leadership . . . but it's there. It's keeping the streets alive. We've never had as much civil unrest in Egypt as we've had in the last five years. And that is good. That is good— but, how will it coalesce? And what shape will that take?[2]

We now have this information—you, my reader, in more advanced form, as you read these words, than I as I race to write them in the summer of 2011. I won't try to guess at what's on your news bulletin today—but whatever shape Egypt is in as you're reading now, this is the story of some of the moments that got us there.

And it's also, in a small way, a story about me and my city, the city I so love and have so sorrowed for these twenty years and more. I am not unique, but Cairo is. And her streets, her Nile, her buildings, and her monuments whisper to every Cairene who's taking part in the events that are shaping our lives and our children's futures as I write. They whisper to us and tug at our sleeves and say: This is where you were born, this is where a man, a boy, first reached for your hand, this is where you learned to drive, this is where the picture in your schoolbook shows Orabi facing down the Khedive Tewfik, this is where your mother says she and your father stood in '52 and watched the fire take hold of Cairo. The city puts her lips to our ears, she tucks her arm into ours and draws close so we can feel her heartbeat and smell her scent, and we fall in with her and measure our step to hers, and we fill our eyes with her beautiful, wounded face and whisper that her memories are our memories, her fate is our fate.

For twenty years I have shied away from writing about Cairo. It hurt too much. But the city was there, close to me, looking over my shoulder, holding up the prism through which I understood the world, inserting herself into everything I wrote. It hurt. And now, miraculously, it doesn't. Because my city is mine again.

Masr is Egypt, and *Masr* is also what Egyptians call Cairo. On Tuesday, 1 February, I watched a man surveying the scene in Tahrir with a big smile: the sun was shining and people were everywhere, old and young, rich and poor. They talked and walked and sang and played and joked and chanted. Then he said it out loud: "Ya Masr, it's been a long time. We have missed you."

〜〜〜

It was evening on Tuesday the twenty-fifth when I realized something was happening back home. On my Jaipur hotel TV, I could only get CNN, but there the Americans were, transmitting from Tahrir, and the whole world was wondering what was going on, and the spokesperson for the Egyptian government, Hosam Zaki, was cheerily dismissing the crowds on the screen and reassuring the world that our government and our people were very close and that the government knew the people and knew what they wanted and would supply the bits of it that it saw fit. This was the line that the regime was unable to let go of; throughout the three weeks of the confrontation, every speech given by (now-deposed president) Mubarak or his vice president, Omar Suleiman, or any member of his party or regime, maintained the patronizing "we know what's best for you" stance that had been so roundly rejected by the people.

What transfixed me so completely was that the picture on the screen was from Tahrir. Unmistakably from Tahrir. Midan el-Tahrir—

I prefer the Arabic word *midan* because, like *piazza*, it does not tie you down to a shape but describes an open urban space in a central position in a city, and the space we call Midan el-Tahrir, the central point of Greater Cairo, is not a square or a circle but more like a massive curved rectangle covering about 45,000 square meters and connecting Downtown and older Cairo to the east, with the river and Giza and the newer districts to the west; its southern boundary is the Mugamma3 building and its northern is the 6 October Overpass—

The Midan has been our Holy Grail for forty years. Since 1972, when (then-president Anwar) Sadat's forces dragged the student protesters at dawn from around the empty plinth at its center and into jail, demonstrations and marches have tried and failed to get into Tahrir. Two years ago we managed to hold a corner of a traffic island in front of the Mugamma3 building for an hour. We were fewer than fifty people, and the government surrounded us with maybe two thousand Central Security soldiers, the chests and shoulders of their officers heavy with brass.

Since Egypt's ruler, Khedive Ismail, established it in 1860—its core modeled on Paris's Étoile, six main roads leading out of its center and a further six out of the larger space surrounding it—control of Tahrir has seemed central to controlling the country. Ismail stationed the Egyptian army and the Ministry of Defense here, and when the British occupied Egypt in 1882, their army took over the barracks and the ministry on one side of Qasr el-Nil Bridge, and they put their embassy on the other. The Americans were to follow suit and put their increasingly fortresslike embassy next to the British. Then in Nasser's revolutionary times, Egypt put a statue of Simón Bolívar between the two embassies; the Arab League building and the headquarters of the Arab Socialist Union went up in place of the British barracks, and the Ministry of Foreign Affairs faced them from the (nationalized) palace of the Princess Nimet Kamal across Tahrir Street.

But as well as housing the symbols of military and political power, Tahrir is home to the civic spirit of Egypt. The Egyptian Antiquities Museum (1902) marks the northern end of the Midan, and when in 1908 the Egyptian national movement founded—through public donations—the first secular Egyptian University, they rented the palace of Khawaga Gianaclis—now the old campus of the American University in Cairo—at the other end. In 1951 all government departments that came in direct contact with the citizens were consolidated in one huge new building: Mugamma3 al-Tahrir. And early in the 1952 revolution, the small mosque near the Mugamma3 was enlarged and dedicated to Sheikh Omar Makram, the popular leader against Napoleon's French Expedition in 1798, against the British "Fraser" Expedition of 1807, and later against Muhammad Ali himself when Sheikh Omar felt the ruler was taxing the people unfairly. Omar Makram died in exile, but his statue is part of our revolution; a meeting place, an inspiration, a bearer of flags and microphones and balloons.

In 1959 the first modern international hotel in Egypt, the Nile Hilton, opened in Tahrir, next to the Arab League. A decade later, on the evening of 27 September 1970, and having just closed the two days of negotiations and arm-twisting that ended Black September and would kill him, President Gamal Abd el-Nasser—whose picture was raised by many during the revolution—stood on the balcony of the thirteenth-floor suite he had occupied for a few nights and gazed at the Nile. He turned, smiling, to Abd el-Meguid Farid, the secretary to the presidency: "How come I've never seen this amazing sight before? Look at it! I'm buried alive out in Heliopolis." Then he went home. And it was from a window in the Arab Socialist Union building next door that, two days later, his wife and daughters watched his funeral surge across Qasr el-Nil Bridge toward Tahrir. The ASU building became Hosni Mubarak's National Democratic Party headquarters—the only building in Tahrir to be torched by the revolutionaries.

The Hilton—now bearing the Ritz-Carlton sign—has been undergoing renovation for years. In front of it is a waste ground surrounded by sheets of corrugated iron—which we will use in the battles for the Midan. This massive space in the central *midan* of our city has been in a condition of ruin for twenty years. We're told it's to do with the construction of the Metro. Also to do with the Metro, we're told, was the removal of the empty plinth in the middle of the garden of the central roundabout, the plinth around which the students gathered in 1972 on the night Amal Dunqul immortalized in "The Stone Cake":

Five o'clock struck
with soldiers a circle of shields and helmets
drawing closer slowly . . . slowly . . .
from every direction

and the singers in the stone cake clenching
and relaxing
like a heartbeat!
Lighting their throats
for warmth against the cold and the biting dark.
Lifting the anthem in the face of the approaching guard.
Linking their young, hopeless hands
a shield against lead
lead
lead.
They sang.

Now the whole country is gathered around that central, plinthless garden. In one of the most moving moments of the revolution—and there were to be many—the people's delegations that had come in from the cities and the provinces of Egypt set up their banners around the garden and set up the chant "El-shar3eyya m'nel-Tahrir"—legitimacy comes from Tahrir.

I drove to Delhi in the morning and, next day, caught a plane that put me in Cairo on the evening of Thursday the twenty-seventh. From the airport I called my sister, Laila, and asked, "Where's the revolution? Should I go to Tahrir?" She said I should call her daughter, Mona, and Mona said there was nothing in Tahrir, but I might, possibly, see some crowds if I went to Midan el-Sa3ah in Nasr City or if I drove through Abbaseyya. But there were no crowds. I saw two charred and overturned Central Security Forces trucks, but the city was, if anything, quieter than was normal for a Thursday evening. The revolution was up and running in Suez and Alexandria; in Cairo it was gathering its breath, getting ready for Friday.

Embaba, on the western bank of the Nile, five minutes and one bridge from my home on Gezira Island. For a long time, all I knew of it was the name of its main bus stop, the Kit-Kat, and attached to the name a black and white image of British johnnies staggering out of shady doorways, drunk, into the street, hushed families watching them from darkened rooms, their faces lined with the light from streetlamps falling through drawn blinds. The Kit-Kat, I seemed to know, was one of the many sleazy nightclubs that had sprung up in Cairo to cater to the Allied forces stationed there in the West's second great war. Now if you say "el-Kit-Kat," everyone thinks of Daoud Abd el-Sayyed's 1991 film, with the opening shot of Mahmoud Abd el-Aziz weaving through Embaba market on his motorbike. A long, ongoing shot—and sometime during the course of it, you realize the biker is blind.

Embaba has a small airport from where you can go gliding. When my first marriage was breaking up, we flew from there, in a glider, I and my just-become-ex-husband. He was at the controls. I can't think why we did that. For clarity, maybe? We—I—didn't find it. Even the amazing spread-out fields below, the river, broad and still and—from here—docile, were dimmed by my unease.

And Embaba is known for three hospitals. One is a specialist rehabilitation center where they taught Ali, the five-year-old son of Um Nagla, our help, to speak. My father snatched him back from the jaws of a "fraudulent charlatan" who, he said, was about to send him off for electric shock treatment—and sent him to Embaba instead. He's now fifteen and speaking plenty. Ali says he'd carry on going to school if there were any use, but he's not learning anything, and the teachers are only there for the cash from the private lessons. The only thing that might be useful now for his life is the revolution. He berates his mother for being prepared to believe that Hosni Mubarak is "sorry" and will give back our stolen money. "Ali," she tells me, "Ali says of Mubarak and all his men: 'Before they open their mouths, they're liars; they breathe lies.' And this," she adds, "is Ali-who-couldn't-speak."

The second is the Embaba Fevers Hospital, which used to rival the best in the world. The third is the new Emergency Hospital, where construction was stopped when its riverfront position caught Mrs. Mubarak's eye, and the government decided to turn it into a luxury residential block. The latest scandal of this kind is the Madin'ti Project, where eight thousand acres were sold at so much lower than market price that the courts estimated the loss to the Egyptian treasury at billions of pounds. Today as our protest passes the hospital project, the crowd starts up the chants against corruption: "A bowl of lentils for ten pounds—a Madin'ti share for fifty p."

We've been walking the streets of Embaba for two hours. My friend Mamdouh Hamza brought me here and left me in a small coffee shop by the local mosque. MH is a celebrated civil engineer who's been in charge of some of Egypt's major construction projects. I'd known he'd been lending his support for a while to some of the revolutionary shabab, the young people. "Something will begin here," he said, and went off to distribute banners. It was the usual pleasant, the world-is-on-pause feel of Friday prayer time, and I watched women chatting in front of shops, the winter sunshine falling on them through the colorful clothes displayed above their heads, men sitting at cafés, others spilling out of the mosque, praying on green mats in the road. In my coffee shop, a young man is sitting in the corner; something about his stillness, his quality of concentration, stays with me.

Prayers finish, but the imam solicits blessings. And blessings. And more blessings. Men start folding their mats, putting on their shoes. Suddenly the young man from the coffee shop is above the crowd, on top of it. People shift and stir, there's a buzz like in the theater at the moment the curtain starts to rise, everyone looks, people come out of shops: the young man's arm is in the air, his hand is reaching to the sky, and then there comes the loud, carrying voice: "Al-sha3b yureed isqat al-nizam!" There it was, no lead-up, no half-measures; the young man on the shoulders of his friends; a loose knot of some fifteen young people: "The people— demand—the fall of this regime!" We start to walk.

Later, we will learn that similar marches started after prayers in every district of Cairo and many other cities. We will know this young man as Khaled el-Sayyed, one of the three hundred young people who organized these first marches. Up there, his still concentration has transformed into energy, his back is straight, his arm movements are precise. Again and again the call goes out, and the crowd responds: "Your security, your police—killed our brothers in Suez." We walk, and the numbers grow. Every balcony is full of people; some just watch impassively, some men look uncomfortable. "Come down from the heights / Come down and get your rights." Most women are smiling, waving, dandling babies to the tune of the chants "Eish! Horreyya! Adala egtema3eyya!" Bread. Freedom. Social justice. Old women call, "God be with you! God give you victory." For more than two hours, the protest walks through the narrow residential lanes, cheering, encouraging, instigating: "Prices up and no one cares / Next you'll sell your beds and chairs." We pass the offices of the Land Registry. In 2008 I'd visited it to get some papers relating to my mother's estate. I failed to get them. At the next window a man remonstrated that this was the fifth time he'd been and that he no longer understood what he was required to do to get the stamp he needed on his papers. Then he lost it: "Yel3an abu Hosni Mubarak!" he bellowed. God curse him curse him curse him! He slammed his files rhythmically on the countertop as he cursed out the man at the head of the system that, here and now, in this local specific manifestation of petty bureaucracy and corruption, was frustrating him to insanity.

"Eish! Horreyya! Karama insaneyya!" Bread. Freedom. Human dignity. Kids run alongside the march: "The *people—demand—* the fall of this *regime—*" In the eighties and nineties, at the time of the big expansion of the Islamist currents, Embaba came in for some particularly harsh treatment. The Dakhleyya (Ministry of the Interior) stopped policing Embaba itself but set up border stations at its exits; every male going in or out was subjected to stop and search. Anyone not carrying his ID was detained, and "detained" meant beaten—sometimes tortured. Several times during today's march, sweeping up people from the neighborhood, the cry rises, "To the police station!" and each time the march's leaders deflect it.

Later I will find out that my sister, Laila, MH, and various other friends are all on this march. But it has grown so big, we don't see each other. By the time we wind onto a overpass to head for Downtown, we are easily five thousand people or more.

As we descend from the overpass, I recognize that we're in Ahmad Orabi Street. This is where my beloved Khalu, my mother's brother, ever present though gone now these eighteen years, used to live. His wife still lives here. I glance up at her plant-filled balcony, and I can't resist. I slip away from the march and up the five floors to her flat, where I find cousins and friends—all slipped away from the march for a few minutes' rest and to find out the news. We'd woken up that morning to find the Internet down, and by eleven a.m. not a single mobile was working. Landlines were all we had, and even there the international lines had been taken down. We knew then that this was a regime fighting for its life. We sat around in Tante Nahed's home and used her landline to phone and check up on friends and family. Most homes had arranged to have one person stay in by the landline and act as liaison. My brother, when I called him, said his daughters wanted to join the action, and would I take them? This would be their first protest. Tante Nahed gave us tea and juice. The last time I'd sat in her living room was two years ago, and I had been looking through the results of a survey she'd just published: *The Problems and Discontents of the Egyptian Citizen.* Unemployment consistently scored highest on the list of people's personal problems, second was housing, and third was education.

4:00 P.M.

My brother, Ala, and his wife, Sohair, and their daughters Salma and Mariam, pick me up. As we drive, we pass protests heading to Tahrir. Ala and Sohair have brought bottles of water and hand them out. Months later my brother—an IT man and an Egyptologist—will, with friends, put together an initiative to dismantle the security establishment, another to overhaul pre-university education, another to set up a national employment bureau. . . . Today this is his and his wife's first action for the revolution.

Salma and Mariam and I decide we'll walk across 6 October Bridge and up the Corniche into Tahrir, so my brother drops us off in Agouza, at the foot of the steps leading up to the bridge. We run up the steps and find ourselves facing a cordon of Central Security soldiers blocking our way. The bridge crosses Gezira Island and passes over the Gezira Club. My nieces, twins, had both been champion gymnasts in their childhood and teens, and the Gezira was their club. Now twenty-two, they could easily still pass for seventeen. I take their elbows and stride up to the line of soldiers: "Excuse us, my daughters are late for their training—" pointing below us at the club grounds. The line opens courteously.

I love these young men. And I don't want them to be part of Central Security. In fact, we've got a case in court arguing that using conscripts for Security is unconstitutional; conscription may be necessary to protect the country against invasion or aggression. But to use conscripts to protect the government of the day against the people cannot be right.

We get to the middle of the bridge before we realize that there are no cars, that the air is dim and fumy, and that the few people around us are not moving forward. There's something of Dante about the spectacle. Isolated figures drift. Smoke drifts. Everything is slowed down and dim. A young man comes up and gives us tissues, then sprinkles vinegar over them. "Hold them over your nose," he says, "a tip from our Tunisian friends." In Palestine they use onions. We can't yet smell the gas. I see a friend, Lena, and her husband, and we drift together, embrace, and stand silently watching a man wearing a large brown paper bag over his head rotate slowly on the narrow traffic island at the center of the bridge. He's turning in slow motion, and as he faces us, we see the slits for the eyes and the large, red question mark starting on the forehead and running down the nose with the dot at the mouth. Later I note this as my first experience of spontaneous, revolutionary street theater. Now it just adds to the weird, dreamlike feel of the scene. A heavy thudding thumps rhythmically through the smog. Lena says it's guns. Across the water, we can see that the real action is on Qasr el-Nil Bridge. We've started to feel the gas, but Salma and Mariam and I decide to follow our plan and run the hundred meters or so to the bridge's exit by the Ramses Hilton, get down, and run along the river to Qasr el-Nil.

Tear gas! This was a gas that made you feel the skin peeling off your face. Later, when we saw the canisters, we found it had passed its expiry date. You'd think that would make it less painful, but apparently it makes it worse. We run blind; I can't even open my eyes to see what's going on. When I do force them open for a second, I see that Mariam, the more delicate of the twins, has stopped in the middle of the bridge, her eyes streaming and shut tight, one of her shoes lost, her arms held out helplessly. She's saying something but so softly I can't hear. Salma and I run back for her. "I can't," she's whispering, "I can't." We find her shoe, grab an arm each, and run. We run down the slope of the bridge and straight into another cordon of Central Security soldiers. They're meant to block the way. We are three women, disheveled, eyes streaming. We run right up to them, and they make way. "Go!" they urge us. "Quick!" Eye to eye with one of them, young, brown, open-faced, Egyptian, I pause, just for a second. "What can we do?" he shouts into the smoke. "If we could take off this uniform, we'd join you!"

Stuck. Stranded. For a moment, as I was running down the slip road with my eyes closed holding on to my nieces, I had the—typical—thought that we might nip into the Ramses Hilton and wash our faces, maybe even get some tea. Down on the embankment, with the soldiers facing us and behind them the Corniche road littered with stones and charred cars and the Hilton dark and shuttered, it is clear that a five-star interlude is out of the question. We run down the embankment steps and jump into a boat: "To Giza, please. Drop us next to Gala2 Bridge." We'll go home.

But: as we get farther from the shore, our coughing and choking subside. We can draw breath, even though the breath burns. And we can open our eyes. And when our eyes meet, we change direction and head, again, to Tahrir.

〃〃〃〃

On the traffic island at the Qasr el-Nil entrance to Tahrir, you turn 360 degrees and everywhere there are people. I cannot tell how many thousands I can see. Close up, people are handing out tissues soaked in vinegar for your nose, Pepsi to bathe your eyes, water to drink. I stumble, and a hand under my elbow steadies me. The way ahead of us is invisible behind the smoke. From time to time there will be a burst of flame. The great hotels: the Semiramis Intercontinental, Shepheard's, the Ramses Hilton, have all darkened their lower floors and locked their doors. On the upper-floor balconies, stick figures are watching us. At the other end of the Midan, from the roof of the American University, the snipers are watching us, too. Silently. Everywhere there is a continuous thud of guns and, from time to time, a loud, intermittent rattling sound. We stand. That is our job, the people at the back: we stand and we chant our declaration of peace: "Selmeyya! Selmeyya!" while our comrades at the front, unarmed, fight with the Security Forces. From time to time, a great cry goes up, and we surge forward: our friends have won us another couple of meters, and we follow them and hold our ground. We sing the national anthem. Eight months ago some young protesters from the 6 April Movement were arrested in Alexandria for singing the national anthem; it was "instigator," the prosecution said. We sing it. On 28 January, standing at that momentous crossroads, the Nile behind us, the Arab League building to our left, the old Ministry of Foreign Affairs to our right, seeing nothing up ahead except the gas and smoke and fire that stand between us and our capital, we stand our ground and sing and chant and place our lives, with all trust and confidence, in each other's hands.

⁄ ⁄ ⁄ ⁄

Some of us die.

⁄ ⁄ ⁄ ⁄

Many of us have not yet truly realized what we are engaged in; what the country is engaged in. We know that Suez has been under siege for three days and people there have been killed. We know Alexandria is up, and news is coming in of other cities. But we are still calling what we are doing "protesting"—and we have been protesting for ten years. I think that over the last decade, every time I've arrived in Cairo—and that's three or four times a year—I've joined my sister and various friends on protests: marches to support the Palestinian Intifada, marches against the war on Iraq, protests against our rigged elections, against our co-opted judiciary, against the plots to perpetuate the regime by slithering Gamal Mubarak into power, against corruption, and against police brutality. The government was vicious in dealing with all of them. It knew that a demonstration for Palestine or Iraq would sooner or later turn its attention to the Egyptian regime, and that a demonstration against the regime would count its role in Palestine and Iraq among its sins.

Looking back now, we see the progression, from small groups collecting medicines for the Intifada, to the civil movement Kifaya hitting the streets, to the massive workers' strikes in Mahalla, to the point where every sector in civil society—judges, lawyers, farmers, teachers, pensioners, journalists, tax collectors—is fighting with the government. And I see it, too, in my family. Like so many politically engaged Egyptian families, it's now in its third generation of activists—and this third generation, in their twenties, are more clever and cool and effective than we ever were. We, the older revolutionaries, have been trying since '72 to take Tahrir. They are doing it. They're going to change the world. We follow them and pledge what's left of our lives to their effort.

FRIDAY, 28 JANUARY, 10:00 P.M.

Four army tanks are on the Maspero[3] Corniche, the run of riverside from Boulac to the Ramses Hilton on the eastern bank of the Nile, five minutes and one (different) bridge from my home on Gezira Island. They're blocking the road in front of the Radio and Television building (also known, through metonymy, as Maspero) where, when I was a student, I had my first job. I played "Laila" who, with her brother "Ahmad," appeared in weekly episodes of a sitcom designed to teach English to schoolchildren. Sometimes we filmed on location, but mostly we worked in a studio in Maspero. This was in the early seventies, and the cavernous and freezing Studio 6 had no editing facilities. Each episode was twenty minutes long, and we had to record it from start to finish without stopping. If someone made a mistake or missed a cue or got the giggles, we had to start from the beginning. And if our booked time ran out, we had to vacate the studio and wait till a free slot came up and try again. So I've spent many, many hours loitering in this area, warming myself, drinking tea and chatting and hanging about and catching up on essays and assignments. And now it is dark and deserted, and there are four army tanks outside the building, and MH is distributing molasses sticks both to the soldiers on the tanks and to the revolutionaries on the street "for energy."

In the weeks to come, I will understand why revolutions and coups always rush to seize the radio and television facilities. Our revolution seized the main *midans* of our cities and went on to deal with the strongholds of the most hated parts of the regime: its party and its brutal security establishment. Next day there was talk of Maspero, but trying to take it would have meant engaging not the police or Central Security but the military.

At six p.m., Hosni Mubarak had declared a curfew. Nobody paid attention. At seven, while the battle for Tahrir was raging, a cry—a jubilant warning—had gone up: "El-geish nezel!" The army had deployed. We saw the first open four-man vehicle arrive on the Corniche by Qasr el-Nil Bridge and just about caught a glimpse of the red berets of the Military Police before the welcoming, co-opting crowds closed in on the vehicle.

Now, at ten, we walk past Maspero and past the darkened Ramses Hilton. In the eighties it was a novelty to zoom up thirty-six floors and watch, from Windows on the World, as night fell and strings of city lights blinked on and light-encrusted boats darted about on that central darkness that was the river. Five days from now the regime will barricade the world's media correspondents in this hotel while it calls in its cavalry and makes a desperate stand against the revolution. But we don't know that yet. Ahead of us a huge cloud of black smoke rises to the sky: the National Democratic Party headquarters has been set on fire; flames leap from its windows and the windows of Suzanne Mubarak's Specialist National Councils. Hundreds of people on Qasr el-Nil Bridge are holding up mobile phone cameras. But next door, around the Egyptian Museum, the young people, the shabab,[4] have linked arms and are surrounding the building, cordoning it with their bodies. When the fire broke out next door, even young people who had left the Midan came back to protect the museum. At this point, none of us knows that the regime's snipers are concealed on its roof. We don't know that the army will use it as a holding pen and a fast-torture location. The young revolutionaries just know that this is their museum and they have to protect it; they will not move until they have handed it officially to the army. They even make the brigadier with his tanks show ID before they'll give him the building.

When I'd gone home to drop off Salma and Mariam and to write and file copy, my aunt Laila Moussa (Lulie) said that Mona and some of her friends had stopped at the house and taken some clothes and papers and that they're locking themselves away in someone's mother's unused apartment. They've managed to establish a connection to the Internet. The young man who hacked through to the Internet is blind. Mona is twenty-four. Throughout the revolution, she will race between Tahrir, her genetics lab at Cairo University where she's finishing her M.Sc., and the secret location where she and her band of friends become the central nerve in the great communication effort that keeps the revolution linked to itself and to its comrades in the world outside. Now Lulie says Mona has phoned on the landline to say that there is a small mosque in the Tahrir area that is receiving the wounded and any-one who can help in any way should go there. Lulie is a doctor, but we persuade her to wait, wait till morning before trying to go out.

MH insists that we skirt Tahrir, so we go down Mahmoud Bassiouny and Talʒat Harb to get to the back of the Midan, and here, as we walk through Downtown, the sense of being in a film hits me: one of those urban apocalypse movies where the famil-iar features of Manhattan—it's generally Manhattan—are eerily recognizable through the flood/hurricane/nuclear destruction. The streets, the buildings are the same, but they're dark and semi-empty. The shops are shuttered. Litter seems to be floating around at knee level. There's rubble on the streets, and the lights are out, and there's no police: no traffic police, no guards on banks, nothing.

In neighborhoods across the country, through the night of this Friday that will become known as the Friday of Wrath, the regime kills hundreds of Egypt's young. Police and Security men drive cars and trucks into groups of protesters.[5] Snipers shoot young men and women from the rooftops of the Ramses Hilton, the American University, the Egyptian Museum, and the Dakhleyya. Troops fire on them with shotguns and rifles and automatics, and the thug militias, the baltagis, burn them with Molotov cocktails and batter them with stones, ceramics, and marble.

Soldiers break down and cry and are comforted by the revolu-tionaries.[6] Families will spend months of heartbreak finding out and trying to prove how their children were killed. Brave doc-tors and lawyers will speak up for them. The Dakhleyya will continue—as I write—to deny responsibility.

Now, in the darkened and derelict heart of our city, we arrive in Midan Bab el-Louq. And because we're out of communica-tions, we don't know that, three streets down, the young people, the shabab, are taking on the well-hated Dakhleyya, attacking the massive, fortified building in Lazoghli with their bare hands, improvised weapons, and the anger of many years.

〜〜〜〜

When my aunt Awatef (Toufi) got married, she moved into a flat in Lazoghli. I was eight years old, and I used to go and stay with her often, and so, alongside Ataba and Abdeen, my childhood landscape acquired the oddly named Lazoghli. Odd because of the tickly effect of the heavy *z* and the *gh* so close together, and because—unlike *Ataba* and *Abdeen*—it wasn't a word that meant anything in Arabic. Soon I learned that *oghli* is Turkish for "son of"; I would demonstrate precocity in front of my parents' leftist friends by saying I was staying at "Lazovitch."[7]

Unlike Ataba (which was always connected with bustle and commerce) and Abdeen (which was the royal and then presidential palace), exclusively Lazoghli for me was the bridal setting-up of a new home, a home that was an alternative to how my parents did things.

When my mother was twelve, she fell ill with rheumatic fever. This meant that she got to lie on sofas and read while her nine-year-old sister had to step into the traditional domestic role of eldest daughter. These roles were to last all their lives: Fatma ("Fifi," later, "Mama Fifi") the brainy intellectual, Toufi the keeper of tradition.

So when she married and moved to Lazoghli, Toufi's flat was a demonstration of the proper way of doing things. Though small, it had a *salon* (drawing room) and a *sofrah* (dining room)—the two pillars, it seemed, of every Egyptian household (except my parents'), and whose very names reflected the two dominant cultures to which the Egyptian bourgeoisie was in thrall: French and Turkish.

The drawing room chairs were upholstered in pale blue bro-
cade, and the windows had soft white cotton curtains—which, a
few years into their marriage, when Toufi and her husband moved
back into the family home to look after my grandfather, had to
be extended by double their length to fit her old windows. When
she died nine years ago, and we had to dismantle the Ataba house,
and I washed and folded the curtains, I realized that the repeated
pattern of three slim horizontal pleats halfway down each curtain
had been her solution to disguising the joining seam. I sat with the
curtain on my knee and the pleat between my fingers and thought
how she had always done that: made do and patched up and fixed
the world with results of originality and elegance.

But Lazoghli, most important, had a balcony where, on summer nights, we had a full view of the screen of the open-air Cinema
Lazoghli. No bedtime, no restrictions on what you could watch—
the absence, when it came down to it, of my father's regulations:
Lazoghli was freedom with a prime seat at a summer cinema every
night. From here I watched *River of Love*, *The Other Man*, *Rumour
of Love*, *A Beginning and an End*. . . .

My aunt, as I said, later moved back to Ataba, and Lazoghli
dropped off my map for decades. Until, in 2000, when Egyptians
started mobilizing in support of the Palestinian Intifada, it came
back: now Lazoghli was disappearances, Lazoghli was torture,
Lazoghli was the Dakhleyya and the State Security Intelligence
Bureau, the Mabahith Amn el-Dawlah. It was also the Coroner's
Office, which habitually covered up the crimes of the Dakhleyya
and the State Security Intelligence Bureau.[8] Now—unbeknownst
to us in Bab el-Louq, three streets down—the young revolutionaries are attacking Lazoghli, and the security establishment, about
to lose the streets of the country, is determined to keep it. Five
snipers are on the roof, snipers whose existence the ministry will
deny despite their images captured on film.[9]

As we stand in Bab el-Louq, I can hear a voice over a *tannoy*.

I can't make out the words, but the voice is repeating them and repeating them, and it sounds like an appeal. It comes from the Midan end of Tahrir Street, where I expect Mona's mosque to be, so I start walking up toward it. It's dark, and the shop on the corner with the best carob juice in town is shuttered. MH has gone to hunt for a truck that will agree to come here and transport the wounded. Men walking down warn me to turn back. I can hear the shots and smell the acrid smoke, but a lesson learned from time spent in Palestine is that unless there's an insurmountable physical obstacle (and that includes a man or woman with a gun), keep going. So I keep going and find that the voice is coming from Amir Qadadar Street to my left: "This is a house of God. A house of God and a hospital. There are wounded people here and doctors trying to help them. You must not attack this house. Your brothers and sisters are here. This is a house of . . ."

It's an entrance you might easily miss. One of the magical architectural features of downtown Cairo is the pedestrian passages that run at street level between or through buildings. My grandfather's house had one of those. You walk through them, under cover, linking from street to street. Some of the wider passages have stalls or shops. This entrance is to a passage that links Amir Qadadar Street to Tahrir. I didn't know it existed, and I only see it because of the knot of people and cars outside it. "This is a house of God— and a hospital—" the voice declares, and there's rubble and smoke, and the only people in the street are around that small entrance almost hidden by a large sign for mobile phones, so that's where I go. I edge past the hurried toing and froing, and I'm inside, and the space is maybe twenty meters long by eight meters wide. If I walk straight through, I'll come out on the east side of Tahrir, but to my left there's a waist-high railing that runs the length of the passage, and the space beyond it—a width of some six meters—is a small mosque. Well, not a proper mosque but a space that has Quranic verses hanging on the freshly painted walls, and a prayer niche to guide you toward Makkah, and rows of prayer mats on the floor, and on the mats lie young men covered in blood, and other young men are running in through the Midan entrance carrying yet more young men covered in blood and lowering them carefully onto the mats, and by the walls figures are stretched out, shrouded in dark blankets and then I see a white light at the center of it all, and it's coming from a slight figure crouched on the floor doing something to the chest of a young man, and the figure has a face of such intent seriousness and compassion that I cannot look anywhere else, and I stand and watch her until she finishes and straightens up and is revealed to be Mona Mina. Mona is the founder of the activist group Physicians Without Rights. She's a friend of my sister and the mother of Salma Said, a fiery and popular activist. As I step toward her, a young man runs up between us and puts his head in my eye line. I say "journalist," but he's already asking: "Is the pellet still there? Can you take it out, or should we leave it? I have to get back to the shabab." The shabab are storming the Dakhleyya. Mona tells me she knows two of the young fighters: "Two weeks ago they were scared to report that their boss was bullying them. Look at them now!"

I look. Wounded young men everywhere. And other young men and women tending to them. Medicines and dressings stacked in neat piles by the walls. People come to talk to me. I write fast; their message is urgent: they're using live ammunition. They're using shotguns. Look: empty cartridges, *Made in the USA*. Look. Look: his legs aren't working. Two others have died. No one wants to go to hospital because they report them and they get taken away. Eye injuries. Head injuries. They're shooting to kill. Then the tear gas floods in again, and the exhortations on the loudspeaker grow louder, disbelieving, angry: "Soldiers of Egypt! Police of Egypt! Your brothers and sisters are in the protection of this house. . . ." Young men try to carry the wounded out into the air through the back. Someone gives me a gas mask. Someone else gives me two empty cartridges. They'll sit on my mantelpiece. "This is what we get from USAID. This is the 'aid' they hold over us." The gas clears. A collapsed Central Security soldier is carried in. He's given emergency treatment, and his weapon is emptied before he's set free. He sobs as an older man pats his shoulder. Weeks from now we'll find out that soldiers went AWOL and lived on the Midan until the military broke the sit-in. I make a list of things the hospital needs: Betadine, dressings, spray anaesthetic, sutures, needles, surgical gloves, painkillers . . .

//////

At midnight I'm standing outside the pharmacy on the street corner opposite my house waiting for the pharmacist to bag the things I've bought and for MH to come back from his search for sutures and needles. We suspect we won't get these because pharmacies are not allowed to sell them except to hospitals. We drove to a couple of hospitals, and they wouldn't let us in. The central twenty-four-hour emergency pharmacy is closed. So we've gone round collecting things from any neighborhood pharmacy that's open. There are no streetlights. And no police.

The Dakhleyya, thoroughly beaten by the protesters in Alexandria and Suez and about to lose Cairo, has pulled all its men from the streets. The accepted figure for the personnel of the security establishment is about 1.5 million. They have received orders to withdraw from duty. Our government has switched off the lights and gone away. Actually, no, they've not gone away: in the dark they've thrown off the camouflage and transformed into the occupying force they always were.

Word is coming through that the Dakhleyya is opening up selected jails and police stations across the country and letting— or even throwing—violent criminals out. In el-Wadi el-Gedeed prison, all the cells were opened except for one that held thirty-

six newly detained Islamists; then the prison was set on fire. A
group of convicted criminals risked their lives to break open the
cell and set the new prisoners free. We'll find out later that General Muhammad al-Batran, the Dakhleyya's chief of intelligence
of prisons, has been battling to keep order. General Batran has a
reputation for fairness. Yesterday he visited Fayyoum prison and
established peace there. It will turn out that at the same moment
that I'm standing here, on the corner, waiting for the medicines,
he's on the phone to his sister. He is enraged. He tells her that
Habib el-Adli, the minister of the interior, has closed down seventeen police stations and is determined to set the whole country
ablaze. Tomorrow General Batran will go to Abu Za3bal prison
and restore order. Then he'll go to Qatta prison and talk to the
prisoners, and they will agree to return to their cells—and then
he will be shot and killed by the inspector in charge of the jail.
His sister, Manal al-Batran, will pursue his killers in the courts for
months—perhaps years.

I glance up, and my balcony, on the sixth floor, draws my eyes
to its light, its trellises and plants. I always leave the light on at
night, so that I, coming home, or someone coming to visit, can
glance up and feel an early welcome. Now I question whether it's
a good idea.

Karima comes to talk to me. She's my age and is the daughter of the greengrocer under my building. He, the greengrocer,
used to sit quietly in the corner all day with a cigarette-full of
hashish while Karima's mother ran the shop and the children.
When I was small, I used to watch their fights from the balcony—
enthralled. They were a mother and a father with two daughters
and a son. Just like us. But instead of the tight lips, the silences,
the "withdrawal of affection" that signaled anger or displeasure in
our household, their emotions and exchanges were all out there:
yells and wails and tantrums, the mother chasing the kids with
a bamboo cane, the kids screaming and running and dodging

behind startled passersby, the street intervening, cuffing them on the head, enforcing peace. I was sure I preferred their style to ours. The parents are dead now, and the brother runs the greengrocer's. He still gets into fights, and the classy glass front he's put up for his shop is often smashed. But Karima owns three hardware and general stores on the street and holds court from a stool on the corner. When her children were young, you saw them stop by her, composed and well dressed and always carrying books.

She comes to talk to me and says she's worried. "They drove round and collected all the guards from the embassies and the banks," she says, "and it's not only that; they've turned their baltagis loose on the streets. How can we live without security?"

"Don't tell me you're afraid?" I joke.

"Of course I'm afraid."

"Well, seriously, don't be. You could take on a hundred baltagis."

The baltagis are worse than the regular forces. They're men— and recently women—with a record of violent crime, who're trained and paid by the Dakhleyya and used for special assignments, like beating up people at elections, dispersing protesters, etc. A baltagi is mercenary and without honor. A baltagi is violent and loud but ultimately a coward; his speciality is bullying the weak. And Karima is not weak.

Two weeks later, when Mubarak falls, she will take off her *galabeyya* and veil and put on a loose trouser suit and a scarf. When I grin, she'll shrug: "Just a bit of a change." But now, at midnight on 28 January, we stand together and watch three young residents armed with sticks take up position outside my apartment block. "Where are your children?" she asks. "They're coming," I say. I don't tell her that I've made my youngest, Ismail Richard, stay put in London to circulate information and help organize the protests there—and finish his M.Sc. But my older son, Omar Robert, is, in fact, trying to come home. Two nights from now he will join these young men at the barricades.

As we'd driven from Tahrir to my neighborhood, Zamalek, to look for pharmacies, news was coming through of the police withdrawal. By the time we'd finished buying the medicines and were heading back to Tahrir, we passed three citizen checkpoints in Zamalek alone. In every district people came down from their homes and set up neighborhood watches, Popular Committees. They invented barricades out of tires and chairs and lengths of wood and blocks of stone and traffic barriers. The characters of the checkpoints varied with the neighborhoods: in the villages they were farmers with axes and hoes; in the poorer neighborhoods they wore *galabeyyas* and carried sticks; in the posh districts they had walking canes and golf clubs; at one Zamalek checkpoint there was a lady in a camping chair holding a glass of gin and tonic. Kids played in the streets.

For a week the city will be policed by Popular Committees. They will have fun, checking ID and licenses and ushering cars through with a theatrical flourish. Everywhere they are courteous and apologize for the inconvenience. And we are courteous right back and thank them for protecting us, thank them for giving us our city back. Everybody ignores the curfew. People, especially women, say they've never felt safer. We joke, seriously, that we can save the eighteen billion pounds the Dakhleyya costs us every year and put it into something more useful. In the daytime the shabab will run the traffic and collect the litter. Revolutionary graffiti will start to appear everywhere and become more confident and more sophisticated each day.

2:00 A.M.

It is quieter at the mosque. I deliver the supplies, add them to the neat mounds that other citizens have brought in, then sit with an exhausted young doctor who tells me he'd come down with four of his friends from Minya to join the protest. They lost each other and, with no mobiles, couldn't communicate. Then the shooting started, and he knew what he had to do. He has been working nonstop for ten hours. I ask if he knows where he'll sleep. My brother, who's come down with more medicines and a car, takes him to the Hisham Mubarak Legal Center, which is now functioning as a shelter and food kitchen as well as providing legal backup for activists. The center was set up by my sister's husband, Ahmad Seif, and a group of friends in 1999 and named after one of the group, Hisham Mubarak, who'd been thirty-five when he died of a heart attack ten years earlier.[10] Tonight its floors and sofas are home to scores of Egyptians from outside Cairo who've come to join the revolution.

Before I leave, I ask the name of the mosque. It is the Mosque of Ibad al-Ra7man, the Servants of the Compassionate.

Hundreds die that Friday night. And thousands are injured, and many will die later of their wounds. Their smiling, hopeful faces will be everywhere. Our shuhada: our martyrs of the revolution, who walked in peace and died before they could live the lives they dreamed of. Their song will become our anthem.[11] We will march in their funerals and promise, "We'll get what they died for / Or die as they died." If we tire or our hope dims, if our optimism for a moment falters, we will open our hearts and they will come to us: their bright faces, their hopes, their lives, their parents, their children. This is now our life's work: we will create the Egypt they died for.

3:00 A.M.

On my way home I walk again through Cairo's darkened streets, through the rubbish, past the shuttered shops and the closed hotels and the smoldering party headquarters and the charred, upturned personnel carriers, and it all seems apt. It's not a film anymore. This is the reality that we've been living for decades, finally risen to the surface. At last our capital reflects the true condition of the country and of our lives: burned and broken and almost ruined. And now we'll have to save it.

I come again to the four tanks on Maspero. The soldiers in camouflage are still standing on top of them; I wonder if they have to stand there all night or if they may at least sit down. Behind one of them is the sign of the Paprika restaurant, and as I look at the restaurant's darkened window I see—so clearly that my breath catches—I see my younger self, ablaze with love and poetry and the stormy, dusty *khamsin* winds, sitting, leaning across the table from the man I love, the man who has followed me from London to Cairo, allowing him to hold my palm to his mouth, to kiss it under the gaze of all the waiters standing by.

~~~~

For our honeymoon we drove up the length of the Suez Canal and discovered we were on a military road only when we hit the first checkpoint and it was too late to turn back. The soldiers fetched the colonel. I gave him our passports, our story, our marriage certificate from the day before. He stared for a moment at the silent foreigner in sunglasses sitting in the passenger seat, then said "Mabrouk" and let us pass. We went through at least ten check-points before the road gave us an option to exit.

Four months later our London wedding, for good or ill, took place on the anniversary of Nasser's 1952 revolution. And my life became Cairo/London, London/Cairo. And both cities changed, but I liked—on the whole—the changes that happened to London: the view from Waterloo Bridge, more exciting every year, the blossoming street markets, the angel alighting once more on the dome of our local theater. In Cairo, every time I went home, home got a bit more bitty on me.

I came home and found the old mysterious villa on the corner of our street gone. One of my classmates used to vanish into it at the end of every school day; now the wrought-iron railings, the dense trees, the lights shining far within: all gone. In its place, this pharmacy.

I came home, and they'd pulled apart my beloved Abu el-Ela Bridge and built the ghastly 15 May Overpass in its place. No more strolls to Maspero, to Boulac, to the Shagara Café. The overpass (named after the 1971 coup—the "Corrective Revolution," with which Sadat consolidated his power and got rid of what was left of Nasser's men) runs across Zamalek and turned its high street into an instant slum.

In Ataba, the other main theater of my life, the changes were more radical. A super-ugly iron walkway circumambulated the *midan*: Midan el-Ataba el-Khadra, the Place of the Green Threshold. Step through the threshold, east into the heart of the old city, west into the heart of Haussmann's late-nineteenth-century creation, both hearts centered on commerce. Everyone here was in small industries and trade. But they used to have style. My grandfather's home was here, his business a five-minute walk across Shari3 el-Azhar. But he was dead, and Khalu, my uncle—because of the Mafia-style practices of the tax authorities—was shifting the business from wood to aluminum. The showrooms and workshops, soon to be sold, were in the massive Italianate terrace on the eastern side of the *midan*. Look at the confidence of it! Of the National Theater, and the Khedivial Post building, and the block that held Matatias's coffee shop, where Khalu played chess every night.

And the house: a solid Mediterranean-style apartment block fronting on a quiet courtyard on Shari3 el-Geish. The fun thing was to approach it from the other side, from the Ruwei3i market. You walked through the busy street past Alf Sanf w'Sanf, the piled-high toy store from which we bought all my toys and my brother's and sister's toys. Alf Sanf w'Sanf furnished me one day with the sudden aperçu that the accurate translation of *Alf leila w'leila* was not the literal "a thousand and one nights" but just "a thousand nights"—or even "lots of nights." Anyway, past the toy store and through the cool passageway that ran under the building, and you emerged in a courtyard with notices and banners hanging out to dry outside a calligraphy workshop, then you turned right into the spacious entrance with the old black and white marble floor and the stately wooden lift. This was the landscape that furnished my imagination and kept me going through the cold years of the Ph.D. in the north of England. When I came back, I fought my way through the Ruwei3i market to find my aunt, Toufi, fighting a battle with rising garbage and falling plaster and smashed marble. The lift had been overpainted with brown lacquer, and street vendors run by the local MP were using the entrance as storage. Of our neighbors, older people were dying, their children moving into the new districts, away from the center, their apartments taken over by local bosses who used them as storage for cheap goods, and baltagis.

Cairo/London, London/Cairo, and Cairo was being constantly downgraded. Despite the new luxury multipurpose blocks, the marble shopping malls, the $15 million apartments, the city was disintegrating. Partly through neglect and partly, we felt, on purpose. Streets were dug up and left unpaved. Sidewalks vanished. Prime and historic locations—like the site of the burned-down Opera House just off Ataba—became car parks. Streetlights dimmed. Nothing was maintained or mended. Old houses were torn down and monstrous towers built in their place. Public transport became a joke. And in a noose around the city, they built luxury gated communities on virtually stolen land, adorned them with water-guzzling golf courses, and called them "European Countryside" and "Beverly Hills."

And through it all, I loved her and loved her more. Millions of us did. We'd wake up one morning and find a just finished underpass dug up again, more marble and ceramics brought in to line its walls. We'd check out which MPs traded in marble and ceramics (the same MPs who would send truckloads of baltagis with marble and ceramic shards to crack open our heads in the streets of the revolution). Traffic signals were burned out and bent, and we'd wake up another morning to find the city had sprouted plastic palm trees festooned with winking red and green lightbulbs. They'd really scored there: not only made money but made Cairo into a clown. We apologized to her. Among ourselves and in our hearts. We told her we loved her anyway, told her we were staying. I felt a rush of love every time I passed the strange, creamy house with the rotting turrets that they hadn't yet pulled down; the great art deco cinemas, flea-ridden and on their knees but still there. The day the Cairo Tower lost its discreet white uplighting and was caught in a net of flashing colored dots, I cried. They dammed sections of the Nile to create new waterfront residences (the ministers of housing responsible are now being tried) and land was sold from under residents' feet to foreign "investors." Cement was poured into every public construction project, including disastrous restorations of thousand-year-old mosques. The cement factories ran on subsidized fuel and made a profit margin of 65 percent. In Muqattam the sewage from a new, wealthy development on the top of the hill eroded the rock on which Dwei2a, the old poor district below, was precariously perched and sent it crashing down the jagged hillside. (The residents are now camped in protest in front of Maspero, their wretchedness displayed for all to see.) A quarter of a million children lived on the streets, and some people set up shelters for them, and some made films about them and some stole their kidneys and corneas. Police officers ran protection and drug rackets. People regularly fell out of windows during questioning or had heart attacks in police custody. There was a video of a woman hanging upside down and begging, begging. . . . there were protests, marches, demonstrations every day. There were flash screenings of torture videos. The top judges of the country stood for two hours in silence in the street outside the Judges' Club with their sashes and ribbons and medals on their chests. We knew then that judgment would surely come.

Degraded and bruised and robbed and exploited and mocked and slapped about: my city. I was ashamed of myself for not saving her. Every one of us was. All I could do was look and listen and stay and march and insist that I loved her. And she acted like she didn't care. She unraveled with bravado. Every thread of that once tightly ordered pattern breaking loose: blue and green and red and black and every shade and texture, all sprung away from the tapestry, in disarray, tangled, knotted, vivid, sizzling, present. The city stayed awake longer, put more people on the streets. It threw up new haphazard districts, and when the government would not supply them with water or electricity, people stole them from the mains. It opened special restaurants and started special services to cater to the new Gulf tourists. Including agencies for seasonal marriages to young, pretty, impoverished Egyptian women.

Small art galleries opened, and tiny performance spaces; new bands formed across the musical spectrum. Mosques and cultural centers clutched at the derelict spaces under overpasses. Green spaces vanished, but every night the bridges would be crammed with Cairenes taking the air. We suffered a massive shortage of affordable housing, but every night you'd see a bride starring in her wedding procession in the street. Unemployment ran at 20 percent, and every evening there was singing and drumming from the cheap, bright, noisy little pleasure boats crisscrossing the river.

Trees that were not cut down refused to die. They got dustier, and some of their branches grew bare, but they grew. We looked out anxiously for the giant baobab in Sheikh Marsafy Street in Zamalek, for the Indian figs on the Garden City Corniche, for what my kids called the Jurassic Park trees by the zoo. If they cut a tree down, it grew shoots. If they hammered an iron fence into its roots, the tree would lean into the iron, lean on it. If a building crowded the side of a tree, the tree grew its other side bigger, lopsided. I knew trees that couldn't manage leaves anymore but put all they had into a once-a-year burst of pink flowers. And once I saw a tree that seemed looked after, that had just been washed: it couldn't stop dancing.

I loved her. I would wake up in my London bed convinced that as my front door opened onto Wimbledon, my garden door opened onto Zamalek. Until one day, when I was neither in Cairo nor in London but in Jaipur, the shabab of Egypt decided they would no longer allow their lives to be stolen, and in every district in the country they got up and walked into the hearts of their cities. They chanted, "We're your sons / And daughters too / What we're doing is for you," and we came down from our houses and walked with them. They marched for bread, and they marched for freedom, for social justice and for human dignity. We followed them, and we marveled at them, and we stood shoulder to shoulder with them, and every so often—more often than they wanted, for sure—we'd grab one of them and hug them and shake their hand and thank them. Yes, we would thank them for lifting the burden of failure from our backs, for ridding our hearts of their load of sorrow, for stepping forward and sweeping away the question that tormented each one of us: *What manner of homeland, what manner of future am I leaving my children? What have we allowed to happen to our country? To our world?* We're taking care of it, they said, just stay with us: "Parents! Friends! Draw close to us!" And we did.

SUNDAY, 30 JANUARY

MH has turned his office into a revolutionary headquarters, and this is a meeting of some of the older figures of what you might call the establishment opposition to the regime of Hosni Mubarak. Most are over sixty-five. They sit in a big circle, and the buffet man goes round with coffee. They talk above each other and listen only long enough to pick up a line and go with it themselves. An unkind thought crosses my mind: *This is the political leadership that failed.* They talk about the necessity of creating a patriotic front to fill the vacuum created by the fall of the National Democratic Party, about the need to call for the election of a founding committee to write the constitution—and the conversation/argument has the same theoretical feel as the ones we've been listening to for thirty years: lists of things we need to do. But our host has promised us a visit from some of the young leadership of the revolution; when they come in, an energy comes in with them. Six young men, all in their twenties. They're like a football team; they huddle and confer quickly, they "pass" to each other with a nod or a look. They're concise, self-deprecating, firm, and courteous. They say that if they claim any credit, it will be for 20 percent of the people who came out on the twenty-fifth; the rest has been spontaneous, organic—as surprising to them as it was to everybody. When the Khaled Said[12] Facebook page received over 300,000 responses to the call to come out on the twenty-fifth, eleven other groups decided to meet and coordinate. They met physically (and secretly) and organized themselves and their friends. They are about three hundred, and no, they don't all know each other. They won't give information about how they operate, but they want to put it on the record that, were it not for all the protests and writings and activism of the older leadership, they would not have been able to do what they're doing now. "We've learned from you," they tell the room, "and we're building on what you've accomplished." There's a silence, and then one of the older people says simply: "Whatever you want us to do, we'll do."

I go out onto the porch. If I walk across Mesa7a Street, to the right, I'll come to a house we lived in briefly when I was three. A memory of riding a blue tricycle down a paved slope into a—living room? My mother at a sideboard wearing a full-skirted dress in blue and white pencil stripes. The walls were ablaze with paintings, and in the living room my parents' friends, the authors of these paintings, all in their twenties, were laughing and arguing and waiting for the mini-sandwiches my mother was preparing at the sideboard. This is the university neighborhood. Just down the road there's the Cairo University Faculty Club—the Union. We used to come with my parents when we were children and play in the garden while they socialized or organized. My parents taught at Cairo University all their lives, and Laila, my sister, followed them—only she specialized in maths. In 2006 she was one of the group that founded the 9 March Group for the Independence of the Universities—and she and her comrades started contesting the Union. As she told of stormy meetings, of regime-rigged elections, of being locked out of the building and holding alternative meetings on the pavement outside, I would try to imagine all this happening in the quiet, lofty rooms with their dark furniture, their rugs, their discreet lighting that spoke so sonorously of stability and scholarship and calm.

And now, just as my eight-year-old self is peeping round a heavy wooden door into a book-lined room, I hear an earth-shaking roar. I look up. Low down in the clear, blue winter sky, four F-16s are dipping and swooping. They circle several times. In Tahrir, I will learn later, people start to dance. "He's gone crazy! He's gone crazy!" they sing, and dance the crazy dance.[13] A man who works for MH comes onto the porch. "Don't go to Tahrir," he warns. "Go home and stay there. This whole story they're talking about inside isn't going to work." I remind him there's a call for a mil-lioneyya[14] tomorrow. He says he has a friend in the innermost cir-cle of the Presidential Guard. "They have a plan for this. They've been getting ready for this for a long time, and now," he says, "they have orders to put the plan into action: they're going to do dirty things, terrible, terrible things. It's going to be over in two days. Please believe me." The wide white steps lead down into a beauti-fully kept garden, where a calligrapher is busy at work on a series of huge banners: IRHAL! IRHAL! IRHAL! Leave!

An hour later in the sky above Tahrir, helicopters circle and tilt, circle and tilt, and on the ground we tilt right back at them, all of us, waving and laughing and holding up our banners for the men in the machines to read.

Mubarak has extended the curfew—but the Midan is teem-ing with hundreds of thousands of people, and more and more are coming in. He announces a cabinet reshuffle with General Ahmad Shafiq as prime minister—and Tahrir chants: "The peo-ple demand the fall of this regime." Yesterday, when he appointed Omar Suleiman as his vice president, the Midan roared: "No Mubarak / No Suleiman / No more *umala amrikan*," agents for America, and on the front of the papers this morning, Mubarak and Suleiman going through the swearing-in ceremony look irrel-evant, even unreal. This is what's real; what's happening here: the citizens flooding into Tahrir, the cheers, the chanting, the waving banners, the sense that we are pushing against something that will give. We don't know when, but it will give.

So we carry on, we chant and we sing and we wave the flag, and then again we're all looking up at the sky because the air around us is growing dim and heavy and the sky darkens and darkens, and then the thunder comes. God's thunder. It rolls and booms above our heads. Again and again it comes, and then lightning cracks the skies open, and the deluge pours down on us. We stand in awe. Thirty minutes of rain fast and fat and furious, and then the sky, the air, the city clears. The sun comes out, and Tahrir sparkles and leaps to life. "Allahu Akbar" rolls across Cairo. God is with us; He has sent us a sign and has cleansed our skies of Mubarak's jets.

And Omar Robert, my older son, flies in. After a nail-biting interlude when they said the plane would not land in Cairo but would fly back to Athens, they changed their minds, and he arrives. It takes us two hours to get from the airport to Zamalek. The army has closed off the section of highway that runs past Mubarak's residence—even though he's in Sharm el-Sheikh—so we have to drive through side streets, and everywhere the Popular Committees have set up their barricades. Omar has his first taste of the revolution. We show IDs and licenses, and everybody thanks everybody. At midnight he goes down to volunteer for the barricade on our street. In a little while he comes back. "I have to have a weapon," he says, "and I don't fancy a kitchen knife." He roams the house looking troubled. Then, leaning against the hallstand, he finds what he's looking for. My son patrols our street armed with my mother's walking stick.

And I am left to remember the times I walked into this flat to find my sons chatting with my mother on the balcony, or in the kitchen being fed, and how we moved from my mother pushing their swings or watching over them by the pool to Omar driving her around the streets of Cairo and—a couple of times—to the little orchard by the Pyramids that she loved so much.

TUESDAY, 1 FEBRUARY

I shall park by the small building that I still think of as the Pocket Theater. In the mid-sixties my mother used to drag me here to see experimental productions of Beckett and Brecht and Aeschylus. I loved the Nile-side neo-pharaonic building in its grove of palm trees, and I liked being part of an evening activity, a "grown-up" activity. But after the already-too-long performances, there would be intense discussions as to whether Brecht should be rendered in colloquial Egyptian or modern standard Arabic, whether Shakespeare's sonnets had to rhyme in Arabic, whether Sophocles or Euripides was more useful for our times, whether you could—in a translation—add a phrase that changed no meaning but fixed the rhythm. I was *so* bored. But something stayed with me— something to do with, shall we say, believing that artistic endeavor matters—that it's worth arguing about, and that it can (should?) have an intimate relationship with the world it happens in. Something to do with responsibility.

There's no parking to be had. The space is crammed; in every nook and cranny there are BMWs, beat-up old Fiat 128s, sleek Mercedes, environmentally unfriendly SUVs, responsible Toyotas; everybody's parked and come to join the revolution. I find a spot down the alley by the Ahli Football Club, cross, and walk past the Andalus Gardens and over Qasr el-Nil Bridge. Families of four generations are walking into Tahrir on a brilliant, sunny Cairo day.

The entrance to the Midan is a tangle of tanks, barbed wire, soldiers, and people. Yesterday the twelve entrances to Tahrir were guarded and the sit-in secured by shabab from the Popular Committees. Today it seems the army's helping. At the Qasr el-Nil entrance, we hold up our IDs as one by one we squeeze through the narrow gaps between the tanks. It doesn't feel good. Soldiers stand above us as we squash ourselves through their hardware. But they look friendly, and on Sunday, after the air force buzzed us, the Supreme Council of the Armed Forces, SCAF, declared that the armed forces would never fire on the Egyptian people.[15] Battalions of people are continuing the charm offensive that started on Friday—they surround the tanks, lean on them, climb onto them, paint them, stick flags and flowers on them, throw their babies to the men manning them; every tank is overwhelmed, every officer and soldier is engaged in conversation, in photo ops. Last night there was a football match—the people versus the army—with a tank as the prize. The people won. They didn't get the tank. But an officer emerged onto the Midan, young, rugged, well-spoken and almost in tears. He made a speech urging us not to leave our positions until we'd got everything we wanted. He was lifted onto people's shoulders and carried round the Midan: "The people! / The army! / One hand! / The people! / The army . . ."[16]

I tell non-Egyptian friends, journalists, interviewers who ask that we're not Greece or Latin America; that the Egyptian army is very much part of the fabric of Egyptian society, and in both 1977 and 1985 it refused direct orders to fire on Egyptian demonstrators. An oath taken by every soldier is that he will never raise his weapon in an Egyptian face. The army says it will secure for us this space where we are carrying out our peaceful, democratic, young, inclusive, open-source, grassroots revolution. My parents' generation warns us; they send messages through their children, our friends: *Take care. Don't trust the army.* My sister quotes the proverb "Harras wala tkhawwensh"—Don't assume treachery, but be on guard! And in any case, what are our options?

Mubarak is holding on. The Dakhleyya is working against us; they have already killed at least 145 people, and news is filtering through of killings in jails, of bodies found on highways, of attempted robberies of state institutions, of arson—all conducted by men officially and unofficially on the payroll of the Dakhleyya. Next-door Libya's erupting, Sudan to our south is breaking apart, and to our east there is Israel, always Israel; Israel, which is declaring its concern for Mubarak and calling him a strategic asset— which we've always known and is a large part of our problem with him. And in between us and all this stands our army: our brothers and husbands and sons. They're not 400,000 men, and they're spreading themselves thin. Since the twenty-fifth, they've had to deploy rapidly through Egypt's twenty-six governorates, and now they have to be in the cities as well. And we believe that they're like the rest of the country: the very top levels were part of the regime and have made millions. The conscripts and soldiers are ordinary Egyptians making a meager living. The officers and middle ranks have the same wishes, fears, angers, ambitions, equivocations as the rest of us, and on the whole would rather not see Egypt on its knees and would rather not be America and Israel's scabby mongrel allowed to shelter and feed as long as it knows its place, and would quite like to have a decent country where we take responsibility for ourselves and work to make sure everybody can have bread, freedom, and social justice.

We know that the army collects a ton of U.S. aid. We know it represents about a third of the GDP of our country—that it is a massive business interest. We know that in the army, as in the government and the state and also outside our country, massive—fine, the biggest possible—interests do not wish us to do what we wish to do, do not want for us the lives we want for ourselves. But right now we have to take the chance that the balances within the army will keep it from harming us. Right now we need to deal with the other forces ranged against us, inside and outside Egypt. The forces that want our land and our location, our resources and our position, and our history and our quiescence, and that want us out of a number of equations in our region and the world. They fasten on to us and feed, they spoon out our brains, our health, and our will. And if we don't fight them off, we shall die not even the death that is a merciful release but the death that is death-in-life: we shall be condemned to a zombie existence where we are emptied of ourselves but continue to perform their "Egypt."

Bread. Freedom. Social justice. How many have come to today's millioneyya? The military say two million in Tahrir. Four million across Egypt. And all these millions look like people who've awakened from a spell. We look happy. We look dazed. We turn to each other to question, to reassure. A man asks, "How did they

divide us? How did they make us frightened of each other like
that?" Another man—with his hand on his son's shoulder—says
to me, picking up the thread of a conversation we might have
had: "Yes, really. I thought so badly of him, sitting all day at his
computer. Now look what he and his friends have done. Respect.
Respect." People have put up tents in the central garden. In one
tent, young women are collecting footage of Dakhleyya torture.
In another, people are stacking bottles of water and dry biscuits. I
lower myself to the ground for a moment's rest and see I've sat next
to the covered wife of a man in the shortened white thob and the
white skullcap of the Salafis. I wonder if they'll mind. He sees my
glance: "Are you looking at me because I have this beard and I'm
smoking?" A wide smile: "I just couldn't afford razors. When he
leaves, I'll buy all the razors I need." We all become instant friends.
And I see old friends, too; as I wander the Midan, I bump into
people I know are living in Brussels, in Doha, in D.C., in London.
Everyone has dropped everything and come home. We're walking
around wide-eyed, pale with emotion. We hug. "You, too? But of
course you'd come," we say, and hug again. For a moment, Omar is
next to me. "Would you have imagined the revolution would look
like this?" he says. All the ills that plagued our society in the last
decades have vanished overnight. Young men, who a month ago
could have been thought a menace to any woman on the street, are
chivalry itself. People offer each other biscuits, dates, water. People
chat, people pick up litter. We revel in the inclusiveness, the generosity, the humor that come so easily to us. Students, businessmen, waiters, academics, farmers, civil servants, unemployed—we
are all here together, all doing what we've not been able to do for
decades: each and every one is speaking, acting, expressing themselves and insisting on being counted.

A group of some thirty fair-skinned young people are gathered
by the central garden. They hand out leaflets written in Arabic,
English, and French. They carry a banner that says: "The Khawa-

gas [Western foreigners] who have made Egypt their home salute the revolution!"

The world's media are here. "I don't know if one should say this," a journalist says, "but it's like—it's like Woodstock." She looks worried, but if there'd been room, I'd have picked her up and waltzed. In an early morning interview, I'd reassured a worried BBC anchor that Tahrir was like carnival. Another journalist is in tears: "For thirty years we've been discussing revolution—and if a revolution can be 'good.' And—here it is; you've just done it." I see Jon Snow and Medea Benjamin. A man pops out of a tree with branches tied to his arms and performs a tree dance. Another improvises a stand-up routine as "the Indian Expert, Mr. Nana," coming to tell us how to run the revolution. Stages have been rigged up and bands are playing.

But there are also black ribbons flying and pictures, pictures, pictures of the young people who were killed by the regime in the last six days. Our shuhada.[17] Together, we pray for them the Prayers for the Absent: "And do not consider those who were killed in the path of Right as dead; for they live in the presence of their Lord, and they prosper."[18]

And the Midan feeds us, nourishes us: this is the Egyptian Museum that holds our ancestors, the museum that our shabab defended—the museum that bears witness to who we are. This is the Arab League—an example of the death-in-life that was to be our fate; we will breathe life into it. This is the plinthless space. What good fortune that no statue occupies this central space, that the absence of a leader is physically manifest in Tahrir, and our leaderless revolution is watched over, instead, from the boundaries, by Omar Makram, Simón Bolívar, and Abd el-Menem Riyad. And the roads that open out from it—Champollion to the great law courts and the unions, Qasr el-Eini to Parliament and the Cabinet Office and then to the great teaching hospitals, Tahrir Street to Abdeen and the Palace and then to the Citadel, Tal3at

Harb to town and Ataba and commerce and then the Azhar, Gala2 to the central railway station and then the Cathedral—and right next to you, running alongside you—the Nile.

In the novel I was working on before the revolution happened, there's a scene that was written in August 2007. "Mada" is talking to "Asya" about the museum:

> "You know," says Mada, "it's unbelievable. It's as if the city doesn't even belong to us. A soldier stopped me walking near the Museum in Tahrir the other day. In the center of Cairo. He said it's forbidden to walk here. I couldn't believe it. 'How d'you mean forbidden?' 'It's forbidden.' I pointed at a whole load of people walking into the Museum. He said they're foreigners. I said, 'So I'm forbidden because I'm not a foreigner? Are you serious? What if I want to go to the Museum?' He said, 'Why should you go to the Museum?' I said, 'Haven't you noticed it's called the "Egyptian" Museum? And haven't you noticed this square is called "Liberation" Square? Do you know who it was liberated from? It was liberated from the foreigners, for us: the Egyptian people.'" "And what did he say?" "He said: 'You'll have to speak to the officer.'"

A great cry goes up from the square: "Irhal! Irhal!" Leave! Leave! Everybody is looking in the same direction: from the sixth-floor balcony of an art deco building, a long banner unfurls, falling gracefully down the front of the building. We read: "Leave! We want to breathe!" Holding it from the balcony is a young woman with streaming curly hair. She is jumping up and down and holding up her hand in a victory salute. The crowd salutes back: "Irhal! Irhal!"

Tahrir is about dignity and image as much as it is about the economy and corruption. It hurts how much this regime has messed with our heads, divided us, maligned us to the world.

"They say we only care about a loaf of bread," a young laborer says. "We care about bread. But we also care about our dignity." Together, in the Midan, over the last four days, we have rediscovered how much we like ourselves and each other and, corny as it may sound, how "good" we are. I sneeze, and someone passes me a tissue. And all the time the chants continue, the demands are articulated, options for the future are discussed. It is not possible to say what will happen next. But I look around, and I know this won't stop. No one, nobody, not one of us, is going to step back into the nightmare.

An Interruption

EIGHT MONTHS LATER, OCTOBER 2011

"It is not possible to say what will happen next. But I look around and I know this won't stop. No one, nobody, not one of us, is going to step back into the nightmare." This is what I wrote eight months ago. And now, of course, we know what happened next: Hosni Mubarak fell on 11 February; we celebrated, and the world—you—celebrated with us. The Supreme Council of the Armed Forces, SCAF, with tanks on our streets, stepped forward, saluted our shuhada, declared its belief in our revolution, and promised to protect it and the people and the transition into democracy. We left the Midan.

But I need to pause while we're still there, in the Midan, to interrupt this account of the eighteen days, to tell you the ongoing story of our revolution. Because the story does go on; we have not stopped, even though we may have fallen off your—off the world's—television screens, for the moment.

This book is not a record of an event that's over; it's an attempt to welcome you into, to make you part of, an event that we're still living. And there are two problems in the writing of it. One is that while the eighteen days are locked into the past, the revolution and the fight to hold on to it continue, and every day the landscape shifts. The other is that you—my reader—are in a future unknown to me, and yet I want to tell a story that will ease the leap you need to make between where this book stops and where Egypt is as you read.

As I write, I think of you holding this book and reading my words, weeks, months, into the future, and I wonder what the reality that you are seeing will be. That reality is what we, today, as I write, are working, fighting, dying in order to shape.

These are the last few hours that this, my text and I, have together; the last few hours I have to write for you, to you. And it's hard to write because things keep happening, pushing my pen this way and that, or making me lay it down as I stare out the window and contemplate.

We've just had word that Alaa Abd el-Fattah, my nephew, Laila's son and Mona's brother, has been summoned to the military prosecutor to face a charge of "incitement and destruction." Alaa is twenty-nine, an IT man, an activist and blogger. He and his wife, Manal, like many of our shabab, like Omar, my son, had been living and working abroad and dropped everything and came home to work for the Egypt of the revolution. When Mubarak was deposed, Alaa and Manal decided the world was ready for their first baby. The first child of the next generation in our family will be born, God willing, on 24 November. Alaa is at a conference in San Francisco. And Manal received his summons to the military prosecutor earlier today, while she was painting the new nursery. So this morning, as I sit down to write, this is what's on my mind.

My family plays musical chairs with dwellings, and I find myself now, after four moves in thirty years, in possession of the flat in Zamalek where I grew up. When I lift my eyes from my desk—my mother's desk, her card still there, in the corner under the glass by my right hand—when I lift my eyes, there's the view that used to meet them when I was studying for my university exams, and before that, for my finals at high school. The view is unchanged except for the 15 May Overpass that runs about a hundred meters to my left. Under it are the traffic lights at the intersection of Shagar el-Durr Street where in '67, as the military were preparing for the war with Israel that they would lose with such catastrophic consequences, they crushed my uncle, Khalu, in his Citroën between two massive trucks. So I stare out of the window and I think about civilians and the military and how Khalu, though he was an only son and so not conscripted, lost an eye, an arm, and a career to them anyway and, in the end, was killed by an infection that entered his brain through an unhealed crack in the skull, a crack that happened in that accident twenty-eight years earlier. I think of Sally, my best friend, and how we sat in this room soon after we met on our first day at university, and she told me that her fiancé, her cousin, serving his conscription, had been captured by the Israelis in Sinai in the war. He was never heard of again.

I think about civilians and the military and how this year and within the revolution, our army started, on 28 January, to grab and beat civilians, and to detain them and subject them to military trials. Six thousand two hundred and thirty-five young people are serving military sentences now. Another twelve hundred and twenty-five are carrying suspended sentences. The army picked up a few here and a few there at every one of the "incidents" that have punctuated our lives since February, culminating, for the moment, in the events at the Israeli embassy on 9 September and the events at Maspero on 9 October.

On 11 February it seemed that we had emerged into a clear open space and that our progress would be swift. Now, eight months later, our landscape is more ambiguous, more confused. I try to describe it, and big, dramatic clichés crowd into my head: the Forces of Darkness, the Battle against Evil. But clichés can also be true descriptions. Hosni Mubarak threatened that it was either him or chaos. Not because that was the natural order of things, but because if we chose not-him, the forces that he represented would work to create chaos. Mubarak and his family were the packaging, the casing that held the Forces of Darkness together, that utilized them, through his National Democratic Party, his security apparatus, his corrupt government, and the corrupt elite inserted into almost every leadership position in the country. Now the casing's been smashed and the Darkness is out there, unchanneled, panicked, rampant, twisting into every nook and cranny as it seeks to wrap around us again.

On 11 February, SCAF became de facto president, but it kept in place the cabinet appointed by the deposed president, and on 26 February the Military Police attacked protesters who were demanding its resignation. On this occasion the army apologized— and appointed Essam Sharaf and his cabinet—but it had taken several young people into military detention, and a path was set. Not one step or procedure that should have followed on automatically from the success of the revolution and the removal of the head of the regime was conceded without a struggle, without protests and demonstrations and sit-ins. And each one of these was punished more severely than the last.

The slow pace meant that the "remnants" of the regime had time to collect themselves, to organize. Mubarak's sons were in jail, but they still had their cash and their connections and their mobile phones. Zakareyya Azmi, Mubarak's chief of staff, lived a normal life after his boss fell, with daily access to his office for two months before he was arrested. Omar Suleiman, Mubarak's last-minute vice president and long-term head of intelligence, continues very much at large and is even being proposed by SCAF from time to time as a serious candidate for the presidency. If twenty corrupt politicians/businessmen are being tried, fifty more are still free. The decapitated regime is still strong, it's fighting for its life—and possibly growing a new head.

Its weapons have always been cash and coercion. For coercion, it used its 1.5 million–strong security apparatus—plus the estimated half million or so baltagis. The minister of the interior, Habib el-Adli, was arrested in February, but SCAF has allowed no one to examine, punish, or rehabilitate the security establishment, so the country is full of armed and disgruntled police and baltagis, short of cash and ready to be used. The regime is still rich. And the old alliance between the regime and the security establishment is still in place.

And so we, the citizens, resort to the law courts and to direct action. Citizens file legal cases to place barriers between the regime and its money: cases against individuals, against companies, against transactions. Citizens propose ways forward for employment, education, agriculture, the Dakhleyya; a few days ago a group of professionals announced their detailed blueprint for its restructuring and reform. Other citizens sue it for murder, terrorism, and torture. And the shabab periodically besiege it and spray graffiti portraits of the murdered shuhada on its walls. Meanwhile we have no effective security, and a sizable number of our police force are working with paid criminals—attempting to cause chaos and disruption.

When SCAF promised to "protect the revolution," we assumed that this meant protect it against its declared enemies: the Dakhleyya, the remnants of the old regime, and the influence of the outside forces that wished it ill; that the military would hold the state in place as we, the people, went through the process of electing a parliament and a president to whom SCAF could hand over power.

We assumed that SCAF would want a guarantee that its members would not be tried for corruption, and perhaps would want an agreement about the position of the military in the future. This could have been something to be negotiated. Quite soon, though, it became clear that SCAF's policy was to conduct a war of attrition against the revolution and the revolutionaries.

Why?

You, my reader, are better placed to answer this than I. From where we are now, we can only guess at where they think they are leading us, and our dominant guess is that SCAF wants the old regime to continue, but with some cosmetic changes, maybe completely new faces. Its members would prefer not to have to impose an overtly military dictatorship to do this. So they will let the elections for Parliament happen, but they will work—have been working—to ensure that the elections do not deliver a "revolutionary" parliament. Then they will insist that the constitution is written before we elect a president. They will remain acting president and will veto any real moves to change the system and deliver on the aims of the revolution. They will also intervene strongly in the writing of the constitution—maybe to give the military a constitutional role overseeing a civilian government.

These are only guesses.

As I write now, we are supposed to be heading for parliamentary elections on 28 November. But SCAF is talking of eighteen months before it hands over power to a civilian president, while all the political forces in the country (apart from the remnants) insist that six months is their ceiling. Meanwhile, paid advertisements by remnant MPs have appeared in the state press inviting SCAF to declare martial law.

The SCAF generals, and Field Marshal Tantawi, repeatedly inform us that they "took a decision" not to shoot us during the revolution. Yet Tantawi has testified in court that Mubarak never gave him an order to shoot the revolutionaries. We know that the military conducted a poll among the field officers very early in the revolution and learned that officers would refuse a direct order to shoot at the people. We also know that the military were completely against the Mubarak plan to insert Gamal Mubarak into the presidency.

It seems, then, that the SCAF generals discussed among themselves, of their own accord, whether to shoot us, and decided not to because they feared a mutiny in the army. In any case, we were getting rid of Gamal Mubarak. They didn't like to see Hosni Mubarak himself go down, but they've been making his fall as gentle as possible. And meanwhile they've been gradually getting their officers used to harming us.

Our story—since SCAF, with tanks in the streets, stepped forward and promised to protect our revolution—has been a story of SCAF impeding, delaying, blocking every practical aspect of the revolution, every possible step toward achieving the goals of the revolution, while paying florid lip service to "the Glorious Revolution of 25 January." It has been a story of SCAF attempting to close down the public space so hard won by the people. And it has been a story of the people taking the revolution into the workplace: strikes and unionization in factories and hospitals, strikes for elections and transparent budgets in universities—ports, banks, law courts, schools. Since there's no "government of the revolution" making a plan that includes everybody, everybody's trying to act out some aspect of the revolution in their own sphere. And whenever possible, SCAF has held up the process. Court judgments to return fraudulently sold national assets, needing presidential ratification, are left unsigned. Officials who negotiate deals with factory workers are fired. A law to impose a five-year ban on remnants running for office is blocked. And more and more and more.

And so it has been a story of escalating confrontation between the revolutionaries and SCAF. Instead of "The people! / The army! / One hand!" it's become "Down! Down with the rule of the generals!"

~~~~

The incidents that mark our progression down the route of confrontation over the past eight months can be generally grouped under the headings "internal" and "external." The "external" incidents focus on the Israeli issue. The "internal" ones focus on division; and to the Mubarak agenda of dividing Muslim from Christian, Islamist from non-Islamist, Egyptian from non-Egyptian, and rich from poor, SCAF has added civilians from the military. Even though it was the people's anger on behalf of the army that led them to protest in front of the Israeli embassy on 20 August when Israeli forces killed three border guards in Egyptian Rafah and wounded three more—all of whom were later to die of their wounds.

Protesters headed to the Israeli embassy to demand an apology, the dismissal of the ambassador, and the lowering of the flag. Essam Sharaf's government did nothing except ask the Israelis for an explanation. The Israelis refused to apologize. The Israeli embassy is on the sixteenth floor of a residential apartment block. At dawn on the twenty-first, a young house painter climbed to the sixteenth floor, took down the Israeli flag, and raised the Egyptian. The crowds celebrated with fireworks and music.

This was not the first time the shabab had demonstrated in front of the Israeli embassy.

Egypt had celebrated when Nabil el-Arabi—in his brief tenure as minister of foreign affairs—opened the Rafah border and brokered a peace between the Palestinian Authority and Hamas. But a few days later, on Nakba Day on 15 May, while people across the world marched in support of the Palestinians, the Egyptian army stopped Egyptian buses crossing into Sinai; SCAF would not allow a peaceful march to Rafah. So the march went to the Israeli embassy—where it was attacked by the Egyptian Military Police; young men were ordered to kneel on the road in front of the embassy and to repeat the chants of Tahrir and were beaten while they did so. Many young men were taken into military detention, and one, Atef Yahya Ibrahim, was shot in the head. He was twenty-two. He would remain in a coma for five months—then die.

The symbolic victory won by "Flagman" on 21 August was quickly dampened when Sharaf's government, in a brilliantly obtuse move, built a gray fortified wall—reminiscent of the Israeli apartheid wall—on University Bridge facing the entrance to the embassy block.

Friday, 9 September, was dedicated to "Realign the Revolution." After songs and speeches all day in Tahrir, the shabab marched to the symbols of the entities they wanted "realigned": the Supreme Court building, the Dakhleyya, the Radio and Television building in Maspero, and the Israeli embassy. The marches were all peaceful, and they were all to demand changes in government policy. At the embassy, they dismantled the brand-new wall. Then several young men climbed the building and brought down the new flag that had replaced the Egyptian one.

What happened next is still under investigation. But what all the stories agree on is that neither the army nor Central Security—and both were present from the start—tried to stop the group that went into the building and broke into the apartment used by the embassy for storage. Only after papers had been thrown out of the windows did the army and Central Security suddenly act. They detained twenty-six people, injured 1,049, and killed three: Mustafa Hasan, twenty-four; Ala Salem, twenty-three; and Ragab Hussein, also twenty-three. Next day they came back and detained a further ninety-two people who happened to be in the area. All the detainees are being court-martialed. In an effort to support them, twenty-one political groups have claimed responsibility for the "embassy events."

Our issues with Israel are issues of sovereignty and of running Egypt in Egyptian interests—both prime movers of the revolution. Until we have a government that we trust with our sovereignty and our interests, the shabab will be again and again put in the position of protecting them. And this will be represented to the world as "chaos" and "irresponsibility." And it will be presented to the army as the shabab being careless of them, cavalier in pushing them into a new war. And a new wedge will be driven between the people and the army.

Consolidating this dangerous division, a new alliance is forming. The military and security establishments, long played against each other by Hosni Mubarak, are coming together. SCAF has refused any restructuring of the Dakhleyya; it declared the disbanding of the Central Security Forces, which then reappeared as the "Anti-Riot Police," and it renamed the State Security Service the "National Security Service." This alliance also embraces state media; the building in Maspero was always protected by the Presidential Guard, and it uses and is used by the remnants—whom SCAF has refused point-blank to remove from any field of public life.

And the tired tactics of the Mubarak era are very much in play: the attempts to sow division, to make people afraid of each other, of foreigners, of "outside forces," of "infiltrators"; the harping on the need for "stability," the need to not frighten investors, to not "sully" Egypt's image abroad, the need to respect the state and its instruments.

Security's tactics are familiar to us: find a fault line and wrench, spread rumors, use cash, insert agents provocateurs—and then attack. And we've been finding their fingerprints everywhere in the military's dealings with the revolutionaries. Looking through our diaries, we agree that the tactical marriage of police and army began with the events of Abbaseyya on 23 July and consolidated in the period till the breakup of the Tahrir sit-in on 1 August.

23 JULY 2011

"This is the hospital where you were born," my mother would say whenever we drove past it. And I'd be mildly annoyed. "I know. You've been telling me since I was born." As I grew older, I made a joke of it. Sometimes I'd get in first, "Mama, Mama, what's this building?" She'd peer over her glasses, then frown at me: "It's the hospital where you were born. And you're being silly." My mother didn't much like being teased. Except by her grandchildren. Well, now that she's no longer here to say it, I think it. Always. At this junction. Always, always, always. This is the hospital where I was born. Soon I might start saying it to my children. Maybe I already do. Now I say it to Sherif Boraie, the friend with whom I'm driving in pursuit of the march: "This is the hospital where I was born."

The march left Tahrir at five, aiming to go through the Abbaseyya neighborhood to the Ministry of Defense on the airport road. There we would hand in our list of demands. Five months after our glorious, wonderful, successful revolution, we continue to protest and hand in demands—now to the Supreme Council of the Armed Forces, our acting president. SCAF members have been dragging their feet on every issue on which we need to move quickly: a schedule for elections, cleaning up state radio and television, reforming the Dakhleyya. And they've been arresting young people on a variety of charges and summarily trying them in front of military courts. There has been a sit-in in Tahrir since the eighth. The demands are a clear job description for SCAF and a detailed schedule for elections to Parliament and the presidency: we want the police officers accused of murder and intimidation by the families of the shuhada arrested; and we want the court-martialing of civilians to stop. Today we're taking these demands to SCAF.

And we have the now-standard paragraph demanding that SCAF and the cabinet time-table a start on establishing social justice programs such as minimum and maximum wages, reexamining the budget, and developing employment policies and pensions and national insurance systems. We know they won't do this; this will be the work of our elected government, but we have to keep the demands on the table. And we have to make sure we get to elect a government.

A statement on Thursday counted the revolution's recent gains: the cabinet reshuffle, the decision to hold the Mubarak trial openly, and the decision to allocate courts to the trials of regime bosses and people accused of murdering the young revolutionaries. All were wrenched from SCAF and the cabinet through escalated protests and sit-ins.

Today's march was planned to coincide with the anniversary of the revolution of 1952, to remind SCAF of the celebratory phrase, the mantra everyone was repeating in February: "In 1952 the army revolted and the people supported the revolution. In 2011 the people revolted and the army protected the revolution."

The march left Tahrir at five, but Sherif said he was driving in order to carry water and biscuits and stuff. Sherif is a publisher of exquisite books. Since the revolution began, he's been the "father" of a core group of activists, looking out for them, supporting them, and often underwriting their projects. I ride with him, and we zigzag through Downtown and arrive at the Gala2 junction, where we see our friends marching past us as we sit in the traffic jam. And facing me, across the march, is the Gala2 Hospital. It's the hospital where I was born.

He was twenty-six and she was twenty-three, and I was their first child. They were living in Shubra and they were poor, because even though they had both graduated with distinction, they couldn't get proper jobs—and certainly not in their university, Cairo University, which was what they wanted more than anything. Except to be together. The university was not allowed to appoint my father because when he was nineteen, he'd joined a Communist group and been jailed for a year. My mother had graduated from the English department, and you couldn't be appointed to the English department unless you were English. Or at least British. So he had a clerical job in Fisheries, and she taught at primary school. They were poor also because both their families had objected to the marriage, and even though the families had come round and were eager to help the young couple, the young couple would have none of it and insisted on living on their own resources. So they rented a flat in Shubra at the very very end of civilization, and my father worked on his M.A. (*Al-usus al-nafseyya l-el-ibda3 al-fanni*—Psychological Factors in Artistic Creativity— which became a classic) and my mother on her stories (which sit, unfinished, in a cupboard in my living room), and they agreed they couldn't manage kids yet so they tried to abort me, but I wouldn't let go; I hung in there till we were over the first three months and my mother surrendered and knew she had to have me.

She had me on the trolley in the reception courtyard of the Gala2 Hospital fourteen months after they married. The doctor who admitted her looked and said, "You have a long way to go," and she said, "No, the baby's coming." And out I came, in this hospital, at the midpoint between my mother's family home in Ataba and the flat in Zamalek that we were to move into seven years later—the flat where I'm writing now.

Depending on the point my mother was making, this was a story about how I was always in a hurry, or it was a story about how she always got things done in record time. She had me in an hour, and she had my sister in the middle of the Ph.D. that she finished in two and a half years. She wrote the last chapters pregnant with my brother, my sister levering herself up against her legs to toddle off into trouble. But that was in London and in another story.

Here, in the Cairo story, the 1952 revolution happened, and the two young graduates were appointed to Cairo University, traveled abroad to study further, and returned to set up the main geographical axis of my Cairo life: Zamalek/Ataba, Ataba/Zamalek. A straight line across Abu el-Ela Bridge, through Boulac, past the wonderful ruins of the Khedivial Stables with the carved horses' heads, past the hospital where I was born, past the magnificent High Court, through Fouad Street with Downtown unfurling on both sides of it, past Midan el-Opera, and past the National Theater and the Ruwei3i, and into the passage under my grandfather's house—which is where my brother was born. Not in the passage—in the house, with Toufi looking after my sister and Khalu playing distractingly noisy games with me on the stairs till the doctor left and I went inside and found my mother in her pink chenille dressing gown with baby Ala in her arms. "Each one of you was unwanted," she would tell us, "till the moment I held you in my arms—and then each one could not have been more beloved."

And now the traffic has moved, and we're driving through Ramses Street and past the Coptic Hospital until we're right behind the three thousand or so people in the march; behind a boy in a lime-green T-shirt with a Dolce & Gabbana logo. I catch a glimpse of Mona, one hand holding a phone to her ear, the other distributing leaflets: "No to Military Trials for Civilians." Marches that went out in Alexandria and Suez on Thursday were fired on. There were arguments throughout yesterday and today about whether this march should go ahead—but the general feeling among the shabab was that we have to keep up the pressure on SCAF. So even those of us unsure about this particular march are here to support and to witness. In the street, we are back to the instigator chants: "Why why why so quiet? All we want is your rights." Again there are the people on the balconies, watching us, but now mostly impassive. The street tries to carry on with its life.

After the Cathedral and by Ein Shams University Hospital, we park. We load bags with water bottles and join the march through Abbaseyya. We walk. Maybe four hundred meters or so, and suddenly we concertina into the people ahead of us, and the cry is coming from the front: "El-geish el-geish"—the army has closed off the road. We're at a dead end. We all press forward anyway to see the army. At the bottom of the access road to the airport overpass, the road is blocked off with thick coils of barbed wire, and behind the wire there are three lines of Military Police, each man cradling a gun. Behind the men there are the tanks. To our right there are people's houses and one narrow lane passing between them; to our left, the iron railings of al-Fat7 Mosque, then the grounds of the University Hospital—at the other end of which we'd parked. The mosque has closed its gates, and a line of soldiers is deployed inside its railings. An imam is holding on to the gate and remonstrating ferociously with the soldiers. People say he's the imam of the mosque and has somehow been locked out. We've come to a stop but there's that seething milling about when a crowd can't get to where it wants to get. The shabab at the front are nose to nose with the soldiers across the barbed wire. It's a standoff, and we don't know what to do. I think a lot of the shabab are actually willing, now, to take on the army. But we won't let them. We chant: "The army's ours / The council's not."

This morning SCAF issued Statement Number 69. It accused one of the most active movements of the shabab, the 6 April Movement,[1] of "special agendas" and of trying to make trouble between the people and the army. SCAF denied that the military used violence in Suez or any other city and urged "The People" to confront this "suspicious plot to destabilize Egypt . . . with all strength." And General Hasan al-Ruweini, the commander of the Central District, i.e., Cairo, who had just boasted that he'd started several rumors in Tahrir during the eighteen days, has warned on TV that "the people from Tahrir will be coming into Abbaseyya from three directions armed with weapons and Molotov cocktails." So the citizens of Abbaseyya are waiting for us, and they're expecting trouble, and because the army has closed the road and we can't move forward, they fear that we will start a sit-in on their doorstep. They stand in windows and on balconies watching us. We stand in the streets and chant: "Friends and neighbors / Abbaseyya / Our protest is selmeyya." But the feeling around us is not positive.

The first stones come from a group of men who've emerged from beside the army line. Then they come from balconies and roofs. The men on the roofs are in string vests. We can't really look up because the stones are flying at us. After the first shock, our young men start to pick up stones and hurl them back. At first some of us rush up and disarm them. "Selmeyya! Selmeyya!" we shout again and again—peaceful, peaceful. But very soon, as the rain of stones gets thicker, and as the stones start to come from the side street as well, it isn't possible to stop the shabab. A mother holds on to her son, who's trying to break free and run to the front lines. He's about ten or eleven. Quickly we're four adults holding him back: *Stay here and be a man. Protect your mother!* A car on the side street bursts into flames. People retreat from their balconies and close their shutters.

I watch our shabab surge toward the mouth of the side street. Leaders try to stop them: defending our position on the main road is one thing, but pursuing people into a neighborhood is another. The buildings are now completely shuttered. All the fighting is in the side street, and it rages on. The army stands behind its barbed wire, cradling its guns and watching. Two young men run out of the side street carrying a third with blood on his face. They run past me, away from the army lines, about thirty meters along, and lay the boy down by the side of the road. Almost immediately a young woman bends over him: a doctor.

A stone lands by my feet. I pick it up. It's not a stone but a chunk of thick ceramic tile. When I hold it in my hand, feel its weight, its jagged edge, I suddenly feel what its impact would have been on my head. I suddenly, for the first time, feel vulnerable, recognize that I'm standing in the middle of the road with tiles and stones hurtling round me. I start to move, but that seems worse, like I'll actually run into one of them. I stop. I'm uncertain.

Then I feel two hands take hold of me; one presses my head down, and the other holds my arm above the elbow. A familiar rasping voice I'd heard often in the Midan says, "Keep your head down, *ya doktora*. Bend." His hands propel me forward, and I feel my speed double with the energy of the friend who's pushing me to safety. I think, This is like planes refueling in midair. I stay under the tree where he's put me and watch the street. Sometimes I see Omar. Sometimes I see Alaa or Mona or Sherif or other friends. Laila is at the front near the army, where a line of young men stand glaring at the soldiers, taunting them. Stones land and skitter on the asphalt. Young men run backward and forward carrying other young men and sometimes women. Sometimes a stone catches one of the young men, and he staggers as he carries his wounded comrade to the makeshift emergency clinic at the side of the road. There are two doctors there now and a crowd around them, fanning the boys who lie on the ground, pouring water over them, trying to call in ambulances and medical supplies over the phone.

I sit on the curb under the tree. I don't know what this is about. SCAF is officially meant to be preserving order and running the country—never mind protecting the revolution—so what's its problem with receiving a set of demands? What's the worst thing we could have done? Chant in front of the Ministry of Defense. Why the baltagis and the stones? Since when does the army use baltagis and stones? This is a disaster; people are getting hurt. And we're losing neighborhood support. I grab Alaa for a second as he passes. He says we put out the car fire. They're telling us it's the army on the roofs, not the locals.

The mosque has opened its gates, and the imam has gone inside. Sherif and other people come to my curb. There's talk of retreat, of pulling the shabab back from the side street and marching together back to Tahrir. Then people come running up from the rear: we're surrounded; there are Central Security Forces, and they're blocking the road we came from. We all run down to look. Central Security is meant to have been disbanded, but here they are: the black-uniformed phalanxes, the helmets, the visors, the shields. And behind them the muscled toughs in civilian clothes. I watch the first Molotov cocktail crash out from behind their lines.

Word of the Central Security trap behind us has reached the shabab facing the army. Their chants rise to a roar, and they grab the barbed wire and start shaking it. The soldiers raise their guns, and I run up so close that I can see the anger in their eyes—anger and threat. I'm struck with fear for the young men. I think the soldiers would like to shoot them. Then my sister steps forward out of nowhere and with her two older women, one with a hijab and one without. They shove several young men out of the way, and they're standing in front of the soldiers with their arms spread wide. "Shoot us then," they say to the soldiers. "Shoot the women. Shoot the mothers of Egypt. Shoot your mothers."

The shabab are running out of the side street and racing down the road to face up to Central Security. It's gone dark. Stones, stones and Molotovs, and then the tear gas explodes in the middle of the road. Alaa runs past me, and I grab hold of him again. I daren't speak to Omar, but I can speak to my nephew: "*Habibi*, this is about nothing. Nothing. What's to win?" Sherif is checking a way through the hospital grounds. We have to leave. We can't leave. But this isn't Tahrir; this is about nothing. "I know," he says. "But we can't leave while one person stays. It's okay. We're trying to collect people." I don't believe him. I believe that it's become a point of principle: if Central Security or the baltagis attack the shabab, the shabab have to win. They can't afford to lose a battle. But what if someone dies? What about the boys lying in the road? What if one of them dies?

Sherif says stones are being pitched from inside the hospital grounds; the baltagis are in there. The mosque's loudspeaker bursts into life. The imam is pleading for peace. He demands that the army protect the shabab from Central Security and the baltagis, that they open a path for people to leave. There's an ambulance now in the middle of the road. One half of a young man is hanging out of it, and several young men are strewn on the ground by the wheels; their comrades lean over them, fan them, stuff clothes under their heads. The imam calls for prayers, and miraculously all is quiet for the duration of evening prayers. Then the gas comes again. The imam pleads angrily through the loudspeaker with the army: "Open a path. Open a path for the shabab. Let them pass in safety. . . ."

It's dark, and the air is smoke and gas. From the army side, there's silence. From the Central Security side, there's a constant roar and flames and the pop of gas canisters. From the mosque, the exhortations continue. I'm sitting on the ground by the ambulance. My scarf is over my nose and mouth, and I'm pulling in shallow burning breaths. I don't know where anyone is. I can no longer open my eyes.

Omar has his arm round my shoulders and is rushing me through the alley that's been opened by the mosque. Inside the circle of his arm, I run with my eyes closed. What breath I have I use to curse. He conserves his.

9:00 P.M.

Back at the sit-in at Tahrir, we're subdued and angry.

One of our friends is missing. His brother says he was taken by baltagis. Many people have been injured. Two are critical. One of them, Muhammad Muhsin Mustafa, a twenty-three-year-old activist from Aswan, will die of his injuries on 3 August.

Everyone swears the sit-in will continue. Everyone is coughing and exhausted. We know now that the Central Security Forces are back and that the army is working with them and with the baltagis. On the news, they're saying we went to Abbaseyya armed with Molotovs and attacked the army. The *10pm Show* calls me, and down the phone I give my account of what happened.

11:00 P.M.

At home I find a mountain of laundry on the kitchen floor. Shukri, who used to be my mother's driver and right hand and is now Sohair's, has brought down all the linen and towels and cushion covers from my mother's summer house on the coast. They need laundering. He's had the house sprayed against flying insects and checked the electricity and plumbing. Normally we do all this in late May and get the house ready for use. My mother used to go up, and we'd all come and go till September. The laundry is in the middle of my floor. I put the first load into the machine. I don't know if any of us will go up at all this summer.

SUNDAY, 24 JULY

Rabab el-Mahdi phones with an initiative to pull together all the "revolutionary political forces" to cooperate for the protests called for Friday the twenty-ninth; it's the only way we can pressure SCAF. Rabab is a young academic and activist and special in that she's liked and trusted by the Islamists despite not being one herself. Friday will be to ensure we all speak with one voice, she says. *And about time, too,* I think. The leaders of the political forces are like cells gone mad; they swim around frantically, they divide, they coalesce with other cells, then divide again; they accuse each other of not being cells at all.

You could say that this is normal, healthy: people are working out what they believe in and stand for—and they're not used to working together politically because anyone who tried to work together politically over the last sixty years was destroyed. So the revolutionary forces are really doing what they're meant to do, and our society is engaged in a process that will take time.

But we don't have time. Because the remnants of the old regime are gathering strength.

So what do we want? We want to pressure SCAF for a time-table for the elections. And we want everybody to agree that the elections should be held soon, and for no one to give SCAF any excuses to delay them, and we want measures put in place to ensure that they're free and fair. Meanwhile we want to safeguard our world till the elections and to try to move on some procedures that would at least indicate that we're heading in the general direction of the revolution's goals. We could, for example, cut part of the fuel subsidy to the cement industry, bring down their profits to 50 percent, and use the seven billion annual saving to institute a 700-pounds-a-month minimum wage. I'm ashamed even to write down "700" when we know the real minimum wage should be 1,436 pounds a month. But there we are: this is a revolution that's chosen to work peaceably and legally—and it's paying a price for peace and legality.

But everyone absolutely has to speak with one voice. Rabab says she has the leaders from the Ikhwan, the Salafis, and the Liberals. We have the Left and the Progressives. Everyone has agreed that Ibrahim al-Moallem of Shorouk should host it—because he has a lot of power and has maintained the same friendly distance from every faction. And that I should moderate—because I've no power at all and have no relationship with any faction.

I make lots of phone calls for this initiative. Our great problem, our maximum vulnerability, is the rooted, knotty, gnarled suspicion between the Liberal and the Islamist political currents.[2] The Liberals will remind you that the Ikhwan had declared in January that they would not join the revolution, that the Salafis held that rising against a ruler was a sin and they would live pure lives without touching politics. But that was the leadership. The shabab had all come together in Tahrir. Through the eighteen days, Liberals, Progressives, Salafis, Ikhwan, Leftists, Gama3at, and those with no affiliation, just the desire for a better, cleaner, happier life, had rebelled together, broken bread together, talked to each other, slept in the same place, defended the Midan, and finally died together—and they had discovered the vastness of the common ground they shared and the myriad meeting points between them and how much work they needed—and wanted—to do together. Many had begun to change, and to note and welcome the changes in themselves and others as they found this ground. But Mubarak fell, and we all went home and the old leaders all started pulling their shabab back into line. Some couldn't go back and broke away—became, as it were, homeless in Tahrir. Some tried to form new groups, and some tried to form coalitions between groups, and some stood alone and spoke truth. Everyone was madly busy. No one had control of anything.

But I make the many phone calls anyway, and we set up the meeting for Tuesday.

And I manage to catch my younger son, Ismail, at home in London, for a few minutes on Skype and to make more inroads on the washing mountain before I fall asleep on the sofa, waking only when Omar comes home from Tahrir while the mosque is calling for dawn prayers. I stumble to bed and sleep till late. I think this is the aftermath of yesterday's events.

MONDAY, 25 JULY

Monday morning at the Gezira Club with my father and my sister, as usual. Mr. Muhammad Adel, one of my father's caregivers, has his right index finger in a big bandage. He is very ambitious and enterprising. His latest venture is a butcher shop. He put his finger in the mincer, and it cut off the tip.

My father is eighty-six. He still runs his research projects, his committees and his clinic, and teaches once a week. He does this through having lots of support and being extremely organized. For the last decade, he's also been writing monthly articles with titles like "Psychological Health in the Absence of Democracy." The revolution has straightened his back and pumped up his voice. He is advising the activists of his college about the upcoming university elections. I think he is—in an out-of-the-self kind of way— living the happiest days of his life.

When he leaves, Laila and I confer about the coalition meeting tomorrow.

3:00 P.M.

Forty-seven Ramses Street, to give a witness statement to TV channels about the events of Abbaseyya.

I meet the mother of military detainee Ahmad Gabir Mahmoud (detained and tried 3 February, sentenced 9 February, moved to el-Wadi el-Gedeed prison 17 February). He was picked up from Hamad Mosque in Faisal Street, not in Tahrir. Accused of throwing Molotov cocktails and breaking curfew. Sentenced to five years. He is nineteen years old. His friend Muhammad Amin Gamal: same case, same treatment. They are both at secondary school, agriculture. "They create criminal records for the shabab," his mother says. "They all had clean records before this. Now each one has a criminal record. Even sixteen-year-olds. Why are they doing this to us? I'm demanding justice for my son. We walked peaceably all the way from Tahrir to Abbaseyya to ask for justice. We broke nothing, we weren't disorderly. All I want is justice for my son."

There are at least eight thousand mothers like her—and that's not counting the mothers of the martyrs, the shuhada. . . .

The young woman speaking before I do is a tour guide who'd been detained in an armored personnel carrier. The military found

twelve dollars on her and accused her of being a foreign agent.
They ripped off her hijab and beat and tasered her inside the truck
and eventually said they would "give her another chance" and let
her go. She speaks very clearly and confidently. I cannot believe we
are back to this.

All afternoon, phone calls about the meeting tomorrow.

8:30 P.M.

Meeting in Simmonds Café with Mr. Hasan Ali, Abu Muhab,
the father of the shaheed, the martyr, Muhab Ali.[3] He has his
daughter, Rahma, with him. She sits silently by her father, giving
me small, encouraging smiles when I look at her. They are the
saddest smiles I have ever seen. Her brother was her best friend,
two years older than her. She's just sat her school finals. She hasn't
done very well. Yes, we all agree it would be best for both the
revolution and the families of the shuhada if the Tahrir sit-in is
suspended—not called off, just suspended. Everybody's tired and
the weather's so hot and there's no progress and ordinary people
are getting annoyed at the closure of the Midan to traffic. The
calls to escalate the sit-in are worrying. Decisions are not taken
collectively; every group has leaders, but there's no joint leadership. But we need a strategy to suspend. The families won't leave
with nothing. They're being harassed, and they want the men, the
officers, harassing them, the officers who killed their children, put
away.

Abu Muhab and his son were together in Tahrir. They left
when the army went into the streets because, he said, he'd lived
through the bread riots in January '77 and didn't want his son
exposed to the military. They went home, and Muhab couldn't
find his memory stick, so he took his hard drive to go to a friend
and download material. He'd changed into joggers and flip-flops

and just popped out to his friend's. There was a small local protest on the traffic island at the top of the road and he joined it, and there they shot him twice in the neck and he died.

Abu Muhab used to represent a pharmaceutical company. Since 28 January, he has dedicated himself to Muhab and the revolution. He says he was responsible for Muhab's politicization. I say we bring up our kids to do what's right. Beyond that I'm silent. I cannot—don't want to—imagine losing a son. He says, "God has honored Muhab with martyrdom and honored me with being his father. He died for the revolution, and I will live for the revolution."

Khaled Abd el-Hameed joins us. He's getting married in a week—to a young Palestinian woman named Tahrir! He too wants to suspend the sit-in, but he's worried about suspending on a promise. "At least let's try to get two concessions on paper," he says. We look at yesterday's demands. Abu Muhab gives me the names and stations of the officers accused by the families: in Marg, Embaba, Alexandria, and Matareyya. Abu Muhab says his greatest sorrow is not for his son, and not for all the martyrs; they live with God and prosper. His sorrow is for what's to come. He says ninety families have bought arms, and if they're not given satisfaction soon, they will use them. "They need something," he says. He says, "I don't know who killed my son, but some of them know who killed their children. And all of us know who's still terrorizing us and pressuring us; their names are right here. Arrest these officers. Put them away for their own safety pending trial."

I go home and hang out some more washing. More phone calls. Alaa is on ONTV. Waleed Tahtawi phones in to the program. He's the brother of Ibrahim Tahtawi, who was killed on the twenty-eighth. And of Hoda Tahtawi, who was shot on the twenty-eighth and died yesterday. He says he wants to understand why this is happening. Why his brother and sister had to die. How the person who killed them lives with himself. What he feels when he looks at his mother knowing what he's done to other people's mothers.

He says he has received offers of money and death threats to sign that his brother died of heart failure. He says he's had to sleep away from home for the last ten days because of the threats. He's being pressured not to submit his sister's body for an autopsy. It's difficult enough to take the decision to have Hoda's body cut up—but to be threatened and offered bribes to go back on the decision is too cruel. The worst of it, he says, is not what happened to us or what happened to the other families—the worst is what's to come.

Nahla Hetta calls me. Physician, activist, entrepreneur, she's a friend of Amr Helmy, the new minister of health, whom Prime Minister Essam Sharaf has delegated to deal with the revolutionaries and the families. Amr Helmy is a "people's choice." She's just met with him and given him the list of demands. He's going to try and push for them over a cabinet meeting scheduled for tomorrow and the day after. Then he'll meet her on Wednesday at five. She wants to take someone sensible from the shabab in Tahrir who will listen to what Helmy brings back from the meeting and whom we trust to evaluate his results and tell him what more is needed. "I am so tired," she says. "What must we do?"

TUESDAY, 26 JULY

Eleven a.m. meeting hosted by Ibrahim al-Moallem at Shorouk. We got everyone round a table, and we've hammered out a deal to issue a statement on the aims and demands of the revolution. There will be joint organization of Tahrir on Friday. The six officers whom the shuhada's families want arrested will be outed in the Midan. No statement will be made now on the sit-in, but they'll aim to suspend it—or at least open the Midan to traffic—from Saturday. The announcement will be made by the shuhada's families.

I wonder how many other groups are meeting like this. Trying to get people together, to push for unity. Tens. Hundreds maybe.

6:00 P.M.

We have a draft of the statement, but our work is foundering on the phrase *al-Irada al-Sha3beyya*, "the will of the people." The Liberals are adamant that the phrase has been co-opted by the Islamists, and they won't gather under it. The Ikhwan insist on it. The arguments get more and more detailed; they're to do with past experience and with what each group suspects of the other's intentions. The Liberals will not sign.

The committee coordinating on the ground seems happy working together despite the problems.

Where is all this tiredness coming from? Beyond seven o'clock, I drag myself around like a wounded creature.

WEDNESDAY, 27 JULY

Nahla calls to tell me she's met Amr Helmy with a delegation of families of the shuhada and the injured.

A Liberal friend phones and spends an hour telling me how the Islamists will double-cross us.

Abu Muhab calls and asks me to apologize to Nahla for the behavior of the families in the meeting with the new minister. I call Nahla, and she says they were concerned and upset but they'd behaved just fine. (In September, Mona will tweet about how the mother of a recently detained young man called her back to apologize if she'd been somewhat abrupt.)

Amal comes round with her tiny little baby, Amina. We put my mother's quilt on the living room floor and play with Amina. My brother comes round and joins us on the floor.

I finish the last lot of laundry for the coast and send it off to be ironed.

THURSDAY, 28 JULY

Wake up to a group e-mail from Laila repeating her testimony about Amr el-Beheiri, the young protester who was taken by the military in the small hours of 26 February minutes after she'd already saved him from them once. A military tribunal convicted him of possessing arms and sentenced him to five years.

Write and file my column. Use half of it for Laila's statement. Stay sitting at my mother's desk. I have cleared one drawer, the top left one. I cheated, because I just moved what was in it to the other drawers without looking. Now I reach and open another drawer, and there, lying on top of everything, is an old *London Review of Books* with two of Ian's poems. Two of my late husband, Ian Hamilton's, poems. I close the drawer.

I make, and receive, many phone calls about tomorrow. Everyone says it's all under control. It's looking good. We'll all be out there and prove we can work together, just like in the eighteen days.

6:00 P.M.

Sohair drops by for tea.

The ironing man delivers the linen.

Shukri is driving Sohair to Alexandria tomorrow so he'll go to the coast and drop it off.

9:30 P.M.

Cannot carry on. Shower and get ready for bed.

10:00 P.M.

I can't go to bed without checking on the Midan.

10:30 P.M.

The shabab guarding the entrance are three lines deep. They are courteous and welcoming as ever as they check my ID, my bag. Women pat me down.

Omar is rigging up his screen as he's been doing at ten o'clock every night since the sit-in began. He has three street-kid helpers, and a tea man has set up his stall near the screen. He and Khalid Abdalla, Tamer Said, and Ziyad Hawwas (part of the Mosireen[4] Collective) have established "Tahrir Cinema"[5] together with Lara Baladi. They've hand-built the large screen and borrowed equipment from home and family. Every night they show footage, clips, film from the revolution. From the first night, it became clear that the material was new to a lot of people: Cairenes had not seen the films from the provinces; people from other cities visiting Tahrir had never seen footage of the action to take the Midan, or the vast protests sweeping into the center from every part of the city. Within hours the cinema became an exchange point for material that volunteers quickly reproduced. Soon they were inviting guest curators to show their films or footage. A young Libyan came and showed a film. Tahrir Cinema was performing the function that the Egyptian state media had been too cowardly or too complicit to perform—even after 11 February. The cinema also helped stage TweetNadwa—the first nonvirtual meetings of the Egyptian Twitter community.[6]

Now the big handmade screen is up, and people are starting to gather and sit on the mats. I go for a walk and to check things out.

And I find something is different. We've always had posters of the shuhada. Now there are also images of "The Hated." I stand and stare at posters of the Mubarak family, of their associates who became symbols of corruption, of the artists who stood against the revolution in its early days. And I think how the delay, the unwillingness of SCAF, the ineffectualness of the older leadership, the failure of the shabab to come forward as one coherent unit—are all conspiring to push the spirit of Tahrir away from the miraculous and into the mundane. But the tents are all there, in the central garden with the absent plinth in the middle of the Midan, each tent bravely displaying its banner and its exhausted revolutionaries. Even at this hour, the weather is clammy and hot. People everywhere pick up conversations, mostly about what they think might happen tomorrow. I keep talking about unity and agreement and how all the "patriotic forces" have agreed to work together. Any tentative mention of suspending the sit-in or moving the tents to the side is referred immediately to the shuhada families; Tahrir has centered itself on the murdered and the wounded.

Mosireen's screen comes alive with the battle for Qasr el-Nil, the battle for Mansourah, and some new footage from Suez. Then we see footage from Saturday, from Abbaseyya. A young man in the audience tells how he went back next day, and people told him the men on the roofs had been soldiers who'd taken off their uniforms, and that baltagis and stones had been bused in from the Wayli district close by. Hundreds of people are watching; they sit on the ground, they stand in a great semicircle. An activist from Qena says people there have to see this material. Someone from Beheira says they need to see it, too. State media are telling people the revolution's succeeded and everything is fine and on course and needs to be left to the authorities. They're telling them that anyone still in Tahrir, anyone who hasn't quieted down and gone back to their pre-January lives, is a traitor or a baltagi or misled and will cause the downfall of the country. They're brainwashing people, they say, and people have grown tired and want to believe them. So the young cinemateers burn CDs on the spot and distribute them to whoever asks.

And as I write this, it occurs to me that the shabab, Omar and Tamer and Khalid, should have asked for donations, just one pound, whatever anyone could afford. The suspicion that there is "funding" for this revolution is taking hold. As the regime was pushing the lie in January and February, so SCAF and the state media are pushing it now. We must be careful of looking as though we think ten pounds is nothing.

I sit on the curb with my sister and Ahmad Seif watching the films. Ever since Omar and his friends set up this screen, I get a hint of that pleasant summer cinema feeling when I come to Tahrir at night. One day, when the revolution is safe, they can start showing the big classics. Revolutionary still, but structured, and of a satisfying length. *The Battle of Algiers*, perhaps, and *Z*, and *el-Ard*. For tonight we watch the footage, and we also watch coaches arrive from the provinces. Each coach delivers thirty or forty men, mostly in shortened white thobs and white skullcaps, mostly with beards and no mustaches. Salafis. They walk in orderly lines, find sheltered spots on the peripheries of the Midan, and lie down and sleep.

FRIDAY, 29 JULY, MORNING

Twitter is ablaze with news of Islamist banners going up, then being taken down. And then with news of Salafi phalanxes hitting the Midan.

Rabab calls and says Salafist banners went up, but the Ikhwan persuaded them to take them down. The joint organization is working.

Rabab calls again and says I must not go into the Midan on my own; the Ikhwan say they can no longer control the banners or the slogans. "Don't go in," she warns, "you may never come out. Come to Beano's by the American University—we're all there."

A friend phones and says that the Salafis have been going round the villages in tok-toks telling people an important thing is happening in Tahrir, and they're busing them in. ("Three pounds a ticket," I hear next day, "from any part of Egypt to Tahrir.") Whenever anyone describes people as "going around in tok-toks," I suspect them—perhaps unfairly—of classism, because tok-toks are the transport of the poor and the provincial.

I arrive in the area as Friday prayers are ending. I catch the Prayers for the Absent. They feel different. I can't quite put my finger on it, but it all feels more down to earth and practical. None of the emotion I'm used to on the Tahrir Fridays.

I enter the Midan from Muhammad Mahmoud Street, passing Beano's but electing to throw myself into the Midan and see what happens. I do not need protection to be in Tahrir.

Well, the crowding is like nothing I've ever been through before. In the fullest days of the Midan, when a woman needed to move through the crowd, there were always men who miraculously formed a human cordon that created a passage for her. Or there were lines of people on the move, and you took your place among them. Here it's like some terrible crush at a bus stop. A heaving and surging without getting anywhere. People behind trying to push past you. Men, it's true, try not to push you and try not to touch you, but it's hopeless. I am hemmed in with the crowd behind the platform on which Sheikh Safwat Hegazi is speaking. He stands on the massive stage with his mouth to a dozen microphones, and one minute he's shouting, "Muslim / Christian / One Hand," and the next minute he's shouting, "Lift your head up high / You're a Muslim."

The crowd surges this way and that, trying to move from behind the platform. Street traders who've pulled up their stands for prayer time are pushing them out again—against the mass of people, penning us against the platform. Men on the stage throw bottles of water into the crowd, but throw them so high and so far that I'm sure you'd be hurt if you were hit by one. A bottle just misses my head, and I cry out. Sheikh Safwat is screaming into the microphones; he praises the army and SCAF. I remember reading somewhere that in these crowd situations you should stop trying to walk; just make sure you don't sink and get trampled. Allow yourself to be carried by the crowd. I try. I had thrown a scarf over my head during prayers, and now it's been dragged off and is throttling me, and I can't raise my arms to loosen it from my neck or drag it back on to my head.

Sheikh Safwat is yelling in great triumph that *iftar* on 5 Ramadan, next Friday, will be in the Midan: "We shall break our fast in Tahrir! We shall pray the Tarawee7 in Tahrir!" He is practically sobbing with emotion: "Then they'll know who we are!" I don't understand what enemy territory he's capturing. People have always broken fast in Tahrir. Tarawee7 have always been prayed in Tahrir. Omar Makram Mosque, in the heart of Tahrir, is the funeral mosque of choice for Cairo. It's not like he's taking the believers to Jerusalem. To be fair, the crowd is not responding to his decibels with corresponding enthusiasm. And there, I've got it, the difference that's been eluding me between this Friday and all the others: it's as though these hundreds of thousands in Tahrir today are—kind of—tourists. I don't feel an energy coming from them, a wish to make something happen. Their purpose is to be here, and here they are. I feel their bodies pushing against me but not their will. But I see the Saudi flag flying in Midan el-Tahrir.

The knot of the crowd that I am in gets beyond the stage, and

I shove and shoulder and elbow my way out of the crowd and out of the Midan and into the mouth of Tahrir Street. It's still massively crowded, but there's room to walk of your own volition. Groups of men and families wander along the street. Many, many of the men are in the white thob and the white skullcap and the beard-but-no-moustache. I walk toward Midan Bab el-Louq. For the first time ever, I walk down this street and forget to even think about drinking a glass of carob juice at the shop on the corner. We used to come specially. Park and honk, and the guy would come out with the big glasses of light red-black liquid on a tray. Now I walk past the entrance to his shop and the street of the Mosque of the Servants of the Compassionate in a semidaze. Groups of people, mostly men, are drifting along the street, looking around like they've never been here before. I remind myself that this is their capital as well as mine.

My back hurts. I find a raised shop doorway and sit down. I might as well be in an alien city. Groups are making themselves comfortable on the pavements. They spread newspapers on the ground and serve food on them out of plastic bags. What conversations I hear are not political at all: he said, she said, money, family, detailed, personal . . . I lean against the shop window and wonder if somebody will ask me to leave.

My younger son rescues me; Ismail phones me from London and says, "Where are you exactly? What's it like?"

"It's their country, too," I say. I'm saved. I get up and dust myself down and describe it all to him as I walk away.

I walk to Sherif's place. He makes me tea, and we sit silently in his air-conditioned study staring out at Midan Abdeen.

2:00 P.M.

Nahla Hetta calls. Can I meet her in Amr Helmy's office now?

I walk up to the Ministry of Health. Helmy says there's been a decision that the Midan must be opened; the sit-in has to end.

Nahla and I tell him the shabab want to suspend, but they won't abandon the shuhada's families. The families are exhausted, but they say they're still being pressured and threatened to make them change their testimonies and drop their cases.

He says he's allocated Agouza Hospital to receive the injured, and he will put a wing there at the disposal of the families; if they suspend the sit-in, they can stay there. We say they really need to see some officers taken off the streets. We have their names.

He says this is serious: SCAF is determined to clear the Midan.

He also says he's looking for a young, revolutionary doctor to be in charge of the injured and the families at Agouza. I put him in touch with Hoda Yousri, the young doctor I'd met in Tahrir the night Mubarak didn't leave.

3:00 P.M.

Nahla's car smells of mangoes. It's just brought back a crop from their farm. Which reminds me that I have to go and collect our fruit as well, from my mother's little orchard, and check on the repairs to the roof. I should really go before Ramadan starts.

We sit in Café Riche, just off the Midan. Sooner or later everybody stops by Café Riche. At a long table in a side room, I see my brother and Ahmad Seif in a meeting with their Initiative to Restructure the Security System. Judge Ashraf al-Baroudi, the revolution's favorite for minister of the interior, is with them. Omar is at another table with his group, and Sherif at yet another. Today Tahrir is operating out of Café Riche. Nahla and I have meetings with several people about the conditions for suspending the sit-in; a compromise suggestion is to move the tents of activists who want to stay and place them by the Mugamma3 near the tents of the shuhada families. To consolidate and tighten the sit-in, vacate the central garden and allow the Midan to open. Most people accept that three weeks is long enough to close down the central *midan* of the third largest city in the world, and that they need to take account of the residents and business owners and shopkeepers of the area who're getting fed up. This compromise would allow the physical manifestation of solidarity with the shuhada families to continue, keep a symbolic presence in the Midan, and undermine the theory—fast becoming popular—that the Tahrir sit-in is responsible for all our ills, from the Cairo traffic jams to the state of the economy. At four o'clock we seem to have reached agreement, and we write a draft announcement. Abu Muhab goes to have a final word with the families. We alert the newspapers and phone ONTV, al-Jazeera, and al-Nil. Their crews arrive and set up. Abu Muhab does not come back. We phone him, and he says they're still in discussion. Time passes.

At six the Salafis pack up and get into their coaches. We're back in possession of Tahrir. Some shabab put on plastic gloves and start collecting the mountains of litter left behind. We find Abu Muhab in the families' encampment near the Mugamma3. There are no lights. People are standing in clusters, arguing, shouting. Abu Muhab holds my arm, steadies me: it's dark and hot and the ground is treacherous. Judge Baroudi appears and begs everyone to understand the importance of unity, of working together. They listen, then resume arguing. Strong voices argue for suspending. Strong voices retort that the closure of the Midan is the only card they have. I think people don't want to go home and pretend their lives are normal when their kids are dead. They need to remain in an "exceptional" state. A woman faints. A young man on crutches tells me he's one of the "injured." He says they're offering him ten thousand pounds. "And what happens to me when they're finished?" he asks. "I don't want money. I want a job." Abu Muhab gives me a folded sheet of paper. It's the draft announcement. Rejected. I phone the TV crews: we don't have an agreement. The sit-in will remain.

SUNDAY, 31 JULY

I steal three hours to go to the orchard. Osta Ashraf has laid palm branches down for the section of ceiling that's collapsed. I climb onto the roof to see his work from above. He urges me to walk on the branches, to jump up and down; the branches, he tells me, are stronger than steel. We're not using a teaspoon of cement in this work. It is so pure, so peaceful, up here that I don't want to come down. If I angle myself. I see nothing except a sea of palm trees. And just beyond them, the Pyramids.

When I leave, I'm loaded with mangoes, limes, mulukheyya, and mint.

MONDAY, 1 AUGUST/1 RAMADAN

I see the tweets at about one o'clock: "Tanks moving into Bab el-Louq. Must be heading for Tahrir."

"We have to open the Midan."

"We have to open the Midan now."

I phone Sherif. He's seen the armored personnel carriers rolling out of Abdeen and is on his way.

I get to Qasr el-Nil Bridge and run into the battalion arriving to control its mouth into Tahrir. They're maybe fifty men. They feel like army—tall and well built and disciplined—rather than police or Central Security, but they're in black. They're carrying long, rough wooden sticks. They're almost forcing cars to drive through Tahrir; they bang on cars that want to turn right at the end of the bridge and push them toward Tahrir—until a boss soldier says to let cars turn right if they want.

The Midan is a massive wreck, a giant tip. They've demolished our small city. Abbaseyya was the first cooperation between the military, the Dakhleyya, and the baltagis. Today is the tryout for the Anti-Riot Troops, the new name for Central Security.

On Saturday, in the burning midday sun, Nahla and I and Abu Muhab stood with ten young people, at an impasse, between the Midan and Amr Helmy's office in Parliament Street. The shabab said, "We can't leave as long as some families and some activists won't go; we can't abandon them."

"So don't abandon them. Move your tents closer to them, and open the Midan."

They wanted to but said there were a few who took a hard line and insisted that the closure should continue.

"Who are these few? Can we talk to them?"

They were mainly independents; they'd become responsible for manning the accesses to the Midan. Some were young activists who'd worked on various campaigns for months; others were new but had worked hard and contributed to protecting the Midan for the last three weeks.

"Please, would some of you—or, better still, the hard-liners—come and talk directly to Amr Helmy?"

They said that for the hard-liners, even that would be treachery. "Please help us maintain unity," they begged.

On Sunday we continued our failed shuttle diplomacy, crowning it with three unprofitable hours with the deputy public prosecutor.

Now the Midan is overrun with soldiers. It's like a scene in a film when an army's been through an enemy village: everything's razed to the ground; the military pass through, and the tents, the flags, the banners, the billboards—everything is transformed into rubbish. Military and Central Security (or, now, Anti-Riot) soldiers are on the move everywhere. Some civilians try to reason or object; some of the families try to go back to their positions; some of the passersby make a point of showing support for the soldiers. We see young men being pushed by soldiers toward tanks, and we see soldiers deliberately breaking up unresisting chairs and tables. Some of the "hard-liners" who'd prevented the shabab from opening the Midan are wearing the vests and headgear of the military over their civvies and chatting comfortably with the soldiers.

The Tahrir Cinema screen is on the ground, broken up by our army, the cables cut and tangled. I see the screen on the ground, then I see a child dragging a blanket behind him and crying. Then I see other children—children for whom the Midan had brokered a truce with their cruel lives and who'd found shelter in the central garden between the tents; the revolutionary shabab had held classes for anyone who wanted to learn to read or write, shared their food with them, and given them responsibilities: the children had spread mats and connected wires and held lights and cameras. All this in ruins now.

I spot Mona and Sherif and other friends on the Hardee's corner and join them. They've just got news of several activists detained by the military. We call our human rights lawyer friends and report what we've seen. A loud voice demands, "Who are these people? Are they Egyptian? Why are they using their phones?" There's something theatrical about the voice, but the atmosphere is suddenly tense. Mona says of course we're Egyptian.

"What are they doing?" voices shout. "Let's see the phones!" "Mind your own business! Move away!" Mona, Nazli and others are shouting back. We're actually scuffling, or being scuffled; somehow we're in a crowd, we're being pushed with shoulders and chests, we're pushing back.

A man looks at me and shouts: "What's this one? Look what she looks like!"

I'm taken by surprise. "Me?" I ask. "Yes, you. I heard you insulting." "Insulting who? Tell me, who did I insult?" I'm shouting at the top of my voice, but it's not carrying as I thought it would. I do it again, above the jostling and pushing and yelling: "Who did I insult?"

His eyes flicker, then he stares straight at me: "I heard you insult the Egyptian people. Yes, you. I'm here and I'm a witness against you—"

My focus narrows right down: I don't know, see, hear anything that's happening around me, it's just me and him: "Me? I insulted the Egyptian people, you son of a . . ." I hear my voice yelling and swearing, and I think I lunge at him. Then there's a military chest in my face and a body of soldiers between us, and the crowd and the military are hurrying us out of the square "for our own good" while we remonstrate: "But did you hear what they said? Did you hear—"

They pushed us gently. Gently out of the Midan. But the next day, when the families tried—not to camp, but just to break their Ramadan fast in the Midan, they were not so gentle.

TUESDAY, 2 AUGUST, MIDNIGHT

At Agouza Hospital, taking the testimony of Mustafa Mursi, sixty-two, veteran of the Egyptian army, father of the shaheed Muhammad Mursi, shot and killed in Marg.[7]

Mustafa Mursi is on a hospital trolley. His shirt is bloody. He refuses to take it off and says he will return to Tahrir wearing it.

He is accompanied by others from the shuhada's families. They confirm he was beaten by the army earlier tonight just after iftar.

Mr. Mursi has a cracked rib and collarbone and bruises to the head and legs, and dizziness. He is diabetic, suffers shortage of breath, and has shrapnel in his leg from service in the 1973 war. He speaks clearly but with frequent stops to catch his breath. He holds up the photograph of his son throughout the testimony.

I said [to the officer] we're going home, son. I was army too and I fought in '73. Swearing and cursing all of them. [Hitting me] on my head and on my chest till I collapsed. They took my son's photo from my chest and threw it on the ground and trod on it. I know them, the two officers. Army. One in camouflage, one in plain. I'll hunt them down. God willing. And I'll hunt down those who killed my son.

I was just saying to them that I am a man who—I am a man—I—my son. My son is now with the Just who never treats anyone unfairly. God forbade Himself injustice. He forbade Himself injustice, but the rulers of Egypt and the corrupt regime in Egypt is unjust. But God is with the downtrodden. I want to follow my son because he's with the Just. Up there. Here, in the world of Egypt, there's no respect for humanity, or for age. The revolution came to clean the land of Egypt. But we still have a corrupt regime. Field Marshal Tantawi—we pray that God forgives him. We pray that God may guide him to the right path. If they wanted to control the situation, two words would do it: *Arrest the officers who killed our children, and the snipers, and try them.* Egypt would straighten out, and the wheel would turn again. But they don't want to. Why? Because there's something in their hearts. Truly. I wish each one of them would sit with his conscience and with God and look into his heart. I hope they do it for the common good.

My heart won't cool until the people who killed our children are arrested. I'm not asking for any of that stuff—they're saying we'll give them this and that. What we have is enough. We lived under injustice and never harmed anyone and what God sent us was enough. But you see murderers and bribe-takers—my son, God knows, before he met God he knew Him well. He knew God. He's in the third year, Information Systems. His name is Muhammad Mustafa Muhammad Mursi. The Marg officers killed him and smashed his head. I'm over sixty now, and we've never harmed anyone. God knows I speak the truth. All we want is that the officers who killed our children are arrested.

The army took me by treachery. I was going home. General Ruweini, when we met him, he said we'll stand by you, yes, stay in your tents. And we'd just arrived at our pavement, and the army came and beat us and pulled down the tents on top of the shuhada's mothers who were preparing food to break the fast. They beat me with such cruelty and such stupidity that I got dizzy and fell. My chest is cracked from how hard they hit me. But God is present. God is here. With us.

OCTOBER 2011, AGAIN

For weeks through August, Central Security Forces occupied the central garden of the Midan. And in September we found out that the regime had been planning to sell Tahrir. They'd been planning to sell the central public space in our capital to a hotel chain, to a foreign hotel chain, because "Hosni Mubarak's government was worried about large gatherings and protests . . . in central Cairo."[8]

I'm not surprised because we knew that everything was up for sale: land, monuments, islands, lakes, beaches, people's homes, antiquities, stretches of the Nile, natural resources, people, sovereignty, national parks, human organs, gold mines, the wealth under the ground, the water in the river, the labor of the people—everything. And yet every time we come across a specific transaction, a specific target, we're gripped again by that surprised horror: They would sell *what*? And it's no use saying, "Well, but we knew they were venal beyond venality, treacherous beyond treachery"—you still feel your heart thump, and the pain in your stomach, and the shiver down your spine: They were going to sell *Tahrir*?

But they would do anything . . . one never really believes that, though, but they would, yes, they would. What could be worse than trying to provoke conflict, war, within the community? That's what the regime has been doing between Muslims and Christians for more than thirty years. And that's what we detect again in what happened in Maspero.

If I had been in Cairo, I would have been on that march on 9 October when thousands of Egyptian Christians and their Muslim comrades demanded the long-awaited "Unified Law for Houses of Worship." But I was in London and sat watching it on fragmented screens: setting off from Shubra, walking, chanting, the people within it, old and young, talking, even laughing. I felt the tension as it drew close to Maspero and then the great explosion of energy and noise and movement: the shooting, the armored personnel carriers zigzagging among the people, hitting them, running them over, dragging them along. I heard the anchor of Channel 25 screaming as the channel was attacked, while state TV tried to incite Muslim viewers with reports of soldiers killed and "Christians attacking the Egyptian army." Twenty-one civilians were killed that night, rising to twenty-eight later. And fourteen hundred wounded.

At my kitchen table, I followed Alaa's heartbroken tweets from the morgue: "Mina's body is here Mina my comrade I can't believe it," "We lost you as you fought for our country may your soul be safe Mina Danial my friend," "I went in and saw them 17 pure bodies and Mina shining in their midst how shall we ever forgive ourselves." But what Alaa and the shabab then did was remarkable: from the morgue of the Coptic Hospital, they took on the entire system. In the face of the priests pushing for a speedy burial and the hospital administration issuing death certificates from "natural causes," they persuaded the stricken families of the shuhada to demand that their children's bodies be cut open. Activist lawyers pressured the public prosecutor to order autopsies. They fetched—bodily—the coroner and his staff and persuaded them to carry out the autopsies in the presence of physicians—like Mona Mina—whom they trusted. And then they made them sit individually with the families and read and explain the reports to them. The hospital morgue had only three drawers, so all the while they treated the bodies of their comrades with ice and fans, and they treated the anger, grief, and suspicion of the families with tears and embraces and explanations.

Back in Cairo, I went to visit the wounded at the Coptic Hospital—and they told me again about Alaa and his friends, Mina's Muslim comrades, who made sure the Christian shuhada were not hastily buried with their blood unaccounted for.

And now Alaa is summoned by the military prosecutor to answer charges of "incitement and destruction."

I can hear Omar on the phone at the other end of the flat, on the balcony where my nanny, who could not read or write, told me stories and gave me lessons in narrative. It used to amuse me that Omar would be working there on a script. These days he works on material for the independent cinema he and his friends at Mosireen are planning to set up—but right now he and Mona are working to put everything to do with the No to Military Trials for Civilians campaign on one website.[9] Back in February, Mona created and spearheaded this campaign, and now she and Omar have their heads together over its papers, as they used to have them together over summer plans when they were younger.

Mona was always the good child, the one who laid the table and helped the smaller children. As a young scientist over the last year, we watched her care for her—"genes"? The things she was growing in the lab that she had to check on every three hours. Serious in her white coat and her spectacles, her hair bunched up, her earrings a gentle, time-keeping pendulum. And then there she was in the revolution—her effervescence stilled into seriousness. And now she peers into her laptop and answers her phone and the campaign in hand now is for her brother when he comes back from San Francisco. Our children.

For twenty years it was school year in England and holidays in Egypt. We would come back, and all the children would fall in together as though they'd never been apart. I built a *diwan* in the playroom, a wide bench that ran the four meters from wall to wall with a window behind it. I furnished it with a giant mattress and bright cushions, and they all gathered on it to talk and play and watch movies and eventually fall asleep in a tangle like a litter of kittens. They ran together in Ataba, in Zamalek, at my brother's and my mother's and the little orchard and the house on the coast. And the first question every grown-up arriving at one of the houses asked would be: "Where are the shabab?" Toufi fed them and embroidered their initials onto their school uniforms, my mother gave them books and listened to them, Lulie treated their cuts and colds, Laila helped with science and maths, Sohair was their confidante, and my brother and Ahmad Seif were the still reference points who made everything special by their presence. And every child had their personality and their role. Alaa was the Guru, who had a detailed and passionate opinion about everything. Omar Robert was the Lord of Games and quizzes and mischief. Mona was the Good Child and the Romantic. Salma was the Organizer, the one who bought tickets and got the family to things on time. Mariam was the Princess, born to be served. Ismail Richard was the Healer; a smile or hug from him made the world your friend again. And Sanaa (Laila's youngest daughter) was the Dreamer, whose off-the-wall comments became family lore. And now they're all working for the revolution. And tonight Mona and Omar are preparing the campaign for Alaa and the newspaper on their table headlines a statement by the Chief Judge of the Military Judiciary: "It is illegal to demand that civilians not be tried in military courts."

What is legal and what is not? The Supreme Council of the Armed Forces, SCAF, makes up the rules as it goes along. The right to protest is enshrined in law, it says. But protesters in front of the Israeli embassy are brutalized and hauled off to military trial. And every one of the incidents that have marked the last eight months has registered a worsening of the relationship between the people and the army.

〳〳〳〳

The big question for us now—the question to which you know the answer and I don't—is, will we have the parliamentary elections scheduled for 28 November? Many of us think the Maspero event was meant to cause enough civil unrest to give SCAF an excuse to declare martial law and postpone elections. It didn't work because Muslims did not respond to the incitement from state radio and television. Will it work next time? Will there be a next time?

"Not one of us is going to step back into the nightmare," I wrote eight months ago. But the nightmare chases us, surprises us, attacks us. So far we have beaten it back.

And the thought is starting to take hold that maybe even elections will not lead to where we want to go.

We are not alone. We were never alone; the feelings, the prayers, the messages that came pouring into Egypt from every place on earth during those eighteen days of Tahrir lodged in our minds and in our hearts and affirmed every minute what we knew already: that the freedom we sought was the freedom the people of the world wanted, for us and for themselves. And what has been happening across the planet since has confirmed and reconfirmed our belief. The first placards raised in Wisconsin, the street signs invented for the City of London, the words we hear from Tokyo to Wall Street, the chants in Oakland, California—all echo the call from Tahrir and Tunis: the people demand the fall of this—entire—regime.

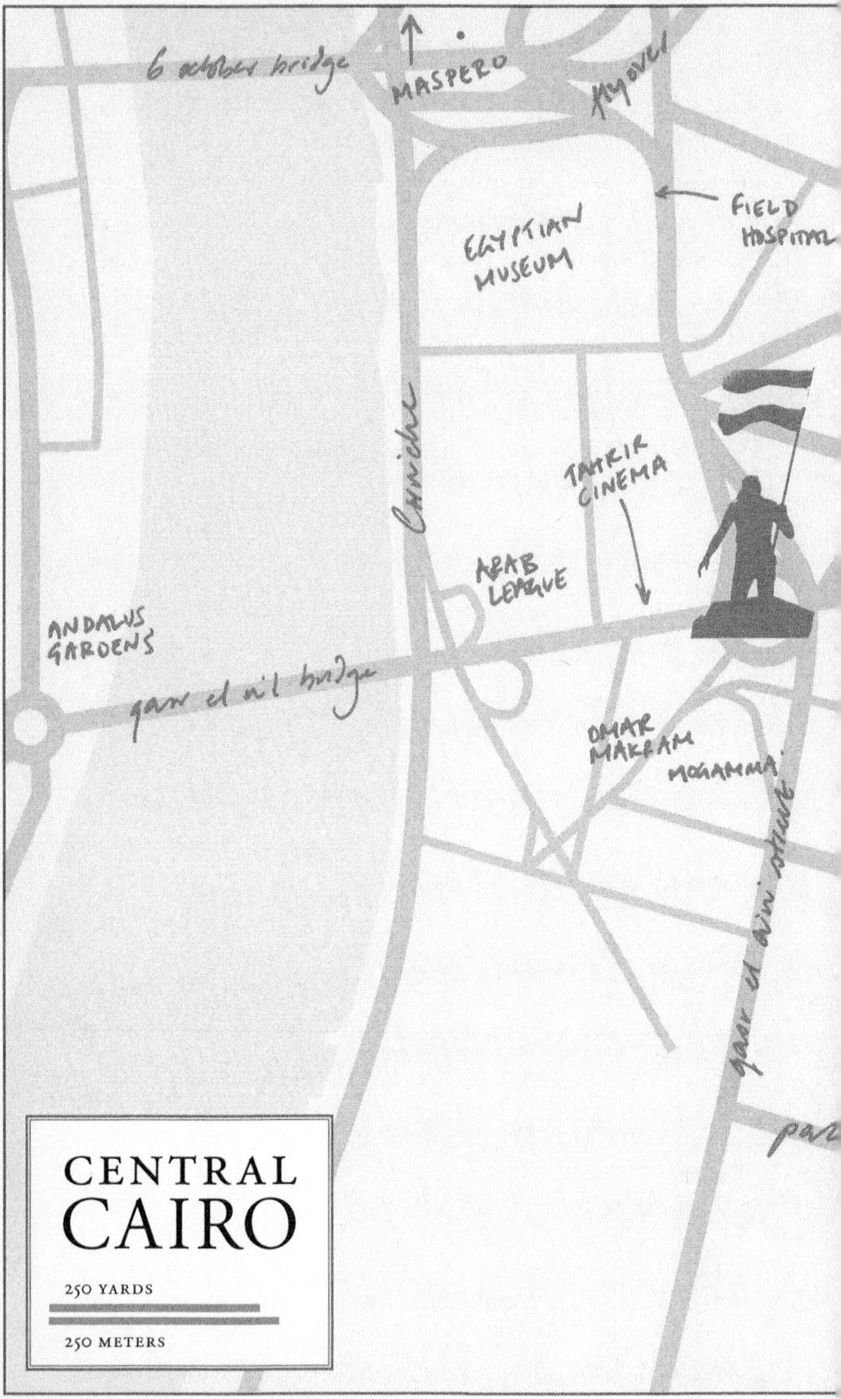

6 october bridge

MASPERO

Mayouci

FIELD
HOSPITAL

EGYPTIAN
MUSEUM

Corniche

TAHRIR
CINEMA

ARAB
LEAGUE

ANDALUS
GARDENS

qasr el nil bridge

OMAR
MAKRAM

MOGAMMA

qasr el ain street

par

CENTRAL
CAIRO

250 YARDS

250 METERS

TALAAT
HARB

CAFÉ
RICHE

...in street

...ELD
...OSPITAL

mohammed mahmoud st.

ABDEEN
PALACE

MINISTRY
of
INTERIOR

...street   LAROGHLI

N

The Eighteen Days Resumed

1 FEBRUARY–12 FEBRUARY 2011

It's getting cold. But there's been an announcement that Mubarak
will speak. We're hoping that he'll resign, and everyone wants to
celebrate with everyone else when it happens. So we stay. We talk
and walk and discuss and chant and shiver. They say he'll speak at
10:00, then 10:15, but it's 11:00 when he starts. There's no screen,
but loudspeakers are rigged up to lampposts, and everyone qui-
ets down. And we cannot believe what we hear. Hosni Mubarak
has simply not understood what has happened. He talks of how
some decent young people have been "led astray" and are being
used by unnamed "political forces," of how we're "living together
through these painful days." He's suddenly aware of everything
that's wrong and pretends that his regime, which has been de-
developing Egypt for thirty years and stealing the bread from our
mouths, is now suddenly equipped to "respond to the demands of
our young people." He's going to create jobs and respect the law
and run clean elections and put the police at our service, and all
he wants is a chance to end with honor his service to his country.
The second he finishes the call rises stronger and more determined
than ever: "Irhal! Irhal!"

2:00 A.M.

I want my mother. I am cold and shivery and I. Want. My. Mother.
I cannot tell you how many people in the Midan have said to
me, Can you imagine if your mother were alive today? How she

would have enjoyed this? I want to ring the doorbell and find her in the living room surrounded by newspapers with the television on loud. I'll turn it down, get some food from the kitchen, and sit beside her and tell her everything that's happened. I want her to be astonished and amazed and indignant and tickled. I want her to interrupt and interject and laugh and question. I want to talk to her, and I want to see her face.

Every night as I've left the Midan, I've thought for a moment I was on my way to see her.

Many years ago, with her living in Cairo and me living in London and the telephone an open line between us, I realized that things I did, or things that happened, never became completely real to me until I had told them to her; until she knew them, too. And I so want her reality imprimatur, her seal, on everything that's happening, everything we're doing now.

Her last summer, 2007, I was sorting out her library while she lay on the sofa watching me, facing the French windows onto the balcony. And at one point I glanced at her, and she had this curious expression, like in a movie when people see a UFO. And I went over and took her shoulder: "Mama, Mama? What is it?" And she kind of shook herself and came back to me and said, wonderingly, "Do you know? I thought I saw a massive storm rolling toward us." She paused. "I'm worried about el-balad"; the country, Egypt.

My mother always had solutions. She always knew what people should do better than they knew it themselves—and told them so. But she was stumped by our condition.

She was worried for our world. And I was worried for her. Ever since I can remember, I've been terrified at the thought of the world without her. That summer she seemed different, less combative, gentler. She'd had mobility problems for a few years. And I think she decided it wasn't going to get better. And she was—loosening her hold. I asked her not to. I really did. And she said gently, "So should I be an old lady in a chair forever?" And

I said, "Yes. Yes. You've always done things for us, not for you. Do this for us." And she laughed and said, "Okay, okay, don't fuss." But I worried. I made her have a brain scan. I was utterly surprised when she submitted. It came out fine. I arranged for an old friend of hers, a psychiatrist, to come and visit. She was vivid and happy, and I'd swear there was a moment when they were flirting. But then they were both quiet, and after a bit he said, "What is it you're worried about? Are you worried about Mustafa [my father, who'd just been ill]?" She said no, he has excellent care—and we're all there for him. "Are you worried about yourself?" No, my children and grandchildren are all around me. "What then?" I'm worried, she said, about el-balad.

When she was six months pregnant with me, her mother told my father he had to make her walk a kilometer every day. The Church of St. Thérèse, la Rose de Lisieux, was half a kilometer from their home in Shubra. So every evening my mother and my father walked to St. Thérèse and back. She told me this when, many years later, my car broke down in front of the church, and I came back amazed at the hundreds of little notices of thanks, the gifts that had been left for the saint on the walls of her church by Muslims and Christians whom she'd healed. There was even one from my favorite singer, Abd el-Haleem. So that summer, when I had to go to Shubra to buy a noticeboard, I went into St. Thérèse and said a little prayer.

But my mother slipped away one night while I was in London. All it took her was fifteen minutes.

Just two weeks earlier I'd seen her and my two boys sharing the massive diwan in the living room, and Omar was reading to her, for a treat, her choice of poem. It was a toss-up between Pope and Byron, but she went for Pope. I used to be unable to gaze full-on at that image of her laughing and repeating choice phrases. Now, for some reason, I can do it. These days I see her constantly, look-ing surprised, looking delighted, looking up every time one of us walks into the room: "What's the news? Fein el-shabab? Where are the young people? What are they doing?" And I tell her: "Mama, you would be so proud of them, of your grandchildren, and of your students and the children of your students. Of all our young people. They are out there: and they are so many."

WEDNESDAY, 2 FEBRUARY

Aches and shivers. Sore ear, nose, and throat passage, and those nightmare suites of consecutive sneezes where you don't have a second to gasp for breath. By the time nine sneezes in crescendo have pumped the air out of me, I am collapsed on a chair in the hall, glad to be told to stay at home and do "media work" rather than go to the Midan.

I knew something was wrong as soon as I woke up. There were car horns. It had been so quiet and peaceful for the last few days that we'd started to see the bats once again flitting in and out of the fruit trees at dusk. And this wasn't even the normal noise of Cairo traffic; this was aggressive, patterned, and constant.

Out of my window I can see bands of people marching across 15 May Overpass, and I realize, even before I see the banners, that these are the "other lot," the pro-Mubaraks. My immediate thought is that they have a right to march. My second is that they're not actually freely expressing their opinion. They are regimented: each band of fifteen or twenty men (always men) accompanied by a honking car; even from this distance, they lack the civility, the friendliness of the protests: they carry sticks, they make provocative gestures at the street, they have obvious leaders, "stewards" even, marshaling and directing them. The banners they carry are the uniform, professional banners we've grown used to seeing at election time.

Why am I taken by surprise? Because we need to believe that

the whole country wants to get rid of the regime? Why am I disheartened? Because I thought the regime had vanished forever after the twenty-eighth and now it looks like it will fight back—and on the streets, which should now belong to the revolution? Because I'm ill?

I am ill. Layers of jumpers, woolly socks, and a hot-water bottle to hug. Boxes of tissues. But it doesn't feel right to just lie down and take it easy; we all have to be useful. The novel I've been working on (and off) for the last several years has gathered itself into a cold little knot in the corner of my mind: is my novel obsolete? My characters, discussing the state of Egypt, the state of the world, acting, working, loving—are they dead? If I think about it, I'll be racked with guilt and self-blame that I did not finish it two, one, half a year ago, when I could have, and then it would have been part of what's happening now, it would have been part of the great turmoil of ideas and discussions that are taking place. But no-o-o-o, no: I procrastinated. I did a million other things when I could have, should have, been writing, and now my poor novel struggling to be born has been left behind, unrealized, unfinished, aborted, irrelevant, stillborn—okay, this is not what I should be thinking about. So work on PalFest instead. The Palestine Festival of Literature, my other baby that took me away from the novel these five years. This year's festival is due to happen in under ten weeks, and still the money is not in place. So, cough and sneeze and write to a potential funder. And cough and sneeze and write to another potential funder—

Omar calls from Tahrir to say that something's different. There are no civilians on the checkpoints, and the military are not searching people or bags or looking at IDs anymore.

I keep an eye on al-Jazeera as I try to work, and suddenly I realize that what I am seeing on the TV screen in the corner of my living room is a camel and horses galloping into Tahrir—yes, indeed: a camel with a colorful tasseled saddle and stirrups—a

Pyramid camel, in fact, decked out to attract tourists and to pose for photographs, and his bright tassels are tossing about, and the horses are prancing and dashing, and people are running and circling round them, and without taking my eyes off the screen, I try to call Omar, but I can't get through, so I call my sister, who has just got in from the airport where she was collecting Alaa, her son (named after my brother), and Manal, his wife, who are coming home from South Africa to join the revolution. She is so happy; I get her typical big laugh that doesn't end when she starts to speak but runs through her words so sometimes you have to ask her to repeat what she's saying—but this time she's so happy and there's so much background noise that she's shouting loud and clear: "It's okay, it's okay," she shouts and laughs. "They attacked us with horses and camels, but we've captured them, and the kids are having rides on them in the Midan, and everything's fine, and Alaa and Manal are with me."

My sister is a force of nature, a rebel child who became the backbone of the family, a brilliant mathematician who dedicated her professional life to saving her students, intellectually, morally and physically; a radical Romantic who has spread her sheltering wings over friends and family and brought up three children who've shone like comets in the skies of our revolution. Over the years, I've tagged along with her to protests—outside the central police station in Garden City, on the steps of the Journalists' Union, Downtown, at the Courthouse in Alexandria—always trying to edge nearer to the center, always cordoned off, blocked by Central Security that was always at least five times our number. I once asked whether she wasn't afraid. And the answer came back simply: no.

Once, on a protest near the university, one of her most brilliant students, fresh back from Britain with a Ph.D. earned in record time, was jostled and pushed, and his glasses were knocked off his face. He got down on the ground to find them, and a Central

Security soldier, smelling blood, moved in on him and Laila just hurled herself between her felled student scrabbling for his spectacles on the ground and the booted kick swinging for his head. "You animal!" she yelled at the helmeted, shielded, jackbooted soldier. "You animal! Have you any idea what that head is worth?" And later, laughing over coffee: "All the years and the effort I put into that boy, and the bastard was going to finish him off for me in a second!" My sister makes a personal investment in everything and everyone who crosses her path.

I nurse a fever, take lozenges with cortisone for my throat, try to write. Egyptian state TV is lying so shamefully, I cannot watch it. We should have taken Maspero on the twenty-ninth, I think for the hundredth time. I follow news on satellite channels and Twitter. The people who last night were listening to music in Tahrir and debating modes of government—my nieces and nephew, my son, their friends, and all the shabab and everyone who has come to the Midan because they want a better life for their country—will now be putting their bodies on the line—again. It's all they have. The Mubarak baltagi militias have sticks and stones, and swords and chains, and dogs and trucks. And the military stand by and do nothing. On the news, I can hear thousands of voices raised in the angry chant: "Wa7ed, etnein, / el-geish el-Masri fein?" One, two, / Army, where are you? And then again: "Selmeyya! Selmeyya!"

〜〜〜〜

Alaa, my nephew, was taken into administrative detention in 2006 for supporting the Egyptian judiciary's move for independence. The regime kept him for forty-five days. He was in Tora, the same jail that had held his father, Ahmad Seif, for five years in the early eighties for leftist political activism. My sister could not bear to visit him. She, so definite and loud and—*there*, she went quiet and blurred and lost. Our nanny, Dada Ziza, old, and wrinkled and losing her sight, berated her in her distress: "Are you happy now? Content? You brought him to this. Every day protests, protests and big talk. Now we've lost the boy because of you." And Laila didn't even answer. Until he came out of jail, no one could comfort her. Now he's back from his job in South Africa with Manal. The revolution is in full swing. Ahmad Seif is running the amazing team at the Hisham Mubarak Law Center (HMLC) and they're at the heart of the practical and legal support for the revolution. Mona is doing her brilliant lab work and her brilliant communications work. That just leaves Sanaa, seventeen, who lives in her head but who's also in the Midan with her friends: taking notes, collecting information. She still has her school finals to get through. Later tonight, she and her friends will take refuge from the fighting in an apartment high up above Tahrir. Over the hours they will transform into the editorial board of *el-Gurnal*, the first independent newspaper to come out of the Midan.

I call Omar, and he says the baltagis are attacking, and there are battles at three entrances to the Midan, and the shabab have formed defense lines. He says that they can see trucks driving up behind the attackers.

There is one useful side to all this: it will nip in the bud any sympathy that started up for Mubarak after the show we were treated to last night. Once again the regime displays its banality; unable to come up with any move that is decent or innovative, it resorts to its usual mix: last night it serves up a sentimental tear-jerker, then it can't even wait for its possible effect but gets right back to obtuse brutality. It is its nature.

Mubarak's baltagi militias attack Tahrir from Qasr el-Nil Bridge in the west, from four streets on the eastern side, and from the main northern entrance that runs alongside the museum. The shabab's first act is to secure the Midan's entrance from Tahrir Street, to protect the little field hospital in the Mosque of the Servants of the Compassionate. The army makes sure to block off one street, Qasr el-Eini, which leads to the ministries and the Cabinet Office. Other than that, it stands aside.

All day long the baltagis swarm the entrances, and the shabab beat them back. Midan Talʒat Harb becomes the baltagi head-quarters for the day, and the whole of Downtown is the scene of running battles as the baltagis retreat from the entrances, regroup, and attack again. For several hours, the periphery of the Midan is a fierce battle zone, while in its heart children have rides on the captured horses and the Midan lives the life it's developed over the last four days. The Battle of the Camel: the same tactics that have been used against us, against every protester over the last five years, the same tactics used at the last elections to scare voters off the streets, have reappeared and with redoubled viciousness. This is the regime that promises to listen to the people and use the com-ing months to put in reforms.

Their next trick will be to say that the young people in Tahrir are "foreign" elements, that they have connections to "terrorism," that they've visited Afghanistan, that they want to destabilize Egypt. But by now the whole world knows what Ali-who-couldn't-speak always knew: that this regime lies as naturally as it breathes.

Omar calls, and I can hear the roar of chaos in the background, and he says, all bored and laconic: "Could you talk to this officer who's trying to take me away and tell him I'm Egyptian and I'm your son?"

"Yes," I say. "Hello?"

I hear a man's voice saying: "I'm not going to talk to anyone. I want you to come with me—"

And then Omar: "You said you'd talk to any relative who—"

"I'm not talking to anyone. I suspect you—"

"Hello! Hello!" I shout.

"We have been arguing for half an hour, and you finally said—"

"I'm an officer in the army, and I suspect you—"

"Hello! Talk to me!"

"Talk to my mother."

"And I suspect you—"

"Talk to ME! TALK TO ME!"

"It's okay. Leave it," my son says into the phone, and the line goes dead. I keep calling him back and getting unavailable.

〰〰〰〰

An hour later I call and get him. The noise in the background is intense. "What happened?" I shout.

"With what?"

"With the army?"

"It's okay, it's okay. I got rid of him. People helped."

7:00 P.M.

Channel 4 News' fixer calls and says they can't send the car they'd promised to take me to the studio because they can't accept responsibility for my safety.

The studio they're using is between the Ramses Hilton and the Radio and Television building, with the entrance in the alleyway running behind the Maspero Corniche. On a normal day it would be a twenty-minute walk from my house.

9:00 P.M.

I know it must seem strange to the garage chaps. I appear out of the darkness, and they have to move cars to clear a path for mine to leave. I apologize. The garage entrance has no gate, and so they've blocked it with a massive black SUV. It has to be moved for me to drive out and will have to be moved again for me to drive back in. I'm putting them to a lot of trouble. "Work," I say, and make a helpless little flutter with my hands. In other words: I am not a mad person driving out into the night in the middle of a blackout and a curfew on a whim.

And so I drive through two neighborhood checkpoints—they apologize for the inconvenience they're causing me, I thank them for the security they're providing—and on to 15 May Bridge. A man on the approach to the bridge taps on my window.

"There's trouble Downtown," he says. "Don't go."

"I have to," I say. "Work."

"Well," he says doubtfully, "take care."

~~~~

From the bridge, I glance down at Maspero and see that the tanks are still in place around the R&T building. I pass my beloved derelict Khedivial Stables with the horses' heads, which seem even more weird and ghostly tonight. I'm asking myself if two minutes on the news in the UK is worth this. But that's not why I'm doing it, really. I'm doing it because I want to be closer to whatever's happening in Tahrir. And because I will not be stopped from moving around my own city. This is the route I used to walk with my nanny when I was eight. Before they put up this overpass. When we used to walk across Abu el-Ela Bridge to buy fresh chicken, and to buy salted fish for Shamm el-Neseem. And later with my friends to walk into town, to the shops and the movies. I miss the old iron bridge, and I hate this overpass, but I won't be made into a frightened stranger ten minutes from my home. I descend into Boulac.

The spookiest thing is the absence of people; how the streets are deserted. Cairo streets are never empty. There are always people walking, men sitting outside their shops, youths loitering, people spilling out of coffee shops and juice shops, gathered around food stalls. Even in the dead hours between three and five in the morning, there will be street cleaners and nightwatchmen and men sitting in the doorways of greengrocers' and bakeries and pharmacies that stay open all night. In winter, they're often huddled around a small fire in a brazier. First-time visitors to the city always think something extraordinary is happening, a fiesta perhaps, to bring all these people out onto the streets. Me, I've never been in an empty street except in London or Washington, D.C. Now the emptiness spooks me. I resist locking my car doors.

There's a barricade at the intersection with Gala2 Street. The young men guarding it look rougher than the ones back in Zamalek. Actually, I'm not sure whether they're Popular Committee or State Security in civvies or even baltagis. But I open the window and show my driver's license and ID, and they wave me through.

Boulac rose against the French in 1798. The French captured one of the leaders of the revolt, Mustafa el-Besheiti. They put down the revolt, shelled the neighborhood, and laid Boulac waste. Then they released el-Besheiti to the people, and the people killed him.

I pass the hospital where I was born and park just before the Ramses Hilton. There are three other cars. The man looking after them says it'll be ten pounds now because it's so dangerous. I don't know if he's the regular guy who parks cars or a baltagi; how can you tell? I'll assume everyone is a good person until I'm proved wrong. Not a hundred meters away, the battle rages. My sister and her children are there. My friends are there. My son is there. I'm sure he's balanced on something high so that he can get a good view for his camera.[1] I shut the image out and phone the fixer, and she says she'll come and get me and not to walk alone. I walk anyway and meet her and two young men, and they take me into the building down through the garage and up the back stairs because the normal entrance is locked and barricaded. Upstairs it's buzzing: several stations are broadcasting out of the flat, every studio is working, and—no big deal—many people have made it here.

Tomorrow the baltagis will arrive on the doorsteps of this and every studio in the neighborhood, and they'll give them a choice: close down, or we'll smash all your equipment. But tonight the studios are telling the world what's happening over there in the Midan.

And what's happening is one of the decisive battles of the revolution. The regime's forces have been pushed back from Qasr el-Nil and all the eastern entrances and now, at ten p.m., are concentrating their attack on this northern approach to Tahrir, the wide road that runs out of Midan Abd el-Menem Riyad and then is flanked on the east by the Franciscan School and some residential buildings, and on the west by the museum. And crossing over the road is a section of 6 October Overpass. The shabab have captured some baltagis, and their IDs showed them to be Central Security soldiers. Anyone they capture, they copy their ID, then turn him over to the military. Now the shabab have beaten the regime's force back from the road itself, but it's taken up position on the overpass—and it has men on the roof of one of the higher apartment blocks by the school. The shabab can see these people. What they can't see are the snipers positioned on the roofs of the museum and the Hilton. But from time to time, they spot a green laser beam shining into their lines. And they suspect that this means snipers.

From the overpass and from the roof, the regime hurls its usual missiles at the citizens: stones and shards of ceramic and marble, bottles and Molotov cocktails. Fireballs land in the midst of the crowd below. The shabab gain access to the roof of the next-door building. Stones and Molotovs are exchanged roof to roof, but the regime has the advantage: it has the higher roof. And on the overpass it is using ambulances and Central Security trucks and civilian minibuses to bring in new cargoes of fighters and ammunition.

The battle is fought across the statue of the shaheed Abd

el-Menem Riyad, the chief of staff of the Egyptian army during the War of Attrition with Israel. Riyad was killed by an Israeli shell, with his men, in Trench No. 6 by the Suez Canal, on 9 March 1969. "A leader's place is with his men," he had said, and now his face is turned toward the citizens defending the Midan.

The citizens have fallen into battle formation. Older people are the supply lines, and they tear the corrugated metal fencing from the mysterious building site next to them and the stones from the pavements. Runners pile the stones into blankets and run them to the front. The shabab on the front line pitch the stones and hold up a shielding wall of corrugated iron. They can't see past their shield so they follow the directions of a maestro standing farther back, high up on the burned-out shell of an armored personnel carrier. A few meters behind the front line, another line stands. These are the substitutes. When a "forward" falls, a substitute takes his place. And a few meters behind the substitutes are three lines of the next "forwards." At a signal, they will step in to give their friends a rest. In the middle of the lines, groups stand on the tops of upturned vehicles; they keep the flag flying and the information flowing. Rations of water and bread pile up. The first lot of crash helmets to be brought in is given to the young women paramedics and the women doctors and nurses giving emergency treatment behind the lines. Bad cases are rushed across the Midan to the field hospital in the Mosque of the Servants of the Compassionate. Anyone who's not busy drums. A loud, energetic, rhythmic drumming drumming drumming on the metal sheets. This is the sound of the citizens, the voice of the revolution. They keep it up all night long. It tells any approaching regime baltagi that the shabab are awake and waiting, and it helps to keep everybody going; it says we're here, we're here, we're undefeated.

On the twenty-fifth, the first day of the revolution, when the regime choked Tahrir with gas and attacked the first waves of protesters with truncheons and shotguns, people found refuge in residents' flats nearby. My friend Ghada Shahbandar eventually decided she would leave her refuge, and a young man volunteered to accompany her to her car. On the steps he told her he was a butcher and had looked at his knives that morning and considered. "But then," he said, "I reckoned we really wanted to keep it selmeyya, so I didn't bring any." He held her arm to run her to her car, and as they ran, he was taken. "I tried to hold him," she says, "but they took him. In Talʒat Harb Street. He was on the ground, and five men were kicking him. Baltagis." Every few meters, she said, there would be a group gathered around a fallen young man kicking his head in.

On the twenty-eighth the regime was taken by surprise. They had not expected to be so comprehensively beaten in Cairo, in Suez, in Alexandria. Now they've regrouped, and they're back. Not with official forces but with their paramilitary thug militias: the baltagis, and some of their soldiers and conscripts in baltagi-type clothing. Later we will discover that one of the organizers of today is the National Democratic Party member of Parliament for Nazlet el-Semman, the neighborhood at the foot of the Pyramids where many of the camelmen and horsemen live. He is also the owner of the massive Ceramica Cleopatra, from whose factory floors come the shards that are splitting our heads open.

The army could stop all this in a minute. It doesn't. At one point a sole officer fires his gun into the air.

I finish my broadcast and hesitate. The shivers and aches are worse. But the battle for Tahrir is taking place not a hundred meters from where I'm parked. Somewhere in there my nieces are manning communications with the outside world, my son is filming the battle. But to go in, I would have to somehow cross the battle line. I phone one last time: Is there anything any of you need? No. What should I do? Go home. Now.

Jon Snow walks me back to my car. How many ways can this government disgrace itself? Would they destroy the country rather than leave?

On Monday the seventh there will be a TV interview with Tarek Helmy, our top heart surgeon. He will say that he's not a revolutionary but had gone into Tahrir tonight because his son was in the sit-in and he wanted to see it for himself. He got caught in a fight between two groups of young men and stepped forward to talk them down. And, just as he thought he'd made peace, stones came flying from the back lines of one group. He shielded himself with a corrugated iron sheet and watched, and he said he had no doubt then who was on the side of right. He said one side fought with courage, and the other, where the peace-breaking stones had come from, was both brutal and cowardly. He said he'd phoned his hospital and asked for medical supplies. His son-in-law filled a car with everything you needed for a field hospital and drove it across Qasr el-Nil Bridge—and the baltagis stopped him and beat him up. They emptied the car. Till that point, he said, he'd thought, *Okay, they have their wounded, too.* But then, he said, they threw all the medical equipment, all the supplies, into the river. He knew then that he would not leave Tahrir till the revolution had been won.

I drive back. I take my time. The streets are dark, but I've gone out and done my thing, and the shabab are holding Tahrir. If we, the pro-democracy movement, win this battle, the spirit that inspires Tahrir will pervade the country. In the Midan, every shade of the political spectrum is represented. The Left is here, and the Liberals. The Muslim Brotherhood, the Gama3at Islameyya, and the Salafis are officially not joining, but their shabab have rebelled, and they're with us, too, making up an estimated 10 percent of the people in the Midan. Our society is rich and complex and varied, and we revel in it. The people here are so way ahead of their government. If you could see the kids on the street telling you that the regime wants to pin the responsibility for this movement on the Islamists in order to scare the West. If you could see the small field hospitals with their volunteer doctors—mostly young women— and the medicines pouring in from well-wishers. If you could see the young men, with their jeans worn low and the tops of their colored boxers showing, form a human chain to protect what the people have gained over the last week in the streets of our country. If you could see my nieces hanging banners from balconies . . . you would know beyond a shadow of a doubt: Egypt deserves its place in the sun—out of the shadow of this brutal regime.

THURSDAY, 3 FEBRUARY

I've woken up much better, and the Internet's working, although it's slow. Our mobiles work, but we can't send messages. The only messages that come through are from SCAF, urging us to behave responsibly! Everyone phones to check up on everyone else. The grocer calls to ask if we need anything, and we ask for bread, milk, tea, eggs, biscuits, cheese. . . .

Lulie is staying with me. We have breakfast, read the papers. I slowly answer some e-mails. Then we get the phone call with the news about Ahmad Seif, Laila's husband, and I send out a last message before we leave the house:

DATE: THU, 3 FEB 2011 13:05:47

A good friend just saw 8 to 12 people being dragged out of No 1 Souq el-Tawfikeyya St and bundled into a civilian microbus while a military police vehicle waited near by. The people were being beaten and the street had been told they were "Iranian and Hamas agents come to destabilize Egypt" so the street was chanting against them. No 1 Souq

el-Tawfikeyya St is the home of the offices of the Hisham
Mubarak Legal Center, the Center for Social and Economic
Rights, and the 6th April Youth.

And, btw, my brother-in-law, the lawyer Ahmad Seif, *is*
the Legal Center.

Please get word out to as many news outlets as you can.

I call Ismail in London to make sure he's got the e-mail and will
get it out. I call my sister, and we arrange to go into the Midan
together, to meet by the Andalus Gardens. Then we head out.

As we park, we meet relatives and friends. Everyone walking to
Tahrir is carrying something: blankets, bottles of water, medical
supplies. Lots of us are taking mobile charge cards for the people
in the sit-in. As we get to the middle of the bridge, three men
come toward us, and we know straightaway they're not friends.
We automatically form into a tight unit. They're grabbing at the
blankets and the first aid bags and shouting that we have to be
searched, that these things have to be delivered to an "official station." We shout louder. In fact, we scream as we beat them off:
"Get away from us! Get away from us!" This is the first time I've
screamed in the street. We're holding on to our supplies and on
to each other, and we keep moving. My sister hits the man who's
trying to grab her bag. She has even less patience than usual today
because of Ahmad Seif and his comrades. We have no idea where
they've been taken. My sister says Ahmad had told her that if this
happened, we should not spend time looking for him but should
concentrate on holding Tahrir, on making the revolution work.[2]

The men snatch at our supplies and call us spies and whores.
Activists run forward from the Midan to help us, and we reach the
shabab's checkpoint, where they thoroughly and politely search
us: men by men, women by women. Two army soldiers stand by.
A young activist asks us to give the soldiers two blankets; he says

the men have been there for two days with no cover. The soldiers demur but eventually take the blankets.

In the Midan the mood is sober, determined, indignant. The disinformation, the smears being spread by the government, is hurting—perhaps more than the wounds and bruises so many people are carrying. That this regime should dare to say that the protesters are agents of Israel, Iran, and Hamas—suddenly able to put aside their differences and work together—beggars belief. This is what people are talking about. This, and the insult of being attacked by thugs on camels and horses, and that women leaving the Midan yesterday were roughed up, insulted, and robbed. And that there's no turning back.

I'm supposed to do a TV interview at 6:30. I phone the recording studio at 4 Gala2 Street, and they tell me they're closed. "They came round," they say, "with sticks. And threatened to smash everything up if we didn't close."

I go to look at the front line of yesterday's battle. The pavements are broken up, and the corrugated-metal sheets are stacked in case they're needed again. "Don't assume treachery, but be on your guard": men lie on the treads of the army tanks to prevent them moving. The regime's baltagis have been beaten back, but they're regrouping on the overpass. Lines of young men with linked arms protect the entrance to the Midan. The clinic that was set up when the baltagis were beaten back hums with activity. Doctors in white coats change dressings on wounds, take details. Two lawyers—in their legal court gowns—take statements. A woman sees me writing and comes up. "Write," she says, "write that my son is in there with the shabab. That we're fed up with what's been done to our country. Write that this regime divides Muslim from Christian and rich from poor. That it's become a country for the corrupt. That it's brought hunger to our door. Our young men are humiliated abroad while our country's bountiful. Be our voice abroad.

Tell them this is a national epic that will be taught in schools for generations to come. We've been in Tahrir since Friday, and the whole Midan was sparkling. Look what they've done to it! But look! Look at that microbus: twelve people on it at all times, and the banners never came down, and the flag never stopped waving. The army stopped the ambulances from coming in, but these young doctors—they sewed up the shabab on the pavement. My son, it took an hour to dig out the pellets from his legs. And then he went back in—" Everybody, everybody here has become an orator. We have found our voice.

The regime has rid itself of one of its central pillars: Habib el-Adli, the minister of the interior, is under house arrest. A new general takes over the ministry, and we get news that thirty-nine more people have been kidnapped. Among them seven of the young organizers of the revolution—kidnapped from the street after a meeting with Muhammad el-Baradei. A friend phones to say many Egyptian Christians have declared three days of fasting: fasting for victory.

My sister comes up with her friend and colleague Hani al-Hosseini. He has blood running down his face. He says he was detained by the military, who refused to believe he was a university professor and beat him up. He says they dragged him into the Egyptian Museum, and there are people there tied up and being beaten. We set about forming a delegation; we find two friends, MH and a surgeon, and our group of five walks up to the tanks by the museum and requests to speak to the officer in charge. A brigadier comes to talk to us. He's totally wooden and persistently denies that anything is going on in the museum. We give him an out by suggesting maybe it's going on without his knowledge. He doesn't like this. We say if he goes in and comes back and gives us his word that there's no one in there, we'll believe him and go away. He says he will, but he doesn't move. Eventually I make a little speech about dignity and iconic buildings and how shameful it is that the Egyptian army should be torturing people inside the Egyptian Museum. His jaw tightens, and he says: "They're not inside the museum; they're in the garden." We go and give statements to the lawyers in the field hospital.

Later we're to find out that the museum was, in fact, used as a holding station for detainees, and they were mistreated. Rami Essam, who became famous for his guitar-accompanied songs in Tahrir, had burns and stripes on his back from the hours he spent there. He was released, but many others went from the museum to military trials and are now in jail.

FRIDAY, 4 FEBRUARY

Morning, and I'm leaving for Tahrir. My family is already there. Omar phoned and said it's fine: the checkpoints are back up and everything's orderly.

It's become a tradition: Friday and Tuesday we get at least a million people out on the streets. Last Friday, the twenty-eighth, was the Day of Wrath, today is the Day of Departure—Mubarak's, we hope. It's also become a tradition that Friday (Muslim) prayers in Tahrir are followed by (Christian) Mass—with everybody joining in both sets of "Amens." This is the first time I am moved by a Friday sermon. Sheikh Mazhar Shaheen, the young imam of Omar Makram Mosque, speaks what's on people's minds and links our actions to spiritual values. He addresses his sermon to "Egyptians" and he speaks of "Christ's example." He ends by praying to God to "make us stand fast. Restore our rights. We want not war but peace. Bear witness that we love Egypt and hold the dust of this land dear. Restore our dignity. Unite us and let not our blood be spilled." Our great communal "Amens" roll through the Midan.

The questions that are being settled on the streets of Egypt are of concern to everyone. The paramount one is this: can a people's revolution that is determinedly democratic, grassroots, inclusive, and peaceable succeed?

4:00 P.M.

Delegations from many Egyptian cities and governorates are here. The regime has stopped the trains running, but people have got here anyway. The flags and banners of Alexandria, Assiut, Beheira, Herghada, Port Said, Qena, Sohag, Suez, and others are flying. The chant is "El-shar3eyya m'nel-Tahrir." Legitimacy comes from Tahrir.

8:00 P.M.

The baltagis have stayed in the side streets. The Midan is well defended and has provided all day—as in the other days of peace we've had—a space for debate. Many ideas for moving forward are being articulated and discussed. Older people are still hopeful of democracy, of clean elections, the representative government they've longed for all their lives. Some of the shabab argue that we're beyond—the world is beyond—the old forms of democracy; that for the last twenty years every movement with energy has come from outside the traditional frameworks; that the static structures of the nation-state and the fluid power of capital cannot coexist without leading to repression. What we have in Tahrir is the opposite of a vacuum; we have a bazaar of ideas on the ground. We are full of hope and ideas, and our gallant young people are guarding our periphery.

SATURDAY, 5 FEBRUARY

Rushing around. Word is that people are being snatched from the fringes of the Midan. Two young women activists were taken by baltagis, but they were freed by two army officers and taken to safety in an ambulance. Six activists have disappeared.

I wish I could stay in Tahrir all day. I'm doing so many interviews, I seem to be talking all the time. I'm tired of my voice. And I can hardly get it out anyway. Thank goodness there are no traffic rules and no traffic police anymore. I just drive the shortest way, park anyhow, run in and speak, then out and start all over again.

I get a transcript of our friend Maysara's testimony. He was snatched by baltagis in Talʒat Harb Street, but it was the military who beat him up—in the museum. And he was moved around other locations and beaten up—in an ambulance. He says they weren't all vicious, and he says they really think the revolution is being pushed by paid outside forces.

I also get a chronology, a history of our new vice president and longtime head of Intelligence, Omar Suleiman. It details his extensive, personal involvement in rendition and torture. The Midan, of course, knows everything: "No Mubarak, No Suleiman / No more agents for the *amrikan.*"

There's no news yet of Ahmad Seif and his colleagues. Or rather, we know that they're detained by Military Intelligence, but that's all we know. While they were being taken, one of them left his mobile on, and a transcript has come out of what was heard. Again, the accusations were all of being spies and traitors: "If you walk out on the street now, the people will kill you: they know what you are."

I know that if I could go to the Midan for a bit, I would feel better and my spirits would rise. But I can't. I finish with the BBC Arabic and race home just ahead of the team that's coming to do an interview for an Indian TV channel.[3] I had suggested I could go to their hotel, but they said they'd been threatened and the hotel had been told not to let them film. I'm uncomfortable, but I welcome them in, and two minutes later my doorbell rings again. It's the concierge's daughter, and she wants to know who the two women are who just came up. I stare: "They're my guests." "This is your home," she says, "and you must do as you please. But the plainclothes have been round, they're asking who lives in each flat, and they're asking about foreigners and about media people, and we have to report to them if foreigners or media people come round. How long are your guests staying?" "They'll have their visit and leave," I say. I close the door, and I make tea. I call Omar, and he says we should sleep at my brother's. When the interview's over, I ask the two journalists to wait. I throw a few things into a bag and leave with them. This flat has been my home, on and off, since I was seven. Now I feel uncomfortable and alien in it.

The garage attendant has to move the SUV again. I apologize and say I hadn't meant to go out again; family emergency: I won't come back tonight. But then it's time for the *Democracy Now!* interview, and I no longer feel comfortable giving it while I drive; I feel I need to be alert to the street. I sit in the dark garage and talk to America for an hour.

TUESDAY, 8 FEBRUARY

There's a small, cracked, black and white photograph that shows my father's family deployed on one of the narrow terraced lawns of the Andalus Gardens. Something keeps bringing me back to this picture: my grandmother, in a demure dark coat, sits with her legs tucked under her, her two daughters one on either side of her. My small father, his hands in the pockets of his short trousers, stands a little apart, in that borderline aloof, slightly arrogant positioning that he is to maintain throughout his life. They were on that step over there, just across from where I'm sharing a sunny bench with Omar.

We're only here briefly, my son and I; a fleeting moment, captured when I said, as he walked me from my car to Tahrir, "Could we go in here for a moment? I don't think I've been since I was ten." "Sure," he said, glancing quickly at his mobile. We clasp our glasses of hot tea and share—though we shouldn't—a cigarette. A limestone Ahmad Shawqi, Prince of Poets, sits pensively to our right. The Nile runs behind us and the sun shines upon us, and we speak of concerts and screenings that could happen in this space. Because everything is possible now; such is our confidence. It's just a matter of time. Hours—perhaps.

For the last twenty years, my main feeling as I pass the Andalus Gardens has been dread; dread that one of the regime's intimates would be able to commandeer it and "develop" it as they've done with so much else in the country. I would search for telltale signs of impending brashness and be relieved to see the dusty old municipal noticeboard still in place. Today the dread has evaporated; suddenly I'm thinking what a great place this will be for music in our new, recovered city.

Omar is answering phone calls. If I get up from this bench and run down the nine steps that dip through this charming amphitheater, and through the narrow fountained rectangle at the bottom, and up another—maybe six—steps on the other side, I'll be right there where my grandmother sits, where my father stands. A cracked black and white photo. Since I was a child, I've been intrigued by it: there's the garden, so distinctive, familiar, unchanged, except that there also is my father, as small as me, a million years ago. Other pictures exist of my father in a Boy Scout uniform in the desert, or with his family posed against the Pyramids, or against a river backdrop. But these things were given, permanent parts of life; you knew you shared them with the whole world since the beginning of history. Is that it, then; that this small, urban, constructed, specific part of my neighborhood should be so unchanged, when change has so marked the four people photographed against it? My grandmother, Neina, old and strict ever since I knew her, and yet—here's a memory: I'm loitering behind her in the kitchen of the Abdeen flat while she whips up a treat for me at the cooker: *sadd el-hanak*, the "mouth-stopper"; flour and brown sugar fried quickly in butter and arranged in spoon-shaped petals on a china plate. I eat it on the small balcony where, angled sideways, I can see the palace that's also pictured in the schoolbook on the table in front of me. There are the iron railings, and behind them the low, far-flung building, and in between the railings and the palace, the courtyard—empty now, but in my book it's teeming with people: on the left stands the Khedive Tewfik, flanked by Sir Charles Cookson and Sir Auckland Colvin, on the right and facing him a melee of troops of the Egyptian army, on horseback and on foot. At their head stands Ahmad Orabi Bey in military uniform, in the act of sheathing his sword. The caption reads: "We are slaves to no one and will be inherited no longer." 1881. That's 120 years ago—and we're saying it again today.

EARLIER

I woke up to voices sounding as though they were with me in the room:

"The army'll stage a coup—"

"They don't need to. They'll wait and take it peeled and ready—"

"Suleiman is army—isn't Suleiman army?"

"Enough military; we've had a bellyful of military—"

"A parliamentary republic—"

"No, no. Egypt has to have a president—a leader—"

In Zamalek I'm on the sixth floor. Here, at my brother's, I'm on the second. In Wimbledon I sleep on the ground floor, but there's never anyone talking outside. Except if they're drunk in the middle of the night and the police come.

Bright sunlight. I get out of bed and look out the window: cigarette smoke rising, keys jingling, a group of men by the front door. I can't get over these open discussions of politics you hear everywhere now. Not just in the Midan but everywhere, the conversations you overhear are political: systems of government, education, public versus private ownership . . . what weight of repression was keeping all this down?

I glance into Mariam's room: a whirlwind of shoes, hairbrushes, tops, necklaces, on the floor, the bed, the chairs; ribbons hanging from mirrors, silver cups on bookcases, hundreds—well, tens—of medals, cups, trophies. Salma's is just the same, with a few extra Egyptian flags: you don't know whether you're backstage in a theater or in a club locker room.

~~~~

I like being at my brother's. Apart from having to stop by Zamalek to pick up clothes or papers—or hairbrushes or necklaces—I like being here; back in the heart of a noisy, argumentative, varied family with lots of friends in and out.

The living room has last night's tea glasses, chocolate wrappers, and orange peel. The cushions are still squashed and scattered from where we sat: my brother in his armchair, Sohair next to him in her upright with the back support, Omar—having inherited from Khalu the ability to simultaneously sleep and participate—stretched out full length on a commandeered sofa, the girls on floor cushions, me perched on the arm of a chair, near the exit, always only there for a minute and about to go and work.

Ahmad Seif and his colleagues from the Legal Center had been released unharmed, the shabab of the Popular Committee were on the barricades outside, my sister and Mona, Alaa and Sanaa were in Tahrir, and we watched heart surgeon Tarek Helmy's testimony about Wednesday's battle reel in anybody who hadn't already been captured by Wael Ghonim.

Ghonim had gone straight to the *10pm Show* TV studio after eleven days in detention, eleven days blindfolded and under inter-rogation. He looked haggard, and he was twitchy with tension. They'd snatched him from Tahrir on the twenty-eighth.[4] He spoke of how for eleven days his parents and wife hadn't known where he was. He cried and collected himself and spoke again. He hadn't wanted it known that he was the admin for the Khaled Said Face-book page, which had got people into the streets on the twenty-fifth. But he'd been outed now, and he had something to say. He started with the shuhada: "I want to say to all parents whose chil-dren have died—they are shuhada with God. I want to say we never thought we'd—even break anything, let alone kill a person." And when the anchor showed the images of Eslam Beker, Hus-sein Taha, Ahmad Ihab, Seifallah Mustafa, and Muhammad Abd el-Menem, he ended, in tears, with the shuhada: "To every mother and every father whose child has died: I swear it's not our doing. It's the doing of the people who held on to power and wouldn't let go."[5] Overcome and weeping, he stumbled off the set. But he'd done enough; he'd spoken with passion about the allegiance of the shabab to Egypt: "We are not traitors—we love Egypt. Don't treat us like we're being pushed by someone." He'd stated again the big aims of the revolution: to restore dignity and a sense of belonging to every person, to end corruption, and to run Egypt for the bene-fit of its citizens. He'd begged us to "put aside the past for a while and think what we'll look like in the future." And he'd restated what we all knew we needed: a new security apparatus, a new constitution, and a transitional government formed by the head of the Constitutional Court moving toward free and fair elections. He sounded like every young protester on the streets of Egypt; this was an authentic voice of the revolution arriving on the TV screen, and we knew it would carry to those who had started to lose heart and to those who, until now, had been unsure.

The day before, Sunday the sixth, the regime had sent out messages: state radio and TV pumped lies into the ether: drugs and "bad things" were happening in Tahrir, the economy was collapsing, the country was witnessing a total breakdown of law and order, the president had promised to consider all legitimate demands, and now the good shabab of Egypt were being led astray by infiltrators from Hamas, from Iran, from Israel, from America—and they were leading the country to its destruction. The new minister of the interior inspected the Central Security Forces barracks on TV and talked of redeploying them. State-run organizations resumed work, and banks opened. The message was, *Okay, we got the message: now, everything back to normal.*

So there's a call for another millioneyya today. I'll go to Tahrir for one o'clock. Meanwhile I'm producing copy and doing phone interviews at Sohair's dining room table. Everybody's gone to work, and Omar's gone to Tahrir. Um Nagla has arrived, and she's clearing up around me, practically dusting my keyboarding fingers, so I stop typing, and she tells me how people are worried because there's no police on the streets, so I remind her what the police on the streets used to do to people, and she agrees but she would still like police on the streets—good police. Well, that's one of the things this revolution is about: good police. And a fair chance for everybody. And health care, she says: her husband was as tall as the door and worked all his life, and when he fell ill, there was nothing. Except for good people who helped her—"yes, indeed." I'm on my soapbox: "Your husband. No health care, no cover. And how come you don't get a pension for all the years he worked? So God's given you health and you're able to go out to work. But what about people who can't work? What should they do? And your daughter, didn't she work in a textile factory? Six days a week, twelve hours a day, for thirty-five pounds a week? Tell me what you can buy for thirty-five pounds. And your son: he's working at a gas station. What do they pay him? Nothing. That's right. They give him access to drivers who'll maybe give him tips. You've tried to educate all your kids. Did they get an education? Is Ali staying on at school? No. Why? So what is a government for? Is it there to steal the bounty of this country, the sweat of its labor—"

"God will punish them," she assures me. "God is with you. Ali says the income of the Suez Canal alone would pay off all our debts. *Yalla*, I'll let you work." She escapes into the peace of the kitchen, and I hear the radio start up: *and I never knew . . . before today-ay . . . that eyes could betray . . . in this way . . . and I never knew . . .*

⁄⁄⁄⁄

Today will be critical. Yesterday Tora Cement and Suez Textiles came out on strike. We're hoping the "back to normal" strategy will backfire and that once people get back together in the work-place, they'll decide to join the revolution. My sister says the academics are going to march. And there will be others.

EARLY AFTERNOON

The entrances to the Midan have been narrowed even more. Sunday night the army tried to move its tanks a few meters into the Midan and fired into the air when people stopped it, and there's a rumor that last night, too, they tried to move. Now they're completely surrounded. People have spread mats and newspapers on the treads and are lying on and around them.

But once you're inside, the Midan is amazing. Even the light in here is different, the feel of the air. It's a cleaner world. Everything's sharper, you can see the leaves on the trees. Badly lopped, they're trying to grow out. Everyone is suddenly, miraculously, completely themselves. Everyone understands. We're all very gentle with each other, as though we're convalescing, dragged back from death's very door. Our selves are in our hands, precious, newly recovered, perhaps fragile; we know we must be careful of our own and of each other's.

The Midan is sparkling clean. The rubbish is piled neatly on the periphery, with notices on it saying NDP HEADQUARTERS. The fence of corrugated iron stands again around the mystery building site and screens newly constructed washrooms. Lampposts have put out wires so that laptops and mobiles can be charged. The field hospitals provide free medical care and advice for everyone. A placard reading BARBER OF THE REVOLUTION guides you to a free shave and a haircut. A giant transparent wall of plastic pockets has gone up. The shabab sit next to it. People tell them jokes, and they draw or write them and slot them into the pockets; a rising tide of jokes and cartoons. A Punch and Judy show is surrounded by laughing families. A man eats fire. There's face painting and music and street theater and a poetry stand.

On Sunday at Christian Mass and Muslim prayers, we all pray together for the young people the regime has been killing since 25 January—and before. Then, in the evening, there is Omar Suleiman: we watch the veteran intelligence boss interviewed by Christiane Amanpour. Earlier in the day he met with sections of the older "political leadership," including the Muslim Brotherhood. But he assures Amanpour that we, the people, don't yet have "the culture of democracy," that the "Islamic current" is pushing us, that the "other people who have their own agenda" are pushing us, that the Internet and social media have "facilitated" our young people "to talk all together but is not their idea [*sic*]; it comes from abroad."[6] Again he confirms: in the eyes of the regime, we simply cannot be self-propelled. The most we can be is a handcart, and anybody can throw their rubbish into us and trundle us along. The country falls on its back and kicks its legs in the air with laughter as he intones, yet again, for his American audience, that el-Baradei "has links" with the "Brother Muslimhoooood" and that "the Brother Muslimhoooood" are pushing us. Why, we ask, does he speak in English at all? Why don't these people respect themselves even if they don't respect us? We watch the old tor-turer, stiff with formality and self-belief, clinging to his simple conspiratorial concepts, holding himself rigid against the tide, the tsunami of us in the Midan and in the streets, his thumbscrews and cattle prods for the moment useless. When he says his mes-sage to us is "Go home. We want to have a normal life," the streets answer with one voice: "Mesh hanemshi / Enta temshi!" We're not going / You go home!

And then, in the Midan, there is a wedding, and then more music, and everywhere there are circles of people sitting on the ground talking, discussing; ideas flow from one group to the other, until the most popular find their way to one of the four microphones on the stages. I pause by one group, and they imme-diately invite me to sit. People introduce themselves before they speak. Three civil servants, a teacher, a house painter, two women who work in retail. They talk about what brought them to Tahrir. In the end, the house painter says, it comes down to one thing: a person needs freedom.

There's word that a cold is spreading; people have been sleep-ing out for twelve days. Everyone coming in brings vitamin C. A travel agent has emptied his office so that it can be used as a clinic. A call's gone out for tarpaulins. People go to check on the

Dakhleyya: the tanks that rescued it from the shabab are still protecting it. The police have locked themselves in and are to be seen
crowded behind their windows staring out into the street.

Tahrir is teeming, and people are still flooding in. There's an
excited buzz as news comes that a march of ten thousand workers is on its way. Laila phones: about five thousand academics are
coming along Qasr el-Eini Street; the army has taken down the
military barricades at the entrance to Parliament Street and made
them go through it and enter Tahrir from Muhammad Mahmoud
Street. I walk across to meet them. I've bought fresh mint from a
child in the street and brought it and biscuits into the Midan. The
courtliness with which people accept the offer of a biscuit! The
dignity with which the hungry try to decline! The bow! The hand
on the chest! We're all princes here, our manners are impeccable. I
walk through the crowd holding a spray of fresh mint in my hand,
and nobody thinks it strange; they smile and help themselves to a
sprig and hold it to their noses. People move between the different
stages and the different speakers, and people pose by the tanks,
and people kiss the soldiers. By the time I get across the Midan
to meet them, my sister and aunt are sitting on the curb at the
American University corner. A Salafi family sits next to us, and
we exchange cakes. My sister says she's going back to check on
Parliament Street because "we've left a couple of thousand people
to take it over."

Lulie and I sit side by side on the curb facing the Mugamma3
building. Lulie had a small medical "event" a few years ago, and
there's a slight drag to her left leg. She is, like all the women in
my family, gallant and raring to go—except her body's starting
to block her. My mother, to stop the war on Iraq, marched from
Charing Cross to Hyde Park in and out of her wheelchair, and I
saw the pain in Toufi's knees bring tears to her eyes as she insisted
on climbing yet another set of crumbly stairs to visit yet another

woman in the Productive Families project. Lulie and I give our bodies a short break on the uneven curb, and we're both thinking about Toufi because for us the Mugamma3 building, there, across the road, is Toufi.

That massive curve, like the beginning of an embrace; you step into it and into a different, darker universe: a huge lobby funnels upward into a massive galleried tunnel soaring up eleven floors and swirling with solid noise, its air heavy with thousands upon thousands of forms and applications and stories and desks and chairs and paper clips and complaints and carbon paper and filing cabinets and cupboards, crowds of people are in a permanent stampede crossing and recrossing the giant lobby trying to find the right staircase the right corridor the right lift and me with my hand in Toufi's waiting in line for the narrow lift that will, amazingly, carry eight people plus me uncounted up to the seventh floor and her office. All the government departments that deal with actual people are in this building, and Toufi works in Social Affairs but she doesn't really do her work in the office but out in the city.

Sitting on the curb, outside the building, I can feel the noise and bustle and jokes and ribbing of the crowded offices, people squeezing past each other to get to their desks, files files files everywhere, the hunt for someone's missing chair stolen by another office, the maps of the city on the walls as everyone in Outreach sets their routes for the day and yells at the "buffet" for their coffee and assembles their cases and finishes their paperwork. We'd always stop by the department boss; tall, gentle, graying Uncle Rashad, whose face I can, oddly, see very clearly as I write these words. He had a smile that only crinkled the lines around his mouth a little bit but filled his eyes. And his eyes and eyebrows were very black, like my grandfather's. He stooped, but maybe that was because I was so small. And everybody would disperse into the streets of Cairo: Tante Zeinab, plump and fair and red-haired and loud and always in the highest of slingbacks, Tante Kawthar, dark, green-eyed, and a little sad. And Toufi, with that swing to her cropped hair and her full skirt and me holding on to her hand. They dispersed into the streets to make good things happen. We walked through alleys too narrow for cars, and we came to the "sa7at sha3beyya"—the People's Spaces—and wherever we went, the kids and the staff were busy around her, and Toufi watched the boys play football and looked into the arts and crafts room and admired the woodwork or sat down to give a quick demonstration of hemming or a neat blanket stitch. She looked at papers in the admin office, and sometimes there was a small musical performance or a play. The high point of the year was the Sa7at Sha3beyya Exhibition, where the great Cairo stadium filled with the kids and their families. President Nasser attended these, and I remember one show ending with a young girl draped in the flag of Egypt holding up a torch while everyone sang around her. This must have been before February '58 because the flag was the green one with the crescent and stars.

My sister says that Nasser is all the proof anyone needs that the "benign dictator" scenario can never work. No one could have been cleaner than him, or more on the side of the disadvantaged, yet he set in motion the practices, the systems, that led, finally, to Mubarak's regime. Omar says, isn't "a girl draped in the flag of Egypt . . . etc." a typical fascist image? I say surely it's fascist only if you're powerful? We'd just got rid of the king in '52, the British in '54—and then were attacked by Britain, France, and Israel in '56. Can't we be allowed a girl in a flag?

Time passes, and I am in those narrow streets again, Toufi heavier now, her hair gathered under a gray bonnet, holding on to my arm over the extra bumpy bits or the bits where we have to balance on narrow ridges between stagnant puddles. We go through entrances and up stairs where we can't avoid brushing the walls with our shoulders even though we walk in single file, and we sit in tiny rooms taken over by the fabrics and the sewing machines that Toufi has, in part, come to see have not been sold or pawned.

Toufi knows the names of all the small children who come and lean against her and knows which fathers, husbands are in work, out of work, invalided, dead. She listens to the women and looks at their hems and buttonholes and seams and makes sure the leaders of the Productive Families project are delivering linen and thread and collecting finished work and paying cash, and she sees which women are ready to move on from sewing to cutting and who wants to do a refresher course at the local center—which is where we go next to check on the preparations for the Productive Families Bazaar: the current high point of the year. The bazaar is held nationwide, but the main one is in Cairo and inaugurated by Mrs. Mubarak, and by the time the ceremony's over, the best pieces have all been reserved by Mrs. Mubarak's train of ladies in power, to be collected by their drivers next day and never paid for. One year Toufi quietly sold off the best pieces ahead of the bazaar—some pieces went to foreign friends who willingly paid three times the asking price, and the money went to the women in the narrow rooms. And word came that if the project could not produce its usual level of work, it would be closed down. So the Productive Families limped along, with its well-wishers buying the indifferent stock and the old-style leaders, Toufi, Tante Zeinab, etc., raising and donating money to keep it afloat.

"Khalas," I say to Lulie, "no one's going to rob the Productive Families anymore."

"My sister, *habibti*," she says, "this city used up layers of her. Her legs, her soul."

We observe the Midan, heaving with bodies, with chants, with flags, with freedom. But where I could see my mother wide-eyed with wonder and delight, I could only see Toufi cautious, skeptical, a little grim, to be honest. A kind of *this is all very well but where's it leading?* "Come on, Toufi, it will lead to clean, honest, transparent government—why not? We'll have clean elections. A government that's accountable to the people, to Parliament . . ." I hear her typical phrase: "Let's hope so."

LATER

Tahrir has spread into Parliament Street. The Qasr el-Eini entrance to the street is a swarm of red berets as the Military Police, wrong-footed, move to block it again. People are streaming in from the bottom end of the street—reinforcements for the two thousand academics. A group of men get as far as the soldiers and sit down at their feet. One man, large, fiftyish, eases himself onto the tarmac, glances up at the soldiers, and comments good-humoredly: "Here we are. Maybe I've sat down on my grave."

Blankets and carrier bags of bread and dates and water are already being stacked by the Parliament walls. We watch the figures moving behind the windows of the Cabinet Office and the Ministry of Health. Two shabab start spraying graffiti on the wall of the Cabinet Office. A cleaner comes out and tells them he's going to have to stay up all night cleaning it. They apologize and put away the spray cans.

Lulie and I sit on the low wall and lean against the railings. Seventeen days from now, on 26 February, at this same spot, Laila and Mona will see Military Police dragging away a badly beaten young man. My sister will rescue the young man from the soldiers and put him in a car that will take him home. Mona wants to keep him till they can take him home themselves, but she's overruled; he's so unwell he's better off going now. Ten minutes later he's taken from the car, and this time it's not possible to save him. Amr el-Beheiri will be tried for "possessing arms" and be sentenced to five years in el-Wadi el-Gedeed prison in the Western Desert.

But today we sit and watch the street fill up. We hear the cheers of the Midan as the workers' march arrives, and they bring news that Lafarge Suez and Cairo Telecom have come out. And now all the diffused noises and shouts and bangs and cries of the street get sucked and unified into one song: the drumming clapping chanting of the Ultras. The White Knights of the Zamalek Football Club and the Ahlawi of the Ahli Football Club, the guys who were at the front of the marches on 25 January and broke the police and Central Security lines. It's always a party when they get to the Midan, and now they're here to seal the takeover of Parliament Street. They drum and swing and chant their way up the road just in time to surround the black limo driving out of the gates of the Cabinet Office. Nobody tries to stop it, but we drum it on its way. And now people sit and talk, and some of the shabab want to occupy the Parliament building, Magles el-Sha3b: "This is the People's Council and we are the People," but the dominant opinion is against breaking into anything. They discuss marching on Maspero, since we're all now aware of the harm that state radio and television is doing us—but again the dominant opinion is not to break into the building and not to push a confrontation with the army.

I look back now at the spectacle of us, us the people, in all our variety, picnicking, strolling, camping, chanting, on the street of the ministries between our Parliament and our Cabinet Office; my aunt and I and a few thousand people are outside the railings. It would be dead simple to go in and occupy them both. And it's not fear that holds us back. How can these shabab be afraid after their attempt on the Dakhleyya down the road—when for three days they surged against that Fortress of Evil facing bullets and gas? Or after Bloody Wednesday, when they defended the Midan against cavalry and Molotovs and snipers and militias? No, we the people were implementing a doctrine of minimum force, minimum destruction. This was a revolution that respected the law, that had at its heart the desire to reclaim the institutions of state, not to destroy them. It was very clear who its enemy was: the Dakhleyya and State Security and the National Democratic Party. Theirs were the buildings the revolution torched. Even the common soldiers of Central Security were spared—because they were conscripts.

Would we have ended up in a better place if we had been more violent?

When we leave the Midan, we walk through two lines of shabab clapping and drumming and encouraging us to sing along: "We'll come tomorrow / And bring our neighbors / We'll come tomorrow / And bring our friends."

On Qasr el-Nil Bridge there are stalls selling grilled sweet corn, cold drinks, peanuts. Soon there will be candyfloss and rice pudding.

Driving home, I find the barricades manned by army soldiers alongside the shabab of the Popular Committees. But the soldiers are, for the moment, wearing the armbands of the committees.

FRIDAY, 11 FEBRUARY, NOON

Osta Ashraf is waiting, as arranged, next to the mosque just after the Pyramid underpass. He'd gently reminded me that life doesn't stop just because there's a revolution: "May God strengthen you all. Our country could be so good if the people running it feared God," then "And are you not thinking of coming out to see the land for an hour or so?" The Land! The Land is the little orchard-cum-palm grove near the Pyramids that my mother bought maybe twenty years ago. It's only about half an acre, but with this being Egypt, Kemet, the Land of the Black Earth, it produces in abundance dates and mangoes, limes and melons, and whatever vegetables are in season. My mother bought it from Hagg Kamal, a retired schoolmaster, and he continued to look after it for her. She

came out every Friday afternoon, and they would sit on the stone
verandah and talk leftist politics, and he would tell her jokes. Soon
after my mother died, at eighty, Hagg Kamal, who was eighty-five,
had a stroke. To receive his condolences for my mother, I visited
him at home, and six months later Ala, Laila, and I were all there
again to offer condolences in turn to his widow and family.

So now my mother's children have to look after the Land, and
now the little house on the Land needs fixing, and Osta Ashraf is
fixing it for us, and that's why he and I are driving along Pyramid
Avenue on this Friday noon after prayers. I know I'm getting old
because as we drive, I'm wondering, yet again, at the changes; at
how this urban sprawl has taken hold in the short space of my
adulthood. I take care not to gaze out the window and say, "Imagine . . ." But it really did used to be green fields on either side, the
fields that fed Cairo.

"He's not gone," Osta Ashraf says.

"No."

"People were devastated last night."

"Yes."

"What's he waiting for?"

Which is indeed the question everyone is asking.

⁓⁓⁓⁓

We had been so sure. Wednesday had brought a rolling wave of
strikes: in Kafr el-Sheikh in the Delta, thousands had besieged
the governor's office, the workers of PetroTrade and the Co-op
and three other oil companies came out against Sameh Fahmi, the
minister for petroleum and mineral resources, the Water and Sewage Workers of Cairo came out, and the Garbage Collectors. The
boss of the National Union of Journalists—a regime man—was
thrown out of his office, and the younger journalists of the govern-

ment mouthpiece, *al-Ahram*, issued the supplement *el-Tahrir,* in support of the revolution. Everywhere people had scented freedom.

Spokespeople and committees had for days been going off to meet with SCAF to propose presidential councils and interim cabinets, and on Thursday SCAF had declared it was in a state of "permanent convention" to monitor developments and plan how to "safeguard the nation, its achievements and its ambitions." The camera, lingering over the generals in their wood-paneled meeting room with the flags and the flowers, seemed to be underlining the absence, for the first time, of the Supreme Commander of the Armed Forces: Hosni Mubarak.

From the afternoon on Thursday, everybody was heading for the Midan. We were certain: today would be it. Time passed and passed. The clock on the Arab League building said 8:30. The Midan, all geared up to celebrate, held its breath.

I'm in front of the "Artists for the Revolution" stage. Like the hundreds of thousands around me, I'm bouncing, waving. West el-Balad (Downtown) are pounding the floorboards. There's no room to dance because we're squashed so close together, but everyone's bobbing and swaying and singing along. The uplifted hand of Omar Makram's statue blesses us all, and so does the half-moon, farther up, nestling—truly—in the fronds of a palm tree. Tahrir is bubbling, bobbing—and so's the whole country. Maybe the whole world. We're waiting. I know my family's in the Midan—but so are a million people. I know we'll all find each other eventually.

Nine thirty, and nothing's happened.

Tomorrow we shall learn that while we, the people, were waiting in Tahrir, our soon-to-be-deposed president was on the phone to his friend, the former defense minister of Israel, Benjamin Ben-Eliezer. For twenty minutes he complained that America was abandoning him and prophesied that "civil unrest" would not stop in Egypt but would spread to the whole Middle East and the Gulf.[7]

A hand on my shoulder, and it's my brother Ala. I've no idea how he's found me, but I hang on to his arm, and we work our way through the crowd, and we find Sohair, and she and I sit on the curb facing Omar Makram. Someone brings us tea, and we clutch at the glasses, cup them, expose as much as we can of our palms to their warmth. Ala is standing with a group of friends who're discussing whether we're actually in the middle of a military coup and the revolution is about to be turned into a sideshow. We need a figure, or a group, to step forward and claim the revolution, in Tahrir and with Tahrir behind them. The one individual who could conceivably do this is el-Baradei, but when he came to Tahrir, he couldn't take it and had to leave after fifteen minutes. He doesn't like crowds. Alaa, my nephew, and many of the young people have for days been trying to put together coalitions, governments. Sometimes they've consulted us, and we've sat in the street forming cabinets. But we're in a catch-22 situation: there is no mechanism for Tahrir to select and mandate a group to talk to SCAF. So separate "leaderships" are taking it upon themselves to do it. And the talks are private, which means that anyone who talks to SCAF now automatically loses credibility with the Midan.

We wait on the curb. We walk. We join an arguing group. Three young women come and ask if I'm me; they've seen me on television and think I'm "clean." One is a doctor, Hoda Yousri, the other two are in the final year of school and want to be journalists. They live in Ma'adi, and they've been collecting files on the people who were killed there on the twenty-eighth. They want a good contact in the media. Hoda also wants a contact who will help her help the injured. They say more than twenty people have been killed in Ma'adi and that the police were particularly vicious and let criminals loose on the people and started using live ammunition straight off. They say there was a sniper stationed near the house used by the Israeli ambassador, and he killed anyone who came within range. The young women have been collecting infor-

mation from families of the dead and injured. They say the area
around Gumhureyya Street is full of posters of shuhada as though
you were in Nablus or Bint Jbeil. We exchange phone numbers as
cries rise from everywhere to "Hush! Hush!"

Hush.

And unbelievably, he does not go. And unbelievably, he has
not understood. And quite believably, he cannot change his game.
In our millions across the country, we listen to him patronize the
shabab, "speaking to you as a father," assuring them that the blood
of "your martyrs," the young people his police and his thugs have
killed—more than three hundred, we think—has not been shed
in vain, promising us that he'll move forward and fulfill legitimate demands—people start angry chants, but the Midan shushes
them; we listen intently. He trots out the tired old "I will not be
dictated to from abroad" trope, and we stare at each other in disbelief; this person who's been doing America and Israel's bidding
for thirty years will not be dictated to from abroad! When he
declares his determination to carry on "serving" his country, we
erupt: "Don't you understand? *Irhal* means depart!" He promises dialogue, waffle, constitutional changes, waffle, he talks about
team spirit and safeguarding the economy, and the crowd yells:
"Thief!" When, twelve minutes in, he starts on the "I was once
young like you" riff, a great collective groan goes up, and when
he ends with delegating presidential powers to the vice president,
we erupt.

The Midan is furious and in tears. What will it take? I write:
"By choosing this path, Mubarak is deliberately pushing Egypt
further into crisis. He is putting the army in a position where
they will soon have to confront either the Egyptian people or the
president and his Presidential Guard. He is also ensuring that by
the time the revolution is victorious, the military will be in a far
stronger position than when all this started. We are on the streets.
There is no turning back." People are on the move. Crowds move

to Maspero but still besiege the Radio and Television building rather than breaking into it. And others start the long trek to Urouba Palace, Mubarak's Cairo home.

⁄⁄⁄⁄

"He still doesn't understand," I say to Osta Ashraf.

"He understands," he says. "He's just obstinate."

I call Laila for news. She says that people, millions of people, people who've never come out before, are moving into the *midans* of all the cities, that Tahrir is full.

"This regime would rather see the country ruined than let go," Osta Ashraf says. He gets out of the car to open the gates of the Land.

When I'm here, I leave the world behind. For a while. Except I keep thinking about my mother. Wishing I hadn't so often wriggled out of coming here when she asked me. What had I done with those few saved hours anyway? Wishing I'd done this refurbishment while she was alive. But she would not have let me. She was opposed to spending money "unnecessarily." But maybe she would. And she always liked what I did when I'd done it. Oddly, very oddly, I'd refurbished our *madfan*, our burial house, just months before she went. I'd wanted to do it for ages, but I'd been afraid it would be a bad omen—as though I were expecting it to receive someone. And then, when my father was in hospital for a while, I had his whole flat decorated and all the furniture reupholstered and restored for when he came home, and I thought that was so life-affirming that I could afford to slip in the *madfan*. We gave it a ceiling of pharaonic blue with a band of gold running between it and the cream walls. We polished all the stone and brick and marble and bought new plants and put fresh netting on the windows. And five months later my mother was buried there.

Osta Ashraf is holding the gate. He's always so neat and clipped and pressed, he could have stepped out of a fifties schoolbook. He wants me to decide how to align the floor tiles. The house is crooked, and whatever we do they'll look slightly off anyway. What I'd like to do is align them to the center and have them be off at the various walls. But the tiler says that can't be done, so I choose, haphazardly, a wall in the kitchen and say we'll align to that.

I go up the ladder to the roof and sit. The Pyramids are there, just beyond those trees. We used to come out to the Pyramids at least once a month. We'd run around in the desert, measure our height against the huge rocks of the lowest rung of the great Pyramid of Khufu, attempt a bit of climbing, and have tea in the King's Lodge. (The king, Farouk, had "lodges" at the Pyramids, Helwan, Fayyoum, all the beauty spots of Egypt, and the 1952 revolution turned them all into cafés for the people.) And always, always, we would stand at the edge of the plateau, looking down toward Cairo, and marveling at the definiteness of the line between the desert and the green valley; the line this little bit of an orchard is on; the line I'm standing on now.

I need to go to our *madfan*. I've not visited for a while. My mother, Toufi, Khalu, my grandfather and grandmother—all there. When Omar made his first film, *Maydoum*, he shot a scene in the *madfan*. They hung up white sheets to reflect the light and weighed them down on the roof with bricks. And a brick came loose and crashed onto his head. Forever now, in bright sunlight, superimposed on the marble sarcophagus of those whom I love but see no longer, I see my son, slowly crumpling to his knees, on his face a look—not of fear or of pain but of intense and interested surprise. Before the blood started making tracks down his face.

I climb down and discuss the roofing. We'll roof the house with dried palm branches. This will be the Big House, the playground and memory-former of the coming generation of our family. Amal,

Lulie's daughter, has given us Amina. Maybe Alaa and Manal will follow. And the others, too. Soon.

Hamed, who looks after the Land, makes me walk to the crumbling end wall. The neighbor children climb over it and steal the fruit. He wants me to rebuild it. I haven't the heart to tell him that the fruit he sends us is so plentiful that, even after it's distributed among the whole family, sometimes a few pieces will rot at the bottom of the fridge. I don't mind the children stealing it. I can't tell him that, though, so I say let's not do the wall just yet; enough expense doing the house.

We walk through the Land and pick juicy limes off a tree. Hamed shows me a palm that's collapsed. Why? Its time had come. "Look at the grace of God," Osta Ashraf says, "a palm tree, even when it rots and falls, will fall into a clear space so it hits nothing." Hamed agrees: "A palm tree will never cause harm."

4:00 P.M.

" 'Bye!"
   " 'Bye!"
   " 'Bye!"

The afternoon is a series of 'byes and doors slamming as Sohair, my brother, Salma, Mariam, and the assorted friends and family who've been in the house go off to Tahrir. I sit at Sohair's dining table and work on the copy that I'm to complete and file the minute Mubarak has spoken. Will he leave?

I am ready to go the minute I've filed. We've all perfected routines, routines and costumes born of five years' experience with baltagis and Central Security. Mine is cotton trousers with zipped pockets over leggings. Actually, the "cotton trousers" are the pants Egyptian farmers and laborers wear under their *galabeyyas*. They're wide and loose but with fitted cuffs. They have zipped pockets and drawstring waists, and they come in all sizes in beige, gray, navy, and white and sell for twenty-five Egyptian pounds. One pocket for my ID card, the other for cash and mobile, a shoulder bag for water, notepad, pens, scarf, and tissues. A tight T-shirt with a loose shirt on top and then a looser cardigan. The layered look—so if you're grabbed, you can shed clothing and not be naked. An elastic band for the hair, shades, cotton socks, and flat shoes, and you're ready for anything.

The phone keeps ringing. London, Montreal, Delhi, Dublin, the world wants to know how it feels to be in Tahrir, and I keep saying I don't know because I'm not there. But over a million people are.

I'm writing and pacing. Writing and hedging. Will it be a piece about how we're free? Or a piece about how we're waiting, holding on? Pacing and answering the phone. Keeping an eye on the TV. Tahrir is the center of the universe, and it's ten minutes away, and I'm not there. I go out onto the balcony. The street is deserted. The bats flit in and out of the mango trees. I write another paragraph. Pace and check my bag and pockets.

6:00 p.m.

It happens. A brief statement delivered by Omar Suleiman look-ing even deader than usual, with a scowling, heavyset man in the frame behind him: Hosni Mubarak has stepped aside; the armed forces are in control of the country. My heart is pounding, and my hands are freezing. I'm so—so full, I think I shall burst. I rush back to the table and look at what I've written. I can hardly read, but I know it won't do. I sit down, screw my eyes shut, and take several deep breaths. Then I start again:

> "In Tahrir Square and on the streets of Egypt the people
> have reclaimed their humanity. Now they will reclaim

their state. . . . As of this minute there is no embezzling
president, no extraordinary-rendition-facilitator
Vice-President, no corrupt Cabinet, no rigged Parliament,
no brutal emergency laws, no—regime! We have entered a
new phase. For two weeks the people have been chanting:
'The People! / The Army! / One Hand!' We will now work
to make this true in the most positive way possible: that
the army will guarantee peace and safety while we put in
place the civilian structures that will help us to articulate
how we want to run our country. . . . In Tahrir I had met
two women in the last stages of pregnancy. They were due
to give birth any day and they wanted to give birth in a free
Egypt. Now they can have their babies. . . . The world has
been watching this struggle between a tenacious, brutal and
corrupt government, using all the apparatus of the state,
and a great and varied body of citizens, armed with nothing
but words and music and legitimacy and hope. The support
of the world came through to us loud and clear, and what
has happened here over the last two weeks will give voice
and power to civilian citizens everywhere. . . . Our work
will begin now: to rebuild our country in as exemplary
a fashion as the one in which we've won it back. To
remember our young people who died that this night might
happen and to carry them forward with us into a future
good for us and good for our friends and good for the
world . . . Look at the streets of Egypt tonight; this is what
hope looks like." Press SEND.

I emerge from Mesa7a Street straight into a traffic jam in
Midan el-Gala2; everybody's trying to get to Tahrir. I sit with my
windows open to the drumming, the happiness. It's a party; joyful
cries ring out constantly, people are dancing and jumping up and
down on the traffic roundabout, dancing on the roofs of their cars,

handing out candy. A man walks around with a tray handing out wedding sherbet. Kids are climbing lampposts to wave their flags from the highest point possible. I call my sister, my father, Omar, Ismail, Lulie. I call Osta Ashraf: We've done it! We've done it! We've done it! We've done it! We only inch forward from time to time, but we don't mind.

You can hardly see the lions on Qasr el-Nil for the kids climbing onto them. All the mobiles are held high; everybody is being photographed in the moment. I'm part of the surge of happy humanity flowing across the bridge. Beneath us, our river, alight with sparkling lights, with fireworks, with song. Then, Tahrir.

You breathe deep when you get to Tahrir. A steady roar rises from it, and there are more fireworks, and a million flags are waving and banners fly: "No More Torture!" "Welcome to Tomorrow!" "Congratulations to the World!" And as I walk into the Midan, the song that welcomes me from every loudspeaker is Abd el-Haleem's 1962 "bel-Ahdan": *In our a-arms, in our a-arms, in our a-arms, in our arms our lovely country in our a-arms . . .* The last time I heard this song was in 2005, in the great auditorium of the Opera House, and the whole auditorium wept in desolation; now I see us all here: we're crying and laughing and jumping and hugging and singing, and then "Watani Habibi" comes on, the pan-Arab anthem that's been forbidden for decades, and everyone knows it by heart and roars along:

> *In Palestine and the rebellious south*
> *We'll bring back your freedom for you*

and more gently,

> *We're a nation that protects not threatens*
> *We're a nation that maintains not destroys*

and now the Ultras are circling the Midan, their energy like an electric current fizzing off the walls of the Arab League. "Everyone who loves Egypt / Come and help fix Egypt," off the Mugamma3 building, "We'll get married / We'll have kids," off the Egyptian Museum, "Lift your head up high, you're Egyp-tian. Lift your head up high, you're Egyp-tian. Lift your head up. . . ."

And in the center of the Midan a stillness. The pictures of the murdered. The shuhada. Sally Zahran, massive blows to the head, glances upward and smiles. Muhammad Abd el-Menem, shot in the head, his hair carefully gelled. Ali Muhsin, shot, carries a laughing toddler with a big blue sea behind him. Muhammad Bassiouny, shot, lies back with his two kids. Muhammad Emad holds his arms open wide and wears a LONDON T-shirt. Islam poses against the Nile. Ihab Muhammadi smiles, but his eyes are thoughtful . . . and more, 843 more. In the triumph and joy and uncertainty of the moment, they are the still center; the young people, the shabab, who walked into the Midan in peace, to save their country and to save us. Our future has been paid for with their lives. There is no turning back.

REVOLUTION II

Eighteen Days
Were Never Enough

OCTOBER 2012

Khaled Abd el-Fattah, Alaa and Manal's son, was not after all—born on 24 November. He was born on 6 December. In the pause between the battles of Muhammad Mahmoud Street and Parliament Street, our family acquired the second member of its new generation, my father his first great-grandchild. And our small corner of the revolution moved into Manal's fifth-floor hospital suite on Roda Island. Omar filmed the baby and the family, edited footage of Alaa in court, and uploaded. Mona typed and tweeted and phoned; the army had taken more prisoners in Muhammad Mahmoud, and the campaign against military trials for civilians was busier than ever. Sanaa worked on her newspaper and the Midan tasks that had fallen to her. The baby's two grandfathers gave media interviews. When Ahmad Seif held the baby, he told the TV cameras that he was going to start a campaign for his right to retire and spend his remaining time playing with his grandson. Laila said if there had to be interviews, they should be done outside, in the street.

The river here is the widest it gets in Cairo, wide and placid, and on this quiet street it's hard to look around and believe a revolution is taking place. Hard to believe the degree to which every space, every concept is being contested, being transformed. But step back into the bustle of our rooms, and it all starts up again. Manal's girlfriends and Khaled's two grandmothers are in and out of the inner room that's being kept quiet and separate for mother and baby. Occasionally Manal comes out to join us. Even in our loving midst and with Khaled in her arms, there's an aloneness about her. We show her the lobby filling with flowers and cards and wishes and chocolates and flags and miniature cardigans with

MY DAD'S A HERO knitted onto them. And Khaled's dad is still in jail.

Alaa, as I wrote back in October 2011, had been summoned by the military prosecutor to answer charges of "incitement and destruction." The summons had arrived at his home on Saturday October 22, while he was on his way to give a keynote speech at a software conference in San Francisco. He came home a week later and sat up late into the night with Manal and his sisters and parents discussing the courses of action open to him. When he presented himself at the military prosecutor's next morning with his father and twenty volunteer lawyers, Alaa had decided to take the most radical course: he told the prosecutor that he did not acknowledge the legitimacy of the court and would not submit to the investigation. Civilians should not be tried before military courts, he said. Also, since the military themselves were an accused party in the Maspero case, they could not bring the case, prosecute it, and judge it. The prosecutor jailed him pending trial. The lawyers argued that he had come back from abroad to stand before the court, that he had a known address and family, and that his wife was due to have their baby soon—he wasn't going to run away. But the military locked him up anyway. They locked him up for the maximum they could: fifteen days renewable.

Alaa had arrived at the Maspero protest after the killing stopped. And he had been in jail when both Muhammad Mahmoud and Parliament Street happened. When Ahmad Seif was asked—again on television—how he felt about his son being in jail, he said he was fine with it: "This way they can't gun him down on the street. I wish they'd take my daughters, too."

His daughters, Mona and Sanaa, were both beaten up by the military in the events of Parliament Street. With the stitches fresh in her head, Sanaa wondered on TV, "Why do they still do this? They drag the shabab away and beat them and the minute they let them go they're back in the protests. Don't they see that it's useless?"

Well, no they didn't. For a long time. Perhaps they still don't. Perhaps that's one of the characteristics of power: its belief in itself is unshakable. Or perhaps they have no option; if they are to prevail, to survive, they have to use violence. Maspero, we now see with hindsight, was one stop in a sustained military campaign that SCAF fought against the revolution.

It had started, though most of us didn't see it, on 28 January 2011, the Day of Wrath, when Salma, Mariam, and I, holding our ground with thousands of our fellow citizens at the Qasr el-Nil entrance to Tahrir, had heard the cry "The Army's here!" and rejoiced at the arrival of the red berets of the Military Police—an affirmation that the Ministry of the Interior was in retreat. But just along the Corniche, possibly just meters from us, a young student was being dragged from his car and beaten—by the military. They tasered him and cracked his head open and kept him in a military jail for sixteen days. And there were others, many others,[1] but, at that point, we had no channels of information to tell us what was happening. Then, on 2 February, at the Battle of the Camel, we watched the military block the approaches to government buildings and then stand by while the regime's baltagis attacked us. On the third we had the first intimation that they were using the Egyptian Museum as a detention center. On 11 February Mubarak stepped down, and General Muhsin al-Fangari read the famous SCAF statement promising to safeguard the revolution and—the icing on the cake—performed a military salute to the souls of our shuhada. Two weeks later Military Police attacked demonstrators in Tahrir with sticks and tasers. They apologized next day for the "unintended clashes between military police and revolutionaries" and promised it wouldn't happen again, but they had detained Amr el-Beheiri and nine others, and they tried and sentenced them to jail—the event that gave birth to the No to Military Trials for Civilians campaign. The military continued to fight the revolution; the places zoom by, the dates gather speed: on 9 March they attacked Tahrir and arrested a hundred people, among them eighteen young women who became the victims of the infamous "virginity tests." (One of the young women, Samira Ibrahim, later took them to court and became a national heroine.) On 9 April the army hit Tahrir again to retrieve fifty of its own officers who had joined the revolution. The officers were in the central garden, and the shabab formed cordons round them, but the army attacked heavily. Two people were killed, the officers were arrested, jailed, and subjected to a program of "re-education." Five of them remain in jail as I write. One, Muhammad Wadie, is a Special Operations commander, a demolition expert; he's also a guitarist and a poet and smuggles his work out of jail.[2] On we go: the Israeli embassy I on 15 May, the Balloon Theater on 28 June, Abbaseyya I on 23 July, Tahrir on 1 August, the Israeli embassy II on 9 September, the Ministry of Defense on 30 September, Maspero on 9 October, Muhammad Mahmoud on 19–24 November, Parliament Street on 16–22 December, Port Said on 1 February (2012), Mansour Street for the next few days, and Abbaseyya II in May.

These events mark the road that has taken us to where we are now: on the first anniversary of the Maspero massacre with thousands taking part in a march of remembrance, vowing not to forget and not to let go.

Now, in October 2012, Egypt has an elected president—who was the first and real choice of only 5 million out of an electorate of 52 million. We have no parliament because it's been dissolved. We have a committee writing the Constitution—but it too might be dissolved because it was elected by the dissolved parliament and, in any case, no one likes the draft articles it's floating. We have a judiciary that's been widely discredited, a police force that's furious and out of control, its long-standing baltagi militias unpaid and unhappy. And we have a political leadership that seems chronically dysfunctional.

Meanwhile the revolution is determined to push toward its declared aims: bread, freedom, social justice. It is also determined to establish its narrative of what happened from 25 January 2011 until the elections of June 2012 and beyond. And vital to both these aims is the need to hold on to the transformations that have taken place in our cities and in ourselves.

Across the country people's landscapes have been changed. In Cairo a new map has come into being; the names of its spaces resonate with new significance and new energy.

MASPERO, 9 OCTOBER 2011

The French Egyptologist's name that had come to mean state radio and television now means 9 October and the military lying in wait by the Radio and Television building to open fire on the vanguard of the unarmed—mainly Christian—protesters who were marching from Shubra to Tahrir. It means armored personnel carriers zigzagging through the panicked crowds smashing into people, dragging them along, running them over. It means State Television itself plumbing new depths of baseness as it urges Muslims to go out and attack Christians to "protect the Egyptian army." Maspero means a young man in a red lumberjack shirt throwing himself on the neck of a commanding officer watching from the sidelines. (Was that officer Hamdi Badeen, the chief of Military Police, at this very moment retired with honors to be Egypt's military attaché in Beijing?) The young man begs him, pleads with him, in his despair he slides down the officer's body till he kisses his feet, imploring him to stop the killing. Maspero is the morgue in the Coptic Hospital and someone's mother screaming, her eyes still wide with disbelief. It's Vivian's grief-stricken face turned to the sky as she presses Michael's cold hand to her heart.

Maspero is Mina dead.

Mina Danial was twenty-three and had the widest smile. Mina Danial had a passion for Egyptology. Mina Danial refused to be ghettoized into "Christian affairs" but insisted on the struggle for everybody's rights. He'd been among the hundreds wounded on 28 January and in Maspero they murdered him with one bullet to the chest in the first few seconds of the killings; the bullet went through lung and liver. Now Mina manifests in varied ways. His stenciled face was the first to appear after Khaled Said's on the walls of the revolution. And in Muhammad Mahmoud, we saw for the first time that same stencil, on a square of red fabric, flying under the wing of the Egyptian flag that danced in great arcs and circles in the smoke of the guns and the tear gas.

Mina's banner appeared when we most needed it. This double flag, the large Egyptian one fluttering over the red square with the now-familiar face and the legend "We are all Mina Danial" became an immediate icon, transforming into myth even as it was real and palpable in our hands—even as the bit of fabric grew tired and tattered. Throughout the year, Mina's banner appeared at the darkest points of our confrontations with the military, at the protests outside Parliament, at the heart of the strikes. It spoke of a courage and gallantry that could never be defeated. It lifted our spirits and put courage in our hearts, because where we saw it rise, we knew that around it, under it, there were kindred spirits and a space that was human and humane and inclusive and clever and free. And Mina's banner appeared in Cairo and Luxor, in Alexandria and Aswan; everywhere where people were expressing an idea of freedom and dignity, social justice and inclusiveness, the red banner with Mina's stenciled face under the Egyptian flag was there.

And the same stencil, surrounded first by a garland of flowers then by a geometric arrangement of lotus, heralded an eruption of innovation in graffiti, the art that—together with poetry and music—most expressed the revolutionary moment. Then Mina was the first shaheed to appear in a full-length portrait—he appeared one night on the wall of the Mugamma3 Building and was soon joined by other young shuhada posed together in a comradely group: Khaled Said, Ali Taha, and Rami al-Sharqawi. A few days later we were dazzled by a larger-than-life freehand portrait of Mina sitting cross-legged on the ground, two huge angel wings springing rainbow-colored from his back.

Maspero was the consolidation of SCAF and the Dakhleyya working together against the revolution. We'd seen their first simple cooperation in Abbaseyya I; now we saw them plotting, daring to kill several people in one event, trying to turn sections of society against each other, deploying state radio and TV to spread lies, silencing independent reports, and co-opting the leaders or elders of the targeted group—in this case, the priests who tried to bury the bodies without proper autopsies. Maspero was also the coalescing of a core revolutionary front that understood that the regime had not fallen with the departure of Hosni Mubarak and that rejected all initiatives or procedures with any connection to the current rulers of the country—the military.

////

At six o'clock on a cold, dark night in early November, Laila and I are walking fast on a narrow pavement by the river in Muneeb, in the southernmost part of Cairo. There's a loud and constant roar of traffic. This is the road that connects Cairo to Upper Egypt, and giant trucks are roaring past us, swirling up dust and exhaust fumes. Our old nanny, Dada Ziza, lives a few narrow lanes off this road. It's 3 November, and we'd been sitting in crawling traffic on the Ring Road for two hours, so we decided to get out of the car and go and visit her as we do at the beginning of every month. We're marching along in silence, because of the noise and because the military prosecutor has just renewed Alaa's imprisonment on remand for fifteen more days and there's nothing to say right now.

Alaa had refused to recognize the authority of the military court, and the military prosecutor had decided to jail him. They'd sent him to the Appeals prison in Bab el-Khalq. Next day three thousand people marched in support of Alaa, from Talʒat Harb to Tahrir, down Tahrir Street and through Abdeen to the prison. There a battalion of Central Security Forces faced us, and we could see more down the side streets. As our chanting and drumming grew louder, the roof of the prison was filled with plainclothesmen peering down at us. We stood for two hours chanting for Alaa and all the shabab held by the military, then we wound back into town. We chanted and distributed stickers and talked to people. Once again we were reclaiming our streets—and waiting to see what effect we would have.

Over the days protests were staged, graffiti appeared, poems were written, leading figures in the country contacted us to assure us that they expected SCAF to let him go soon. And Alaa stayed in jail.

So today we'd been in S28: the Military Court, way out in the Fifth Tagammuʒ on the southern section of the Ring Road. We got there at ten in the morning and joined the group of fifty or so of Alaa's comrades chanting outside the court. At midday the military took our IDs and mobiles—that's to say, the IDs and mobiles of the family and the lawyers—and let us in. We waited in a large courtroom. Thirty-two young men wearing the white training suits of prisoners on remand came into the room. They were handcuffed to each other. One of them was Alaa. He was handcuffed to a guard, and he was smiling at us and already talking to us, telling us quickly about the other prisoners, who they

were, and the ways in which they were being set up. The lawyers
started moving among them, taking names and contacts, so officers came and took us away and into a courtroom on our own.
They took the handcuffs off Alaa, and the guards went and sat at
the back of the room, and we all sat round him, Manal on one side
and Laila on the other, Sanaa and me opposite. His father moved
between the family group and the lawyers. Laila kept her hand on
her son all the time. Occasionally she would rest her head, for a
brief moment, against his shoulder. They had cut his long hair but
allowed him to choose the barber. He was shorn and beautiful. He
talked about the terrible conditions in the Appeals jail, about the
men held there unjustly, about his take on what was happening.
He asked me to deliver a message to Amr Helmy, the new minister
of health: *The Appeals jail is crammed with injured people. Their
injuries, untreated, will affect them for life. This doesn't need to happen; they can be treated well and seriously in jail.*

When the court came in, we stood up. Alaa was asked to stand
in front of the bench. The military prosecutor read out the list of
charges:

1. Taking by force weapons belonging to the Armed Forces.
2. The deliberate sabotage of the property of the Armed
   Forces.
3. Attacking public officials of the Armed Forces in the
   course of their duty.
4. Using violence and force against the Armed Forces.

The judge asked for Alaa's lawyer, and twenty-three lawyers
stepped forward, men and women from the Revolutionary Socialist end of the political spectrum right through to the Liberals, the
Brotherhood, and the Salafis, all in solidarity. Seven of them made
statements, and when they'd finished, Alaa said that he would like
to speak. He reminded the court that he had been imprisoned on

remand for forty-five days back in 2006 when he'd supported the Judiciary's bid for independence; he had no doubt that his imprisonment now, as then, was meant as a punishment. He pointed out Manal; surely his place—in the last days of her pregnancy—was at her side? He listed all the reasons why the authorities could be certain that he would present himself to the court when required. He spoke naturally and courteously and with such genuineness that I was sure that they would let him go.

They adjourned. And we encircled him again, and our lawyer friends brought us tea and biscuits, and it felt like one of our normal family gatherings except for Laila sticking so close to her son. And then suddenly our little group fragmented, and there were shouts—"Quick!" "Move!" "Down the stairs!"—and we were jumping out of our seats, and a tight posse of soldiers was moving away fast, and in its center was Alaa, and we were all running after him, and Manal couldn't run but her arm was stretched out, and she was holding a book and shouting "His book! His book!" and someone, it might have been me, grabbed the book from her and tore down the stairs because now the most important thing in the world was to give Alaa back the book he'd brought with him, the book he was in the middle of reading. So we hurtled down the stairs and out into the sunshine and saw him being bundled into a military transport and threw him his book, and they locked him in. We stood around calling, "We're still here. Can you hear us?" And he said, "Yes. Get information about the others." So we went to the other young prisoners: "I don't even know what I'm being charged with," "Don't forget us," "Your campaign is our only hope," "Do you have any campaign stickers?" And suddenly again the shouting: "The building's shutting down. Everyone out. Out. Quickly. Out." From inside his solitary transport, Alaa called out to us to find a way to let him know the decision of the court.

Because that's how they did it, you see. They waited and waited for the phone call that was to instruct them what their decision would be. Then they grabbed their prisoner and locked him up, dispersed family and lawyers onto the street, and announced their decision to an empty courtroom. And when we were in the car, crawling in the traffic on the Ring Road, one of the lawyers called Laila and told her the military were keeping Alaa for another fifteen days.

Now, as we walk, Laila is saying something. I lean toward her, shout into the traffic: "What did you say?"

"I'm going on hunger strike," she shouts back. "From tomorrow."

We stumble headlong on the ruined pavement, the trucks thundering past us, and she shouts that she believes they have it in for him and she's going to pull out all the stops. Total hunger strike, nothing but water. I say, "You can't look like you want special treatment for your son." No, she says, she's going to fast until the whole Maspero case is removed from the military and referred to a civilian court. A friend said once that when the sky's about to fall and crush us, Laila Soueif appears and holds it up. And this is what she's doing; she's trying to keep a terrible evil away from her son and the other young men in the white training suits. I'm at a loss. I say, "Should I join you?" She says no—or not yet, anyway. I say, "Is there a chance you'll die?" She shrugs. I say, "You won't tell Dada Ziza, will you? Because it'll kill her—after she's killed you first."

~~~~

Mona's blog three days later:

> Sanaa goes for a nap in the car. My uncle goes to buy us
> some cartons of juice. My dad and Tante Sohair (my uncle's
> wife) sit on the kerb solving a sudoko together. Tante
> Ahdaf drags a chair away from the shade and suns herself
> while she writes on her laptop. Mama and Manal read the

newspapers and mark every item connected to Alaa. Azza and Rasha have vanished for the moment. I'm chopping up a salad. My cousin, Omar, is filming all this. This was not a scene at the club; this was the first day of Eid on the pavement opposite the wall of Tora Istiqbal Jail. It could look strange to a lot of people, but to my weird, wonderful family it was totally normal.

It was the Eid and every prisoner was allowed an extra visit. And so we'd become one of the many thousands of families spending their Eid morning camped outside the gates of a jail that holds a loved one.

We'd come to visit my brother. All jails permit a maximum of three blood relations to visit at any one time, but we're a family that loves to crowd together and make a lot of noise so eleven of us came along and were so surprised when they wouldn't let us all in!

When they wouldn't let us all in, we formed an assembly line to pass the bags we'd brought him to each other, through the security scanner, and to the rest of us till they got to the soldier at the door. Two young officers stood at a distance watching: pillows, blankets, soaps, shampoo, fruit and vegetables, fruit and vegetables, books, books, books—they intervened. They had the books carried over and bent to look through them: novels, graphic novels, comics—one of them looked up at me and Sohair, his face alive with interest: "Who is it you're coming to visit?"

"Alaa Abd el-Fattah."

His face broke into a wide smile. He turned to his colleague: "Didn't I tell you?" And back to us, still with the big smile: "You are very welcome here. I knew it! Who would be bringing these kinds of things to jail? You can't take them in, though. They're too many." We negotiated. Half the books went in, the other half we took back, for next time.

~~~~

As the days passed, the list of charges against Alaa grew. He was charged with destroying an armored personnel carrier and stealing the weapons it was carrying. A witness was found to say she'd seen him do this. She was the mistress of a general who was the former head of psychological operations in the Armed Forces. When Laila asked—in an open letter in the papers—why the army hadn't raided Alaa's house if they believed he was in possession of a mini-arsenal of automatics, why they had waited till two weeks after Maspero to summon him, another witness came forward to say he'd seen Alaa run away with the weapons and throw them into the Nile.

~~~~

Alaa's article, "Your Solidarity Is Not Enough," smuggled out from jail and published on *Manal and Alaa's bit bucket free speech from the bletches* on 7 November,[3] urged everyone, of every political color, to take to the streets on the eighteenth, to remove legislative power from the hands of SCAF, and to insist on elections on the twenty-eighth and a swift handover of power to the elected Parliament. No one knew how he smuggled out his articles. Manal, Laila, and Mona went to Tora jail every visiting time. Sanaa did a food, newspaper, and laundry run every day. Ahmad Seif, unwilling to use the family allocation, visited his son as his lawyer. On the eighteenth, *Shorouk* published Alaa's "The Hostage State," in which he added his voice to those insisting that the Constitution must not be written under the supervision of SCAF.

SCAF had gathered around itself a collection of old politicians, judges, academics, and experts various. I would not accuse them of betraying the revolution; I think that for them the revolution had been an excellently useful event to sweep away the Mubaraks. But now that that was done, it was time for order to be reestablished. For them, it was always the state that mattered, not the people. They could not see "a people" operating outside the known and accepted framework of the state—they saw us as a mob, mindless, and bent on chaos. It was natural for them to gather around the military, around SCAF, the one pillar of the state that seemed unshaken. Perhaps it was even their consciences that guided them to help SCAF fight the revolution.

Since August the leaderships of all the political forces—the Left, the Liberals, the Salafis, the Muslim Brotherhood—had been holding meeting after meeting trying to reach an agreement on basic principles to govern the Constitution. SCAF too had been doing its work, and a document produced by Dr. Ali al-Selmi was the military's contribution to the debate. It proposed that it was now SCAF—not the people or their representatives—who were the "protectors of revolutionary legitimacy." And it gave SCAF authority over the larger part of the country's budget and sole authority over military budgets and over any legislation that affected the military.

For most people, the "Selmi Document" was proof that SCAF was trying to steal the revolution, and that it was getting help from sections of the judiciary and the old political elite. The country was in an uproar.

Alaa's "Maybe I'm Confused" is representative of the concerns of the street; it engages with the processes of elections and constitution writing but knows that these are, finally, the instruments, not the aims, of the revolution. Alaa calls on his friends and supporters to carry on working on several fronts. He urges them to join or create neighborhood or workplace Popular Committees to protect the revolution; to join campaigns like No to Military Trials for Civilians; to organize TweetNadwas; to investigate and publish information about the remnants of the old regime; to support the electoral campaign of "The Revolution Continues"—the group of parliamentary candidates coalescing around the revolution's aims of human rights and social justice; to follow up the initiative to set up a People's TV Channel and the Let's Write Our Constitution project. All this, and to not abandon direct action but to join the millioneyya called for on the eighteenth.

The eighteenth had been declared the Millioneyya of One Demand: *tasleem al-sulta*, the handover of power—by SCAF to an elected civilian body, by April 2012.

MUHAMMAD MAHMOUD STREET, 19–24 NOVEMBER 2011

There are an estimated eight thousand people that the police, the military, and their baltagis have injured to a point where they are not able to resume their normal lives. Sami Emile is a young geographical surveyor. He had just married the woman he loved, a lawyer. They owned their apartment. His life was set. The army smashed his leg, and he now drags it behind him and has to pay for the physiotherapy that just about keeps it from withering away. I met him at the Coptic Hospital when I went to visit the Maspero injured. His leg had been smashed—not in Maspero but in an earlier clash with the military in March. He was just visiting. He was incredibly gentle. Soft-voiced. His eyes kept filling with tears as he asked why. Why was all this happening? As I was leaving, an older man who was very ill with a bullet in the stomach called me over. I sat bent close because he was whispering to me. He said, "If you can do one thing, do it for Sami. He's the one who needs it most."

Another: Randa S. is a nurse. The doctors in the field clinics always got her to do the stitching because she was so good at it. On 28 January she was suturing the heads of the shabab, and a Central Security Officer beat her so badly that she was paralyzed. In fact, he would have killed her, but she stabbed him in the hand with her needle. She's in the rehabilitation unit at Agouza Hospital—the one where we took Abu Mustafa's testimony on 2 August—and she's giving them hell. She's in a wheelchair but has got back the use of her arms, and she plays revolutionary music and organizes her fellow injured.[4]

Some of the injured are still fighting, and some are broken, but all need long-term provision. They need a plan; they need jobs that they can do and that can support them. The majority of them are responsible for households. One of the things that this revolution has revealed is how many young people—young men especially—support parents, how many have dead fathers and look after their mothers, how many fund their sisters through college or weddings and need to see them settled and safe before they can carve out their own lives. A lot of their injuries—particularly the people shot in the eyes—could have been rectified. But after they were given emergency treatment in the field clinics, they—if they were lucky—went into our abysmal public hospitals. Many doctors opened their clinics and treated people for free, many doctors came from abroad to help, but there was no system in place to ensure that patient and doctor found each other. In fact, there was no official will to take care of them at all. What care some got was philanthropic, through individuals and civil society actions. The government, under SCAF, was content to issue statements—crass at the best of times—about compensating people to the tune of X for a leg and Y for an eye, or—with more enthusiasm—about how imposters were trying to take advantage of the government's generosity and posing as injured.

Some of these injured had started a sit-in in Tahrir on Friday, 11 November, to demand that the government give them medical and practical provision. General Fangari of SCAF—he who had performed the military salute to the shuhada in February when the military promised to "safeguard the revolution"—now scoffed: *Let them go to the Midan with their demands. See if it'll do them any good.*

A week later, on Friday the eighteenth, hundreds of thousands of us went into Tahrir to insist that elections had to happen on the twenty-eighth and to demand that SCAF set a date for a handover.

Manal was one week away from the due date of her baby, and despite everything—despite Alaa in jail, her furniture in cargo from South Africa, her flat topsy-turvy, and the nursery unfinished—she was radiant. Laila was on day fifteen of her hunger strike, and people—hundreds of people—came up to talk to her, to put their arms round her shoulders, and to kiss her head. I stayed close by, pestering her with my concern. "Listen," she said, "I really feel the same as in the days when I used to eat." Fifteen days without food, and the only change I could register was that her voice was more quiet. She submitted to some organ function tests set up by Lulie, and they seemed okay, but I was worried. I tried a tangential approach: "Isn't it hard for Alaa knowing you're on hunger strike?"

"No," she said. "That's our relationship: we trust in each other's strength."

And it was Alaa's birthday: today he was thirty. His friends brought a giant birthday cake to the Midan, and we all lit sparklers and sang happy birthday to him in front of the Mugamma3, in the area where once again the families of the shuhada and the injured were congregating.

Tahrir was back. SCAF's attempt to control the writing of the Constitution had galvanized everybody, and the call to protest had gone out from all the parties, the coalitions, and the movements. The Midan and the streets surrounding it were full, spirits were high, people were in a good humor, the Ultras were out in force, and the sky was lit up with their fireworks. The plan was that everyone would leave at the end of the day, and most people did. But as usual, when the shabab are in a position where they feel they'll be abandoning the injured or the shuhada families, some of them can't do it. Around two hundred people decided to stay.

Next day, Saturday, Central Security Forces moved. They tore down some tents of the sit-in and set fire to the others. They beat the injured. Supporters rushed in to Tahrir to help fight them off, and by nightfall, when I went down to the Midan, there was gunfire and smoke and tear gas and hundreds of Security Forces with guns and sticks and hundreds of protesters hitting back at them with stones. The military stood by. From time to time they covered the Security Forces.

The Security Forces always entered Tahrir from Muhammad Mahmoud Street; this is their route from the Ministry of the Interior in Lazoghli, some seven hundred meters away. So it was on Muhammad Mahmoud that the protesters intercepted and eventually managed to stop them. For four days the shabab protected Tahrir and held off the Security Forces in Muhammad Mahmoud. The battle was presented by state media as "revolutionaries and baltagis try to storm the Dakhleyya building," but what the shabab were doing was once again protecting the Midan—unarmed. Fifty meters was the distance between relative normality and war. And the shabab taking a break from the front told us that soldiers had waved and indicated "peace" so they could change shifts and attack them again, and they told of the attacks breaking the traditional prayer-time ceasefire. A residential block caught fire, the shabab climbed to help the people inside, and Security shot them as they climbed. I learned later that Omar had come within inches of being shot when he and Aida, another young filmmaker, were trapped against a doorway in Falaki Street trying to hide from approaching soldiers. He turned his back to the street and covered her with his body, and they heard the soldiers come closer and closer till they came to a stop next to them. As they heard the clicks of the shotguns, she leaped out from behind him shouting, "A girl! There's a girl! I'm a girl!" and the soldiers didn't shoot.

At six p.m. on 23 November, I wrote:

> I've just read this tweet: "Eat a good breakfast. Take a ruck-sack with a gas mask and swimming goggles. Write your name on your arm. Write your details into a message on your mobile. And go to the Midan."

Tuesday was declared a day to "Save the Nation," and people across the country once again demanded the abdication of SCAF. Tuesday night as the news cameras concentrated on Tahrir, the Army and Police were attacking citizens in other cities: in Alexandria, Assiut, Aswan, Damietta, Ismailia, Luxor, Mahalla, Mansoura, Sohag and Suez. And yet, of course, in this age of televised spectacle it was the images of Tahrir that were most relayed: Midan el-Tahrir teeming with citizens, decorated with flags, and clouded with tear-gas.

All day that Tuesday thousands had poured into the Midan. In the small hours of Sunday the little field hospital in the small mosque of Ibad al-Rahman had been pleading for a stethoscope, a blood pressure gauge, betadine, cotton wool. By Tuesday afternoon there were seven field hospitals around Tahrir stockpiled with equipment and medicines—all donated by the people coming in. Omar Makram Mosque and Qasr el-Doubara Church cross-referenced specialisations. On a wall between them someone had written: "We are the Midan: A Church, a Mosque and a Parliament."

On Tuesday two hundred young doctors walked in to the Midan together in their white coats and distributed themselves among the hospitals—in a few hours one of them had been killed.

The revolution is using what it learned back in January/ February and adding to it. Signposts, information, directions. Young men on motorbikes ferry the injured from the front lines to the field hospitals. The spontaneous, organic organization is breathtaking. And the creativity: when Malek Mostafa—a popular, newly married young activist had his eye shot out by the Army, one of the great bronze lions on Qasr el-Nil Bridge suddenly sported an eye patch.

In a flat on the 10th floor above Tahrir we were weeping under our gas-masks, the smell was so strong.

The protestors are unarmed. When the Army/ Police attack them they fight back bravely, using stones from the street, lobbing back gas canisters, keeping up a constant chanting and a constant drumming on the metal lamp-posts and street-signs, occasionally shooting fireworks. The Midan is well aware of the contrast between their drumming and fireworks and the deadly thud of the teargas canister and the treacherous silence of the sniper.

We're saying these are "ayyam el-farz"—the days of sorting. The situation is very intense. Just now, at that flashpoint on Muhammad Mahmoud where a truce was brokered at 3 and broken at 5, the Army/Police have shot the protestors at sunset prayers. The field hospitals in Qasr el-Doubara Church and Omar Makram Mosque are calling for neurologists; the motorbikes have brought in 50 cases in the last 10 minutes—[5]

In the events that radiated across Egypt from Muhammad Mahmoud Street, 3,800 young people were injured and 42 killed in Alexandria, Cairo, Ismailia, and Marsa Matrouh. Ahmad Sur-our was one of them, killed on the morning of the twenty-sixth, when a police car hit him and dragged him fifty meters down the street. His mother: "When they knocked on the door they said he's just injured in hospital I said he's in the morgue. I know my son. My son won't be laid low except by death. At the [Israeli] embassy he took two bullets and he never flinched. He kept them. Last night I told him: Enough. Enough! You're lucky nothing's happened to you so far. He said how can we be men and leave it now? My son. He helped everyone, he would help the stones on the ground if they asked, and now they've killed him."[6]

Forty-one more mothers lost their children over those four days. The young dentist, Ahmad Harara, who had lost one eye on 28 January, lost the other on Muhammad Mahmoud. Friday the twenty-fifth was declared Shuhada Friday and Last Chance Friday. An unprecedented number of citizens filled the Midan to repeat their demand for the immediate abdication of SCAF and the handing of power to an interim president. No waiting till April now. The street would accept any one or combination of three presidential candidates: Muhammad el-Baradei, Abd el-Moneim Abu el-Futtouh, Hamdein Sabahi. Chants and banners demanded the trial of Hamdi Badeen, the head of the Military Police. The anger and demands of Tahrir were replicated across the country.

But in Cairo, two alternative protests appeared. The Muslim Brotherhood declared against Tahrir and set up its own protest, at the Azhar, the seat of Sunni Islam in Fatimid Cairo. (The grand imam of al-Azhar, for his part, stepped away from this and sent a representative to Tahrir to demand the trial of the murderers of the shabab.) The Brotherhood named the day al-Aqsa Friday. The al-Aqsa—Islam's third holiest mosque—has been under periodic Israeli attack for years, but the Brotherhood claimed they just happened to choose this Friday to show solidarity for the beleaguered mosque. The Palestinians were quick to denounce the naming and accuse the Brotherhood of cynicism and of using the Palestinian cause to undermine the Egyptian Revolution. And in Midan el-Abbaseyya, near the Ministry of Defense, the first demonstration in support of SCAF appeared. This gathering of a few hundred, presented by state TV through close-up shots as the equivalent of Tahrir, became the nucleus of the campaign for the military's candidate, Ahmad Shafiq, in the presidential elections. Some Abbaseyya residents said the "protesters" were mainly police and army conscripts in civilian clothes.

On Muhammad Mahmoud, the army piled up great cement blocks in the middle of the street. As with the Israeli-style wall they had built in May at the end of University Bridge, they now built one cutting across the middle of Muhammad Mahmoud, truncating the street. To protect, they said, the Ministry of the Interior from the revolutionaries. And the street miraculously transformed itself, from a somewhat characterless thoroughfare connecting Midan el-Tahrir to Midan el-Falaki, it became the spiritual home of the revolution. People came to look, to see the wall the army'd built, to take in the place where so many had fallen to protect Tahrir. A group of young artists came up from Luxor, and Mina Danial's cross-legged angel appeared. Then groups of angels in gas masks rose from the pavement into the wall of the American University downtown campus. Pharaonic scenes, Muslim symbols, poetry, and Coptic icons—great vivid murals bloomed onto the walls. In December, when Sheikh Emad Effat fell, he reappeared on the wall of the Greek School luminous with energy. Angel wings burst from his shoulders, and from his extended hands flowed the Quranic verse "And they said Lord, we obeyed our masters and our elders and they led us astray. Lord, double their torment and curse them forevermore."[7] Later in February, when the Ultras fell, it was here that they were celebrated. The street grew plastic chairs and modest tea stands. People sat with their friends, their books, and their laptops in the company of the shuhada. The colors from Muhammad Mahmoud spilled over into Tahrir and into Downtown. General Muhammad al-Batran—killed by the police in January 2011—appeared in his police uniform with angel wings and so entered officially into the ranks of the revolution's martyrs. Through the dark, cold winter, the walls on Muhammad Mahmoud erupted into huge images of celebration, lamentation, and commentary. The army dismembered Downtown with six more walls, and all the walls they built were turned into views from submarines, fantasy beaches, trompe l'oeils, and miragelike street scenes.

They were beaten. Just as they were beaten on 25 and 28 January, the Security Forces were beaten in Muhammad Mahmoud and retreated behind the walls the military had provided. By the end of the Battle of Muhammad Mahmoud, SCAF head Muhammad Hussein Tantawi had pledged that elections would start on the twenty-eighth as scheduled; he had accepted the resignation of Essam Sharaf's cabinet, and he had transferred the Maspero case from the military to the civilian courts. My sister ended her hunger strike. All talk of the people and the army being "one hand" was over, and it became mainstream to chant "Yasqot yasqot 7ukm el-3askar"—Down, down, with military rule.

∼∼∼∼

I keyed my ID number into the election website and found my electoral number and polling station. I keyed in my sons' and Um Nagla's and got their electoral numbers and polling stations. I felt as though some corner had been turned. There were almost forty thousand polling booths across the country, and people filled them: not the 80 percent plus who'd turned out for the referendum in March, but close to 60 percent.

Our polling booth was right by our house, in the school next to the pharmacy where I'd talked with Sitt Karima late on the night of Friday, 28 January, the school I'd never been inside before, the rival to my own school just down the road. On 28 November I took my place in the line waiting to vote. Many of us were in black for the shuhada, and in Zamalek the mood was one of determination to not let the Brotherhood in rather than to celebrate the democratic process. But we were out there, going into polling booths and voting, and no one was beating us or stopping us, and there were arrangements in place to make sure the vote we cast was counted.

But by voting, were we honoring the shuhada of Muhammad Mahmoud and Maspero? Or were we disrespecting them? The progressive Left split. The group that had decided after Maspero that SCAF had lost legitimacy to run elections and run the country was hardened in its resolve to boycott after the killings in Muhammad Mahmoud. Many joined them. They believed that by taking part in elections, people were according the military the legitimacy they had forfeited, and since the military had shown themselves to be against the revolution, by voting people would be, in fact, impeding the progress of the revolution for which the shuhada had died. But the majority still felt that elections could be a way of getting rid of the military and moving forward.

Personally, I do believe that it would have been best, it would have been more true and honest, if every one of us had boycotted the elections, if we had all stayed home and sent a vote of no confidence to SCAF and made their position untenable. But the boycott would have had to be total, and the country leaned toward dialogue, and the people in general preferred to avoid the shedding of blood on the way to their goals.

The elections did not conform to the arrangements laid out in SCAF's Constitutional Declaration, which had stipulated that two-thirds of the seats would be contested by parties and one-third by independents. When it came to it, the parties were allowed to contest all the seats, with the independents contesting their third only. (After the elections, a case was, in fact, lodged with the Constitutional Court charging that the elections had contravened the law.) This gave an unfair advantage to party candidates, and the only parties with a real presence and real organization were the Muslim Brotherhood ("Freedom and Justice") and the Salafis ("al-Nour," the Light). The Liberal parties had been too busy campaigning for elections to be postponed until after the Constitution was written to organize or acquire a presence on the street. The Left—while very high profile in the campaigns and initiatives and struggles that fed the revolution—was disorganized and had absolutely no funding but scrambled at the last minute to field young candidates under the slogan "The Revolution Continues."

When the results came in the Muslim Brotherhood had won 47 percent of the vote and the Salafis 24. The Liberals got 15 and the Left got 4. The heartening surprise was that not a single candidate believed to have a connection with the Mubarak regime was returned. And that when people managed to find a candidate from the revolution, they voted him in.

PARLIAMENT STREET, 16–22 DECEMBER 2011

On November 24 Tantawi announced his choice of Kamal el-Ganzouri as prime minister. Ganzouri had, from 1996 to 1999, been Mubarak's prime minister, and the appointment was greeted with whoops of derision. Accounts of the rash of massive and unpopular sell-offs of national industries that he had brokered during his tenure exploded in the media. I was crossing and recrossing the Midan all day to al-Jazeera, CNN, the BBC—and I didn't hear a good word for him anywhere. By evening, young revolutionaries had set up their tents outside the gate to the Cabinet Office in Parliament Street to stop the new prime minister gaining access. So now, while elections were being held across the country, a new sit-in started in Parliament Street, besides the continuing sit-in in Tahrir.

On August 1, when the military broke up the July sit-in, they had occupied Tahrir. Soldiers stood to attention all day in the blazing August sun—just as they used to stand along the sides of roads when Mubarak traveled on a Cairo street. They kept it up for a few weeks, then withdrew and turned instead to the slyer methods of democracies. If Tahrir was our Holy Grail and the symbol of our revolution, we could have it. Its electricity would remain disconnected, its traffic lights wouldn't work, and it would never be cleaned. It would be infiltrated, and drugs would be found there. Baltagis would make trouble with business owners and residents, and state media would talk about how scummy the revolution had become, how prostitution and drugs were rife in Tahrir, how the people there were no longer the "honest shabab" of January but baltagis and agents of foreign enemies. Discredit Tahrir, discredit the revolutionaries, discredit the revolution—while pretending to honor them all.

And the message was getting through to the people: the Midan was being held responsible for the worsening of the economy, for bad security, for traffic jams, for everything. We tried to end the sit-in and to mount a PR and information campaign for the Midan. We tried to enact the vision of the revolution in the small encampment near the Mugamma3. One tent became a walk-in clinic; another became a play center. We held meetings with veterans of societies that worked with street children to see what we could offer the children. The flags of different cities flew above us. We asked a calligrapher for five huge banners that spelled out the demands of the sit-in: as usual, support for the injured, restructuring the Dakhleyya, and restructuring state media, and now also an investigation into the Muhammad Mahmoud killings and rejection of Ganzouri's retro cabinet.

But Tahrir was becoming chaotic. Fights broke out between "revolutionaries" and street vendors, groups accused each other of being infiltrators, and no one was sure who was securing the space. Rubbish was not collected, and the area around the Mugamma3 smelled of urine. Strange characters appeared, with aides-de-camp and followers, and commandeered spaces where they presided over mobile-laden tables. Mona discovered a "prison" in Tahrir where some alleged thieves were being held. My sister and Sanaa and Sherif Boraie went to the rescue, argued through the night with their captors, and set them free. But the practice had started and would continue. It became one of Sanaa's self-appointed tasks to sit vigil with prisoners to make sure they weren't harmed. Sometimes she was able to negotiate their release, and sometimes not. Sometimes the bosses in charge of them released a few as a gift to her. The quantities of medicines left over from the field hospitals and stored in Omar Makram Mosque became a problem; some people claimed that the mosque was trading in them, while others said no, it was using them to pay off baltagis who were protecting it. Mona Mina took a team of young doctors and went in and did a stock-taking of everything that was held, and a decision was made to remove the medicines to the Doctors' Union.

The street now wanted the Midan opened. Again and again Abu Muhab and the activists among the injured and the shuhada's families tried to end the sit-in, or to contain it in the area by the Mugamma3 so that the traffic could flow through. And again and again they were overruled by self-styled "security." We felt that the same scenario that had happened in July was playing out again. Once again it came down to individual efforts to get vulnerable people out of the Midan and into the Parliament Street sit-in. While sitting on a pavement by the Qasr el-Eini entrance wait-ing for the ladder we were going to use to hang up our banners, I watched a friend, media figure Buthaina Kamel, try with a small band of followers to open the cordon blocking the Midan, and a young woman leaped up out of nowhere to hit her in the face.

Sitting there on that pavement, I got talking to a young man who said his name was Hasan. He was here with his friend, Mahmoud. They were from a village on the southern periphery of Cairo and had been friends since they were three. They'd shared a wedding and now each had two children. Neither young man could read or write, and Hasan had broken his leg when he was fourteen, and it hadn't mended properly, and sometimes the pain made him cry like a child. But they'd worked hard at anything available and eventually got enough money to rent a coffee shop, which they ran together. In the last months business was bad, and the coffee shop owner had raised the rent by 20 percent. They struggled but couldn't pay. They gave up the lease and hired themselves out as day labor, but wages were down to fifteen pounds a day (that's three U.S. dollars), and a house couldn't survive on less than twenty. They'd had to move back in with their parents, and they were embarrassed. "My father worked all his life to support me," Hasan said, "and now he has to support my children, too?" So they'd both left home last week and come to join this revolution that spoke of social justice and the right of everyone to work for a decent life. It also promised health care for everyone—Hasan had been told that he needed a scan on his leg and that it cost 750 pounds. So here they were, standing on the periphery of a dark Tahrir, ready to do the revolution's bidding. I was certain that within days these two young men would be either dead or added to the twelve thousand in military jails. I persuaded them to come with me to Parliament Street, vouched for them that they were not baltagis sent to infiltrate the sit-in, found them blankets, and got them on the rota for the meager bits of food that were being distributed from time to time. All across the Midan, other people were doing the same.

The Parliament Street sit-in was in much better shape than Tahrir; it was contained, and it focused on what it was there to disrupt: SCAF's new cabinet. It had an entrance at either end of the street, and between them, in a row down the center, the protesters had arranged cardboard coffins bearing the names and pictures of the shuhada of Muhammad Mahmoud. There were debates and discussions, musical rehearsals and manifestos. Eskenderella came and played. One night they tried out an early version of a new song. We made them sing it twice so we could all learn it and sing along. The military inside the Parliament compound came closer to the railings, and the band reoriented themselves so the soldiers could hear. When the band left, the shabab and the young officers tried to talk to each other, but the shabab were bitter about their murdered friends, and the military were adamant that any activity other than elections was destroying the country and that the shabab were being misled by a "third party." Their superiors called them back from the railings.

Manal was there that night—the night Eskenderella played to the Parliament Street sit-in. She was supposed to have gone in for a cesarean section and kept postponing it in the hope that the civil court would set Alaa free. But on December 6 she checked into hospital, and Khaled was born, and once again a birth in our family was linked to a jail. A few days after giving birth to me, my mother had held me up outside the Citadel Jail so her brother, who was imprisoned for belonging to a leftist group, could see his new niece. Now Manal rose early from her confinement and took her newborn child to prison to place him in his father's arms. And as I had gone with my sister in '86 when she went to show Mona to Ahmad Seif, so Mona went with Manal to show Alaa his baby. Alaa had thought it would be at least a week after the birth before Manal would risk coming to see him. Mona writes that when, from far away, he saw his wife and the bundle in her arms, Alaa started to leap up and down. I had seen him leap up and down with the agony and the anger of Mina's death, and I'm glad to have this other image: of my nephew jumping with joy at the arrival of his son.

On the ninth he wrote:

On his third day of life Khaled visited me for half an hour. I held him. My God! How come he's so beautiful? Love at first touch! In half an hour he gave me joy to fill the jail for a whole week. In half an hour I gave him love I hoped would surround him for a whole week. In half an hour I changed and the universe changed around me. Now I understand how I will resist: my prison cannot stop my love. My happiness is resistance. Holding Khaled for a few moments is carrying on the fight.

I was not alone for a second in my resistance; I'd become used to receiving telegrammed tweets in my jail: congratulations for the Eid and for my birthday, I also got congratulations for the return of the revolution to the Midan. But Khaled was something else! A huge amount of telegrams, most of them from people I don't know and might never have the honour of meeting; they wrote to tell of their joy at Khaled's arrival and their love for him. They wrote introducing themselves, the names of the members of their families, their addresses, their jobs, their cities. They wrote that Khaled has family in hundreds of homes everywhere in Egypt. . . .

Half an hour in which I did nothing except look at him. What about half an hour in which I changed him? Or half an hour in which I fed him? Or half an hour in which I played with him? What about half an hour for him to tell me about his school? Half an hour for him and I to talk about his dreams? Half an hour to argue about whether he should go down to a protest? Half an hour for him to give me an impassioned speech about the revolution and how it will free us all? About bread and freedom and dignity and justice? Half an hour for me to feel proud that my son is a brave man carrying the responsibility of a country before he's of an age to carry the responsibility of himself? How much happiness in half an hour like that? In that last half hour the father of the shaheed spent with his son?

Prison deprives me of Khaled except for half an hour. I'm patient because we shall spend the rest of our half hours together. Why is the father of the shaheed patient?

The shaheed is immortal, in our hearts, in our minds, in history, and in paradise. But does his immortality bring happiness to his father? His heart will burst with love for the remaining half hours of his life. Will he pour out that love into the arms of history? I am resilient as I wait for my release. What does the father of the shaheed wait for?[8]

On December 15, I went home at midnight. There had been a debate at the Parliament Street sit-in, and then I'd stopped at a meeting in Tahrir. A lawyer/activist friend had managed to bring together a group semirepresentative of the Midan, and we were formulating a statement that basically declared the Midan open. We thought that if the shabab were unable to actually open it, the statement would at least mean that the revolution could no longer be blamed for keeping the Midan closed. I took the document home to key it in, hone it, and format it, and it was about three o'clock when I sent it back to the group to send on to the media. I flicked on Twitter one more time before I switched off my laptop.

Within twenty minutes, I was parked and hurrying down Parliament Street. Young men tried to stop me. "There's trouble down there." "I know. That's why I'm going." I get to the trouble. In the dark street about fifteen young men are hurling stones and insults into the railings of the Parliament compound. They're in T-shirts and singlets, sweaty, sooty, and very angry. Behind the railings, out of the reach of the stones, armed soldiers watch them. The young men have set up barricades either side of their small group. A few fires burn on the road. There's no point hurrying anymore. Some older men are standing at the periphery, watching, and I stand with them. A young man breaks off from the group. He's scanning the ground and finds what he's looking for almost at our feet. He squats down and starts breaking up a loose paving stone. I start talking: "What are you doing? What's the point in what you're doing?"

"Go home, ma'am." He doesn't even look up.

"But what's the point—"

"Go home, ma'am. It's dangerous here for you."

"You can't even reach them—"

"Because they're hiding—the cowards—"

A man joins us, adds his voice to mine: "What you're doing is useless—"

The young man starts gathering the stones he's broken, loading them into his arms. He's glistening with sweat and soot, and he's tied a white bandanna round his head: "So what should we do?"

"Move away from them. Don't put yourselves in pointless—"

"You didn't see him," the young man says. His glance takes us in properly for the first time. "You don't understand. You didn't see him. They gave him back to us finished. Ruined."

With his armful of stones he lopes back among his friends and starts hurling.

"Him" was Abboudi, one of the Ahli Ultras. It was said that his father was rich and owned many shops downtown, and that Abboudi had broken away from him and joined the revolution. And in the sit-in on this street, he had become a leader. This evening, at this spot where the young men are attacking the shadowy soldiers, he'd challenged an officer standing beside an unmarked white vehicle. He'd told the officer that he believed this was the vehicle that had been used to kidnap several activists over the last few days, then soldiers surrounded him and dragged him into Parliament. Two hours later they threw him out. Finished. Ruined.

Abboudi's friends hurl stones, and the soldiers watch from the shadows. I step back. A young woman comes running up and asks if anyone has a car—there's an injured kid who should be taken to hospital. I run back with her. We get the kid into the back of my car, and a young doctor comes too. We get to the back entrance of Qasr el-Eini hospital, but the boy panics and won't go in: "Just back up. Back up. I'll get off here." The doctor tells him he thinks his leg might be broken. "I'm not going in. They'll kidnap me. I'll get out here. I'll get someone." We leave him leaning against a wall, fumbling for his phone, and drive forward again to the hospital.

Dim lights. Dirty green walls. Misery. The main teaching hospital of Cairo University. The clerk at reception has closed his admissions register and is swearing he won't work and he won't be blamed for Security taking away people wounded in Tahrir. "What do they still want?" he shouts. "A prime minister's been named. Why don't they calm down and let him do his work?" In the corridors, patients are wheeled about on tilting, rusty wheelchairs; ordinary people, needing repair. Rasha Azab comes toward me, one of the bravest of our young activist journalists: "You've come to see Abboudi? Come. He's bad." I follow her. Abboudi is on a bed in a room teeming with people. His friends are all around him. His ears are torn, his eyes are sealed shut, his face is caked with blood. It's so swollen that it doesn't even look like a face.[9]

A personnel carrier is in the ambulance driveway. The soldiers in it stare at Rasha and me as we leave. We stare back. We stop at the all-night pharmacy on Qasr el-Eini Street to get some dressings and painkillers and antiseptics. We figure the field clinic at the top of Parliament Street is going to need them. I've been to this pharmacy before, so the pharmacists give me a 10 percent discount and ask for news. I think it's strange that they need news of what's happening a hundred meters down the road, but I tell them anyway. We drive down Qasr el-Eini with men flagging us down to tell us there's trouble. "We know," Rasha keeps repeating, "we know. That's why we're going there."

This was the opening salvo in the attack on the Parliament Street sit-in. Later on, on that Friday, 16 December, Sheikh Emad Effat, a beloved presence in the Midan and a high-ranking researcher and academic at al-Azhar University, is shot dead. Alaa Abd el-Hadi, in his fifth year of medical school at Ein Shams University, has been providing medical help in Tahrir since the beginning of the revolution. When news of the trouble in Parliament Street broke, he writes on his Facebook: "I'll go see what's happening. May God protect us all." Alaa is trying to help Sheikh Emad when he is shot. His mother, worried about him, phones. A stranger answers her son's phone and tells her to "bring someone with you and come to the hospital." She says, "We got to the hospital and I heard them say go to the morgue and I fainted. I never saw my son again."

The Parliament Street events last for five days. In my Arabic weekly column in *Shorouk,* I write:

> Blood runs down the streets of downtown. At four o'clock every morning the valiant Egyptian Armed Forces swoop down on Egyptian civilians in the heart of our capital, they kill and wound and kidnap, then retreat behind the cement walls they've built in the streets that lead into Tahrir; they rest and regroup and get ready to attack again.
>
> Over the course of the week, we've seen the military seduce the shabab into a small war, angering them with insults and gestures from behind railings and from the tops of roofs, pelting them with stones and bricks and Molotov cocktails and furniture and china and oil paintings and glass

panes—as well as their more traditional missiles of bullets and buckshot and gas canisters.[10]

We've seen the vicious beatings of young men, and young women being dragged to places of detention inside the Parliament and the Consultative Council buildings. We saw them come out beaten and electrocuted, one of them with the letter T carved into her head. And we saw the burning and the attempted burning of public buildings like the Egyptian Academy, and the military hurling bricks at the shabab trying to save the books.

Then there was the spectacle that went round the world in seconds: the young woman separated from the young journalist she was talking to. He gets beaten, and we see a soldier jumping on his fallen body more than once. She is dragged along, her clothes lifting off her. A soldier's foot thumps into her blue-bra'd breast. We see an older woman beaten by soldiers when she tries to help her.

At seven o'clock on Monday morning a thread, a line, a fifty-meter trail of blood: the fifty meters along which Muhammad Mustafa bled as his comrades of the moment raced to carry him to help. Muhammad Mustafa, a student of Engineering at Ein Shams University, whom the soldiers of SCAF shot, now lies in the Hilal Hospital. A fifty-meter trail of blood; the shabab marked its path with stones then someone filmed it. A simple, truthful action, awesome in its symbolism, clear in its message: Blood is dear; every drop of it has a price.[11]

Both Sanaa and Mona are taken into Parliament and beaten. One piece of footage shows a young woman doctor, Farida al-Hussi, being hunted down. I've watched it again and again, and each time I see an image of a hunted deer falling in slow motion.

Another: Ghada Kamal. Another: Azza Hilal. Each one of them, as soon as she is released, gives her testimony on television—on the private channels that have somehow become the forum for the revolution. And a few days later, Hend Nafe3, a student at the University of Banha, becomes famous when she throws Tantawi out of her hospital room. The military had beaten her up and given her a massive head wound. Then, in that strange way they'd developed, they gave her medical treatment: they took her to hospital, handcuffed her to a bed, and sewed up her head with twenty-five stitches.[12] "Her face was as badly bruised and swollen as Abboudi's—her whole body was bruised. And then Tantawi comes to visit the wounded in hospital. The state TV producers choose to start with her. The cameras come in first and set up their angles to capture Tantawi's entry, but Hend ruins the whole show by screaming her accusations at him as he comes in.

On 19 December SCAF hold a long press conference in which they deny every accusation leveled at the military and repeat again and again the claim that a "third hand" or an "invisible party" is working methodically to create division and destroy the state.

The same day a coalition of groups and campaigns—6 April, No to Military Trials, Mosireen—and others hold their own press conference where they present documentary footage and witness statements to prove that SCAF are lying. Anger and grief fill the room. A young activist, Lina, shaking as she speaks, holds up the blood-soaked cloth with which she tried to stop Muhammad Mustafa's wound. From this is born "Kazeboon" (Liars), a people's street campaign against the military. The Mosireen collective— and eventually others—will create footage and post it, and activists will download and screen it. It is a great exercise in utilizing cultural commons. Nobody owns or runs the campaign. Individuals will hear of it, form a group, download material, and screen it. The screenings are sudden and unannounced, they take place in densely populated areas and on the walls of public buildings across the country. Sometimes fights break out. But the movement will grow and gain immense credibility and be crucial in stripping the military of popular legitimacy.

And on Tuesday three thousand women march through Downtown. In the first months of the revolution, we refused to highlight gender issues; even radical feminist groups insisted that the struggle was to create a society in which there was no discrimination on *any* basis, including gender. Now, in the face of the images of women being beaten, dragged, and stripped, in the face of the methodical return of harassment on the streets and the news of the "virginity tests" carried out in military jails, we are marching as women, and our challenge to the existing powers is clear: "Where's the field marshal? The women are here," "Where's the Brotherhood? The women are here!" "SCAF stole our revolution / The women of Egypt will bring it back!" Men, trying to be helpful, link arms around the march, so the massive bloc of women is moving in a kind of protective noose of men. At one point the men, bursting with emotion, start a self-castigating "Where were the men? The women are here!" After they repeat this a few times, the women thunder back their comfort: "Muhammad Mahmoud will bear witness / our men there fought like lions." The women's march is brilliant in its subtlety. It is a demonstration of womanpower, but it seeks to enlist and implicate men, not to alienate them. "Beat me! Strip me!" we chant, "my brother's blood will cover me." For we never lose sight of one fact: the overwhelming majority of the murdered are male. Like Muhammad Mustafa. Like Alaa Abd el-Hadi.

In the years leading up to January 2011, when the 9 March Movement—one of the many movements whose separate campaigns came together in the revolution—was calling for academic independence and administrative transparency in the universities, Ein Shams University was famous for the corruption of its administration. When, for example, the movement won a court order banning police from the university campus, the administration set thugs wielding bicycle chains on the faculty to teach them the value of the police. After the revolution, therefore, Ein Shams was very quick to revamp its articles and run proper elections. Its first elected president was Professor Alaa Fayez, a celebrated pediatric surgeon who was known to be pro the revolution and pro his students. When Alaa Abd el-Hadi was killed trying to tend to Sheikh Emad Effat in Parliament Street, the new president consulted with the student union, and the university mobilized. Two professors from the medical school attended the autopsy. The dean of the law school filed a case of murder, and Professor Fayez himself described on TV how the bullet entered Alaa's body below the heart and exited through his skull—indicating that his killer was extremely close to him. The university organized buses for the students who wanted to attend their friend's burial and the president and professors attended the funeral.

The walls of Ein Shams Medical School flanked the events of Abbaseyya I in July 2011, and the Security Forces used its grounds as a base from which to attack the protests. In April 2012, during the events of Abbaseyya II, Professor Fayez will discover that the medical school grounds are once again being used by Security Forces to launch attacks on protesters. He will order the grounds shut down. Next day, on May 1, on his way to inspect new university buildings, his car will be hit by a truck coming from the opposite direction on the ring road. His driver and secretary will sustain massive injuries, and he will be killed instantly.

But this is all to come later, in the run-up to the presidential elections. And later yet we'll learn that the university is used as a trade hub for drugs and small arms.

Back in December 2011, we go down every day to the intersection of Parliament Street and Qasr el-Eini Street, where soldiers of the Egyptian army have commandeered the roof of the Cabinet Office building and, from that vantage point, pee on Egyptian citizens, where the army pelts the citizenry with the embossed china place settings of Parliament and ceremonial shields from its walls. Once a metal filing cabinet comes crashing down. Glass panes are common. A lot of the time the army fights street children, whom the revolutionaries try to hold on to, to hold back. "Every couple of days the government takes me," a child says, "they take the money I've made and do bad things to me." He says he is twelve, but he looks more like eight. They all look small, these kids, because they're undernourished and because they can't ever sleep properly so they can grow.

By the end of "Parliament Street," seventeen more people have been murdered, and a further nine hundred seriously injured.

END OF 2011

On 15 December a civil court set free all the young men detained by the military in the Maspero case—all except Alaa. The next time Alaa appeared in court—ten days later, on the twenty-fifth— he was released. And the judge ordered that a charge of perjury be brought against the two people who had borne witness against him. I was in London, doing Christmas and Boxing Day with Ismail Richard and my London friends. Omar texted, "He's out," and I raced back on the twenty-seventh. On the last day of the year, we held a belated Seventh Day party for Khaled.

We swept and cleaned the house I'd refurbished in my mother's orchard. We laid out tables and chairs and strung up colored lights and strings of Egyptian flags. We set up a barbecue, and all our family and friends and friends of friends came and brought lots of food. We played music and danced and carried Khaled in a satin-lined sieve into every room and into all the dark corners so he would know his way around and know there was nothing, ever, to be afraid of, and we sprinkled the seven seeds in his path so he would always have plenty, and we sang to him the old instructions to obey his mother and his father and added that he must never ever obey SCAF or a government. My mother's orchard was teaming and buzzing and radiating love and light. And just before midnight, we all drove to Tahrir—the biggest family home in the world. And despite the dark days, Tahrir was full of hope and joy, and there was music and song and a church choir and people all the time gathering round Alaa and talking talking talking about the future and about what we need to do.

And while we were in Tahrir and unknowing, two men showed up and parked their motorbike and went around waking up the people in the houses near our orchard and questioning them about who'd been to our party and what had been said and sung and chanted. They went round to 3amm Hamed's house, but his wife wouldn't let him come out and speak to them because he has a weak heart and a strong temper. So she parried them and held them off and in the morning called Shukri who told Sohair who told me. Next day Alaa and Ahmad Seif and I went back to the orchard and talked to our neighbors and paid a visit to the local police stations, where we told the superintendent that we'd be happy to answer any questions he had and there was no need to send plainclothes round to inconvenience our neighbors. He was adamant he knew nothing about the two men. We asked if someone could operate like that in his district without him knowing? He said yes.

From jail, Alaa had written:

We need to be vigilant: they do not kill us to restore their state; they kill us because killing and jailing are normal behaviors in their state.

Remember their state: it wasn't only the police of their state who let us down; didn't the deans of their colleges run over our children? Didn't their bakeries and gas depots let us down? Were we not abandoned by their "wheel of production" that lavishes millions on the director and the consultant even when it's standing still but can't spare a crumb for the worker even when it's turning? Were we not let down by their state's economy that closes down the textile factories while the cotton is piled high in the farmers' homes but keeps the fertilizer plants pouring poison into our river? Were we not let down by its football clubs that permit their Security to brutalize the fans if they cheer too noisily but intervenes to shield players when they carry guns? We are let down by all their state's institutions and every leader in it, and tomorrow we will be let down by its parliament and its president.[13]

✓ ✓ ✓ ✓

The Second Palestinian Intifada at the end of 2000 brought Egyptians out onto the streets. The next great protests came in 2003, against the attack on Iraq. We came out in protest at the rigging of parliamentary elections in 2005 and to support the judiciary in its fight against the regime in 2006. After that we never quieted down. The protests over the six years preceding the revolution were big industrial strikes, as in the textile factories of Mahalla, or else were initiated by the secular branch of the national movement: the Kifaya Movement, the civil and legal and physicians' groups, university students and faculty, small leftist parties, farmworkers, and the professional syndicates. A repeated pattern was that the secular organizers of protests—fully aware of the numbers that the Brotherhood commanded—would try to persuade them to make common cause against Mubarak's state. Time and again meetings would be held, the Brotherhood leadership would commit to putting large numbers on the street—and then the numbers wouldn't show up. Or a couple of thousand Brothers would come out and then vanish at five o'clock, leaving their secular comrades to be beaten up and detained by government forces and baltagis. Some individual Brotherhood members always acted according to their conscience, and some—like Muhammad Abd el-Quddous at the Journalists' Union—played a crucial part in nurturing the burgeoning protest movement, but they were acting outside the remit of the Association. Some younger Brothers came to feel over the years that they could no longer adhere to the principle of obedience that the Brotherhood exacted and went through the trauma of breaking away. But on the whole, the Islamist branch of the national movement did not have an appreciable input into the street dynamics that ultimately became the revolution of 25 January.

On 25 January young Salafis and Brothers did not wait for directives but simply and naturally joined the marches into the centers of their cities. And they were there again on the critical marches of the twenty-eighth. Their leadership did not announce a clear position with regard to the revolution, but when the attacks on Tahrir started on 2 February, the Day of the Camel, the leadership mobilized its network, and Brothers poured in from the countryside to protect the revolution in Tahrir.

But from 11 February, when SCAF and the military took overt charge of the country, the leadership of the Islamist current tried to pull back their young members from street action. Just as they had never been keen on confrontation with Mubarak, now they were clearly not keen on confrontation with the military. The worst manifestation of this was in the four days of Muhammad Mahmoud. The absence of the Brothers and the Salafis from the street, the fact that they stayed home while the Security Forces attacked Tahrir and killed young people who thought they were comrades, left a bitter taste in every mouth.

To the Islamist leadership, the revolution had become a matter of politics and elections and gain, and the Brotherhood, the Salafis, and the Gama3at leadership—now released from jail— swung into political action. The Brotherhood set up the FJP, the Freedom and Justice Party, the Salafis formed the Nour Party. Organization mattered, and numbers, and experience. The Salafis had numbers, the Brotherhood had numbers and organization and experience. Both were present in towns and villages across the country, and both had a membership that did what it was told. Together, as we've seen, they took home 71 percent of the vote.

REVOLUTION, YEAR TWO: 2012

On 23 January 2012 the elected Egyptian Parliament sat for the first time. The country expected it to start acting in the interests of the country. To legislate, for example, for a minimum wage. To act against remnants of the Mubarak regime that were still in position and working against the revolution. To order serious investigations into the murder of protesters and legislate to protect civilians from the military. To start work on legislation for human rights. To deal with the Ministry of the Interior. In other words, we expected and demanded that our elected representatives should start the country moving seriously toward "Bread, Freedom, Social Justice" through the legislative channels now in their power.

The country also expected Parliament to recognize the exceptional circumstances in which it had been elected and to rise to them. We had succeeded in protecting the new constitution from being written under the influence of SCAF; now we were entrusting Parliament with choosing the founding committee that would draft that constitution. For ten months the Islamists had refused to commit to any joint document of "governing principles," protesting again and again that they understood that the constitution had to be a document that spoke for the nation as a whole, not the particular group that happened to be in power. We expected them to grab this opportunity to show good faith and choose a founding committee that was balanced and serious and popular and representative.

So on 23 January, to remind their representatives of all this, thousands of citizens marched toward the Parliament building from different points in the city. Ultimately, the message they were bringing to their representatives was that they should remove SCAF and act as the legislative body of the revolution. If they acted for the people, the people would be their protection and their support. Workers marched from the trade union headquarters. No to Military Trials for Civilians marched from the Supreme Court. Just Retribution [for the killers of the shuhada] marched from the Shaheed Abd el-Menem Riyad Square. I walked in the artists' march from the Opera House. Not one of us managed to reach Parliament. The military had put up an artful series of barricades to protect Parliament from the people: walls, barbed wire, railings, and hundreds of Security Forces.

On 25 January, the first anniversary of the revolution, millions marched across the country calling for the transfer of power to Parliament and declaring "the revolution continues." The Islamist representatives so badly didn't want to hear this message that they encircled the building with a cordon of young Muslim Brothers, drafted in from the countryside, who stood ready to beat us off with sticks and belts. In Tahrir fights broke out between protesters and Islamists. The Islamists' position was unshakable: demands for the transfer of power to the Parliament where they held 71 percent of the seats were a conspiracy to cause a rift between them and the military. The Brotherhood was staying close to power—as it saw it. They did not even seem to recognize that *they* had become the power. They certainly didn't think that we, standing outside in the street, were the power—or at least we were not the power they wanted to align themselves with. Parliament had declared for SCAF.

So the revolution declared the twenty-seventh of January the Second Friday of Wrath. We marched from the four corners of Cairo to Tahrir, and at the mouth of Qasr el-Nil Bridge some of us diverted toward Maspero. Kazeboon projected one of its bloodiest documentaries directly onto the walls of the Radio and Television building. When the lights came on in the windows of the Ministry of Foreign Affairs next door, they spelled out "Thawra": Revolution! Cheers rang out in the street as the message of the activist/diplomats registered. The protesters in Maspero settled down for a sit-in. We would concentrate on the state's media machine and the Parliament. And despite the fact that a representative legislative body was now in place, we still chanted "Down, down with the rule of the military!"

PORT SAID, 1 FEBRUARY 2012

On 28 January the Cairo-based premier league football club, Ahli, played the Arab Contractors Club in Cairo Stadium. The Ahli supporters, Ultras Ahlawi, as you remember, together with their traditional rivals, Zamalek White Knights, had been at the front of the marches that broke police lines in the first days of the revolution.

Ultras Ahlawi were formed in 2007 and from the start had a problem with the police. They were the unofficial fan base of the club, and the police made a point of harassing them and would often round up groups of them and keep them in cells to prevent them attending a match. In July 2010, after a particularly fierce clash with police, they went on strike and stopped supporting their teams. When the Ahli football club board asked them to return to the stands, they demanded protection from the police—which the club tried to ensure. So when the revolution broke out, they were there for it.[14] They roused the Midan and gave it heart, and their cheer for freedom—four short claps and then "Horreya!"— became a punctuation mark for the chants during marches and sit-ins.

Muhammad Mustafa, who'd been killed in Tahrir, and Abboudi, who'd been brutalized in Parliament Street, were the latest Ultra victims of the police and military. Playing the Contractors football club on 28 January, Ultras Ahlawi raised their martyred friends' images and sang against the police throughout the match.

He was a failure
all through high school
just scraped through
fifty percent.
With brib'ry now
the man's a scholar
got a degree
from a hundred schools.
You raven nesting
inside our homes
why d'you ruin
all our pleasure?
We won't do
what you want.
We don't want
to see your face.
Frame us, frame us
lock us up, jail us.
That's the way

of the police.
Catch me, call me
international terrorist.
I play with fireworks
and sing for Ahli
and
freedom . . . freedom.

On Wednesday, 1 February, there was a meeting at the Saqia Culture Wheel in Zamalek to discuss the unpromising performance of Parliament so far, and to develop a strategy to influence the formation of the Founding Committee for the Constitution. We'd taken our seats; I was between Alaa my nephew and Ibrahim al-Moallem, and we were chatting and the meeting was just gearing up when Ibrahim got a message on his phone. Ibrahim (my publisher and the boss of Shorouk publishing and *Shorouk* newspaper) used to play water polo for Ahli and for Egypt, then sat on the board of the Ahli; he's been affiliated with the club all his life. That night the Ahli were playing Port Said FC in Port Said. Ultras Ahlawi had gone up to support, and nobody doubted that Ahli would win. As it happened, they didn't; they lost by two goals to nil.

But the message Ibrahim got was that there was trouble in Port Said and an Ahli supporter was hurt. "But why?" he said. "Port Said won." In the time it took him to say the words, another message came through: three supporters had been killed. And instantly another message: the number of suspected victims was now being put at eighteen. "What's happening?" he kept repeating. "What's happening?" We got out of the hall and stood at the entrance to the Saqia, under 15 May Overpass, meters from my home, and I watched him and Alaa on their mobiles. Twenty-seven supporters dead—no, thirty-six supporters . . . As the numbers rose, we raced to his office at *Shorouk* and switched on all the monitors. People crowded in. The screens and the telephones were registering the rise and rise of numbers.

At midnight Alaa and I left Ibrahim in his office and headed to Cairo Railway Station in Rameses to wait for the train that was bringing the Ultras home. Hundreds had had the same impulse, and there was a mass of people arriving at the station. The huge hall echoed with chants. Just before the revolution, the regime had once again surpassed itself and redecorated the beautiful, austere building with garish gilt pillars and giant metal plants. The scaffolding was still in place, and now it was covered in young men. They were on the scaffolding, on the stairs, the escalators, the balconies. The hall was full of mothers, shabab, sympathizers. It was an ocean of waving flags. At three in the morning, the train chugged in; a third-class train, it had taken five dark and cold hours to make the journey from Port Said. Hundreds rushed to meet it. The train arrived at the platform submerged in people; people on top of it, clinging to it, walking alongside it. The chants died down when the young Ultras who'd been on the train appeared. They looked pale and shrunk, their clothes were torn and bloody, and their heads, arms, and legs were bandaged. They leaned on each other and limped. Some were carried.

Seventy-two young men had been killed.

Mysterious buses had arrived at the stadium, their passengers allowed in without tickets. The governor and the chief of police, both of whom attend all Port Said Club matches, were absent from this crucial one. As the match ended, all the lights went out. Security Forces parted to let groups of men through, and they rushed the away team's terrace. Ahli supporters tried to escape but found the gates soldered shut. Some young men were killed with a quick snap of the neck; others were thrown from the top of the stadium.

We said it in the stadium and we sang it to the crowds:
In Port Said the victims were betrayed before they died.

They plotted hard against us they were vicious they were mean,
They murdered our best mates and they murdered all our dreams.

We somehow couldn't quite believe it. In towns and villages, thousands gathered to bury their friends and mourn them. The Ultras cut across class, profession, geography.

Hey SCAF, hey bastard Council,
What were you paid for the martyr's blood?

Tantawi sent a military plane for the players. In a brief appearance on national television, he said, "I don't understand why the people are letting this pass. Everybody has to take part." Once again the authorities were trying to instigate people against each other. For days the media tore into Port Said's "heroic" label—earned when the city bore the brunt of Britain, France, and Israel's attack on Egypt in 1956—and painted it as a place of evil. The people of Port Said went on protests, described how they had tried to get to the visiting fans but were blocked by Security. An investigation was started.

Ultras flags and banners flew in every street. Wherever there was an injured Ultra, his friends were camped outside his door. Ultras White Knights Zamalek joined Ultras Ahlawi in protest marches, and their banners flew together.[15] Groups of young people gathered outside the homes of murdered Ultras to sing Ultra songs while artists painted their images on the surrounding walls.

In the midst of the grief and the anger, the young men began appearing as angels on the walls of Muhammad Mahmoud. Anas, fourteen, the youngest Ultra, who'd skipped off to the match behind his parents' backs:

I'm wearing a red T-shirt
And headed for Port Said

Came back my shroud was white
And in my country I was martyred

Kareem Khuzam, whose father soon died of a heart attack:

Paradise for the martyrs
And the revolution's born anew

Amgad Aslan, Hasan Taha, Islam Tolba, Basem Osman, Muhammad Ghandour . . . seventy-two young men.[16]

DOWNTOWN

From dawn on 2 February, the streets around the Ministry of the Interior became scenes of running battles. The shabab threw stones and fireworks, the police shot live ammunition, and the army started replicating the wall it had built in Muhammad Mahmoud in November. Seven walls in a small part of downtown Cairo: Qasr el-Eini, Sheikh Rihan, Mansour, Noubar, Falaki, Muhammad Mahmoud. Cement walls, barriers, barbed wire. The walls blocked traffic and irritated residents and antagonized the shabab, but most important they provided cover for the police and army officers when they went out hunting. Now they could come out to the middle of the street and shoot at the shabab in comfort, their backs covered. The shabab pulled down one wall with nothing but steel levers, rope, and coordination.

Once again the small field clinics appeared. Once again the smoke and the tear gas and the crowds and the motorbike ambulances carrying the wounded wedged between two riders. Some newly elected parliamentarians proposed a law to officially allow the troops to shoot protesters. Others threatened to go on hunger strike until the shooting stopped.[17]

On the street the protesters this time looked poorer, less privileged. Laila Soueif and Hani el-Hosseini established a roster so that "an adult of standing" was always there to bear witness. A young man stopped me in my tracks. "Don't step here," he said, "not here—" He had his arms spread out wide, protecting a patch of pavement, about one square meter, and as people surged and heaved with the shooting and the stone throwing, he held everyone off from stepping on that square meter. "Someone died here," he kept saying, "Someone died here. Don't step on his blood."

On the fourth a Mothers' March headed for Parliament. Practically every Egyptian woman I've ever known was there; we ranged from women of eighty to girls of fourteen. We crowded the railings and called, "Give me back my country. Give me back my son." An army officer came out, a paratrooper, flanked by his men, his eyes behind shades, and said, "What do you want? They're dead. What do you want now?" Some parliamentarians came out to where we could see them; they were the independents, and they were wearing the yellow scarves of No to Military Trials. Security men were busy taking photos of us. Lulie stuck out her tongue at the camera.

In the evenings, visored officers went well into the streets to shoot at people. Mosireen were out there filming, finding cover wherever they could and filming. Salma Said was sheltering behind a metal electricity box. As she peeped round the side with her camera, an officer shot at her. Within hours, as she was lying in hospital, Mosireen had put out a film on YouTube: a girl's face with five buckshot pellets: one in the right cheekbone, one four millimeters below her left eye, the third by her nose, and the fourth and fifth in the dimple of her chin. An X-ray image of a leg powdered with thirty-three pellets. She tells the story from her bed. The masked soldier had seen her filming and shot. He hit her in the face, and she fell. He shot her again as she lay on the ground. And he shot the third round as the shabab lifted her and ran. More than fifty pellets were embedded in the young woman.[18]

ABBASEYYA, 11, MAY 2012

Through the rest of February, through March and April, there were constant marches and protests. People tried to implement the aims of the revolution in their own lives and workplaces. The students organized, and so did schoolchildren, teachers, doctors, and workers. New independent syndicates and unions were formed. People worked on the campaigns to end military trials for civilians, to expose the lies of the military, to reform the Dakhleyya. The universities held elections and installed new deans and presidents. Everywhere there was movement. The street demanded that the military step down, but Parliament did not step up to the demand. The majority parties were too busy dividing up the house committees among themselves and trying to form the Founding Committee for the Constitution. The first committee they formed was so clearly both biased and below par that they had to dissolve it and start again. The second one was still flawed, but it countered that it would have satellite committees, and advisers, and groups to collect input from the people everywhere.

And the country was heading for the last "procedural" hope of pushing the revolution forward: the presidential elections. Political parties were formed. Coalitions came together and disbanded again. Candidates put themselves forward, and supporters campaigned to get them the endorsements they needed. The revolution's dream ticket was a coalition of Muhammad el-Baradei, Hamdein Sabahi, and Abd el-Moneim Aboul Fotouh, but we could not get them to work together. El-Baradei even withdrew from the contest altogether. The Elections Committee disqualified the old intelligence chief, Omar Suleiman, and the Muslim Brotherhood boss and millionaire businessman Khairat el-Shater. But it refused to disqualify Mubarak's last prime minister, Ahmad Shafiq. Salafi candidate Hazem Abu Ismail was disqualified because his mother had held an American passport. His supporters refused to accept the committee's decision and held demonstrations at the military's Cairo headquarters in Abbaseyya. The demonstrations turned into a sit-in. When they were attacked by baltagis, people who would never have voted for Hazem Abu Ismail went to help.

Atef el-Gohari was one of the revolutionaries who went to the aid of the Salafis. You can see a video of him speaking in Tahrir, surrounded by children: "What's most important," he says to them, "is that shabab have died; they've died for justice."[19] He says it in that voice with the built-in rasp I'd recognized when he ran me to safety in Abbaseyya in July; the voice I'd heard so often in the Midan: "Ezzayyek ya doktora?" Do you need anything? And I'd known that if I did need something, he'd find it for me. Another video clip shows him handing out breadsticks from a plastic bag during Muhammad Mahmoud. "Anyone hungry?" he calls. "Anyone hungry?" The Midan, the revolution, had been Atef's personal responsibility. He'd gone to Abbaseyya to help keep the peace, to help protect the protesters, even though he was totally against their ideology. On 3 May, on their last killing spree before the presidential elections, the army murdered him. You can see a photo someone's posted of him with his mouth and chin and throat blown away.[20]

THE PRESIDENTIAL ELECTIONS, MAY 2012

A tweet on Wednesday, 23 May: "Intermission for the Elections, then we continue the Revolution."

You could say that more than half the population boycotted the elections. The 80 percent of the electorate that had turned out in such orderly and optimistic fashion to vote in the March 2011 referendum had seen how that exercise had been used to consolidate the grip of the military and divide the country. The 54 percent who had persevered and voted in the parliamentary elections had watched in dismay for four months as Parliament anxiously tredded water and bickered. The revolutionary core that had refused to take part in the elections for Parliament after the army killed protesters in Maspero and Muhammad Mahmoud had gained strength after the killings of Parliament Street, Port Said, Mansour Street, and Abbaseyya II.

The turnout for the first round of presidential elections was 43 percent.

One little pocket of revolutionary activity was the candidacy of Khaled Ali, the young lawyer who was the one candidate truly born of the revolution. Ali only got some 130,000 votes in the end, but he provided a nucleus for an innovative and radical revolutionary group. Working on his campaign, they developed a small network of professionals who put together a detailed economic and social program for the country. This program now provides the basis of the positions of the secular Left in the national discussions we insist on having.

Of the top five candidates, three were very clear in their backgrounds and ideologies: Muhammad Morsi was the candidate of the Muslim Brotherhood and the Islamists in general. Ahmad Shafiq was the candidate of the Mubarak regime remnants and the military. Hamdein Sabahi appealed to seculars and Central Left. The remaining two were more ambiguous. Abd el-Moneim Aboul Fotouh was a veteran of the Brotherhood leadership but had recently fallen out with them, and his international and economic politics seemed well to the left of Morsi and the Brotherhood in general. And Amr Moussa was a statesman of the old regime but famous for being at odds with it, and he had been very careful to publicly support the revolution—although in a "but finally we have to be sensible" kind of way.

The military, the remnants, and the Islamists commanded networks and practices and funds well beyond anything remotely available to the others, but even so, the results of the first round were

Muhammad Morsi: 5,764,950 (24.78 percent)
Ahmad Shafiq: 5,505,327 (23.66 percent)
Hamdein Sabahi: 4,820,273 (20.72 percent)
Abd el-Moneim Aboul Fotouh: 4,065,239 (17.47 percent)
Amr Moussa: 2,588,850 (11.13 percent)

The inability of the candidates of the Left, Sabahi and Aboul Fotouh, to work together cost us the elections, and the two powers heading for a run-off in the first elections after the revolution were the Muslim Brotherhood and the Mubarak regime.

There was a maelstrom of political activity as Shafiq made triumphal appearances and gave presidential addresses. Hamdein Sabahi charged that nine hundred thousand of Shafiq's votes had been fraudulently obtained. Morsi wooed the various secular parties and coalitions and made them sweet promises about how he would be the president of all of Egypt, not just of the Brotherhood.

Hours before the runoffs, SCAF issued a new law giving military forces the right to legally detain civilians. At the same time, the Constitutional Court decided that this was the moment to consider the four-month-old charge that the parliamentary elections in November had contravened SCAF's Constitutional Declaration. They found for the charge and announced Parliament illegitimate.

For the non-Islamist revolutionaries confronted once more with the ballot box, the choices were terrible. You could either vote for Muhammad Morsi, or you could spoil your ballot. And if you spoiled your ballot—or boycotted—and Ahmad Shafiq won, how would you live with yourself? After everything we'd done, after our friends had been killed and maimed, after so many lives had been ruined—and also after the freedoms and the gains and the new spirit we had achieved—we would have allowed the regime to come back. But if we voted for Morsi—if we betrayed the shuhada of Muhammad Mahmoud and Parliament Street, if we forgot the cordons round Parliament and the commandeering of its committees, if we forgave the nonsense spoken in the Islamist Founding Committee for the Constitution, we would still be voting for a religion-based party, and an economically and politically conservative one to boot. But then the Islamists had also been part of the revolutionary current, the current for change, and their young people had shown an ability to be open, to be persuadable—and to make us listen. The trajectory of history suggested that we had to pass through an Islamist phase sooner or later—maybe we'd be able to come up with a different model for that, an Egyptian model. And Morsi would not allow people to be shot on the street, would he? While Shafiq would. Ahmad Shafiq would come in precisely to make sure people were shot on the street, to make an end of all this nonsense and get right back to business as usual—with a new set of faces, more agreeable to the military.

As for "freedoms" there probably wouldn't be much to choose between the military and the Islamists. Around fifteen million people had voted the Islamists into Parliament, and only five million had come out and voted for Morsi. Maybe by the next elections we would vote them out. At least with the Brotherhood there would *be* next elections—or would there? Well, with Shafiq there certainly wouldn't. Every day of these past fifteen months, everything each day had held, everything each day had meant, would all be for nothing. For worse than nothing: Egypt would have voted to bring in a corrupt military dictatorship.

I stood behind the curtain with the pen in my hand. I had been all set to write "The Revolution Continues" right across the ballot. But I put my tick in front of Morsi's name and went home ill and miserable.

Close to three million extra voters took part in the runoffs. And almost one million people could not stand the choice and ruined their ballots. Muhammad Morsi was returned with 13,230,131 (51.73 percent). Ahmad Shafiq got 12,347,380 (48.27 percent) and fled Egypt for the Gulf.

What everybody pointed out, when the results came in, was that the difference between the votes in the first and the second rounds, the extra 7.5 million who voted for Morsi and the extra 6.8 million who voted for Shafiq, were not voting for either man or his program; they were voting because they hated or feared the alternative. Finally, more voters hated SCAF and the old regime.

〰〰〰〰

We will not forgive. Every minute of every day was an opportunity for the military to do the decent thing: even to secure what ill-gotten wealth they already had and still do the decent and the honorable thing and help preserve our bright, shining revolution and the new retrieved spirit of our people. And instead SCAF and its army targeted and killed and imprisoned and tortured and insulted and degraded. We will not forget, and we will not forgive.

AND NOW?

Once again, as I write the last words of this text, at the end of November 2012, I've no idea what will be happening in Egypt as you read it.

In November 2011, Muhammad Mahmoud Street became the place we went to for emotional and spiritual sustenance. We would sit surrounded by the graffiti that had been midwifed by the terrible events that took place here, the drawings and texts that rose above this street to create an art that spoke of our shuhada everywhere, and that spoke to us of Egypt and of the revolution and reminded us what it was we were fighting for.

Ten weeks ago, late at night on 18 September 2012, government workers protected by Security Forces descended on Muhammad Mahmoud and started erasing the graffiti. People gathered and protested. Soon the Presidency, the Ministry of the Interior, and the municipality all denied ordering the erasure! Meanwhile the brushes and paint had come out again. Next day a mischievous face with a shock of black hair appeared; the young man was laughing and sticking out a long green tongue. Within days a whole new set of graffiti went up.

Who owns the wall on Muhammad Mahmoud? Who owns the city? Who owns the revolution? The country? This is now the struggle.

On Friday, 12 October 2012, there was a call for a Friday of Accounting. Muhammad Morsi had been president for one hundred days; so how well had he done? Thinking in terms of two simple axes: an Islamist/secular axis, and a conservative/progressive axis, we knew which pole Morsi came from; how far had he moved toward the other? And did he look like he was heading for some balance? There were always going to be two tests: whether he had managed to rise above party politics and be a president for all of Egypt; and whether he was guiding the country toward the aims of the revolution: Bread, Freedom, Social Justice.

"Bread": The world is now debating the ideology of economics. The Occupy movement in the United States and the protests in Britain, Spain, and Greece are all about the ideology of economics. In Egypt, we find that the economic ideology of the Brotherhood is not very different from that of the Mubarak regime; essentially a free market, capitalist ideology that favors the corporation over the citizen and the rich over the poor. Where it differs is, possibly, in its attitude to the poor; where the Mubarak regime discounted the poor, the Brotherhood sees them as objects of charity—and useful foot soldiers.

But the revolution demands a radical restructuring of economic power relations in the country.

At the moment the most visible argument is over loans from international financial institutions. The Morsi government is negotiating a loan from the IMF. It is deeply unpopular; people know that even if the overt terms of the loan are favorable, its underlying requirements will lead to more privatization and less public spending—while the country is looking for more public ownership, more public spending, and big developmental projects to utilize Egypt's enormous, underused human resources.

Social justice: while no political party will declare itself to be against social justice per se, the question is how this "justice" is to be defined, and how it is to be achieved. The Egyptian revolution wants every child to be born into equal opportunity. And for this you need good free education, universal health care, good public transport, and affordable housing. All this is achievable if you privilege the poor and the majority, if you think in holistic terms of a sustainable way of life for ourselves and our planet.

Freedom: The report put out a few days ago by the al-Nadeem Center for the Rehabilitation of Victims of Violence makes for terrible reading. The shootings, torture, and detentions continue. Not one of the hundred days of Morsi's presidency has been free of some human rights violation by the state.

Muhammad Morsi has not enthroned our shuhada in a place of honor at the heart of revolutionary Egypt—even though his first visitor at the presidential palace was Khaled Said's mother. He has not set in place an emergency commission and fund to support the injured, even though he has instituted a fact-finding committee to investigate their issues. He has hosted a delegation of American businessmen that included every major arms manufacturer in the industry. He has not adopted any of the existing initiatives to restructure the security establishment, and people are still dying under torture in jails and police stations, but he has retired the top generals of SCAF. Whether the medals he gave them will make them immune to prosecution for murder remains to be seen.

In Tahrir, on 12 October 2012, the people raised the following demands:

1. Re-forming the Founding Committee for the Constitution to achieve more balance. We need more women, young people, Christians, seculars. The Constitution is a constitution for all Egyptians.
2. Restructuring the Ministry of the Interior, the Dakhleyya.
3. Providing justice for the shuhada and the injured.
4. Instituting minimum and maximum wages.

So what has changed? Well, us, and the way we see our problems. We see now that we were never going to clean out the residue of forty years of degradation and corruption in eighteen days, or a year. The failures of our state and the ills of our society are coming out for all to see. And this is necessary if we are to put things right. We're finished with smoke and mirrors. We see that we are divided, and that we have to make a huge and imaginative effort to forge a new common ground. We see that our institutions are hollowed out and that we have to clean and rebuild them. We see that we have to clean out the corruption that has eaten into every aspect of our public life. But we see that there are very many good people among us who are dedicated to bringing about the change the revolution demanded. And we see that even though the state is more or less failed, Egypt itself continues to function. Real crime rates have not gone up, shops are open, and people still crack jokes and sit in cafés and take the air on the bridges. This is a testament to the amazing solidity of our society.

As I write these words, in late November 2012, the revolution itself is in many places. Here are some of them:

1. Gaza: while the new Israeli attack on Gaza ("Pillar of Cloud") was under way, five hundred Egyptian activists traveled to Rafah and sat on the border until they were allowed through.[21] They talked with our Palestinian neighbors, gave blood, shot footage, and collected lists of needed medicines . . . this could not have happened any time in the last forty years. Now the people of Egypt will stand—literally—by Palestine.

2. The Nile University in Cairo has been fighting an unfair takeover of its building by the government, which had decided to gift the building to the Egyptian Nobel laureate, physicist Ahmad Zuweil. The students and faculty took the case to court, conducted a sit-in for over two months, on the pavement outside their university, and held classes and exams right there, on the street.[22] Two days ago the judge found for the university. They will keep their building.

3. Qorsaya is a lovely island in the Nile at the southern end of Cairo. It's a farming island, marked by Gamal Mubarak's "Cairo 2050" development project, which would have got rid of the thousands of people living on the island and turned it into a luxury development. This project and several like it were paused after the revolution. Now they seem to be starting up again. But the people won't have it. Three days ago they fought off the army trying to take a piece of the land.[23]

4. In every hospital in Egypt, the doctors have been on strike for sixty-five days now. They demand transparency, an allocation of 15 percent of the country's annual budget for health care, and the tools with which

to deliver decent health care. In a desperate attempt to
get the government to pay attention, they've emulated
the football fans and created Ultras White Coats,[24]
they've appropriated the Ultras' songs (but made them
less rude), and now they bring the streets alive at their
protests.

There is not a day that passes without a spontaneous public
protest of some kind. Workers protest the manipulation of their
factories and the denial of their rights. Mothers protest the absence
of vaccines. Doctors protest the lack of equipment and resources
in hospitals. The work of the revolution now is to attach itself to
each one of these actions and so to politicize them and draw them
together.

Only connect.

And the connections are happening. Not just within Egypt, not
just among the Arab peoples, but across the world. When Wisconsin was first to raise the Tahrir banner in its own protests in early
2011, Tahrir revolutionaries ordered a delivery of pizza to the protesters there. The protests in Spain last month used the rhythms
of the Egyptian chants. In Egypt we're watching Greece carefully. And across the world, hundreds of thousands of civilians are
marching for Palestine. As the systems that oppress and exploit the
people have become global, so our resistance is becoming global.

None of us is alone.

REVOLUTION III

Postscript

31 JULY 2013

I am writing this by the sea, waiting for Armageddon. Hoping it won't come.

We have persuaded ourselves to take three days out of Cairo; away from the jingoism and army-worship of a Tahrir where we don't, for the moment, feel we belong.

Everything here, seventy kilometers west of Alexandria, at my mother's beach house, is unchanged. The sand is impossibly white, the sea many, many blues. When from the road I first caught sight of the colors, I felt as if I were slipping back into the past. But Khaled is not the past, and he's here: eighteen months old, stepping determinedly through the sand, staggering a little, pointing, beaming smiles into our faces, picking up shells and the plastic covers of juice cartons with heartbreaking delicacy. His father, Alaa, still has a variety of court cases hanging over him—new ones brought by the Muslim Brotherhood (MB) government joining the old ones brought by the military—but right now he's waist high in the gentle waves, settling his son into the bright yellow swimming ring Manal is holding out for him.

Ahmad Seif is reclining in the shade of the wide bamboo parasol. He's getting stronger every day after the heart attack that nearly killed him two months ago. The blue kite he's been teaching Khaled to fly bucks and rears and dives up above our heads, tethered to the rim of the parasol.

Back in Cairo, hundreds of thousands of Muslim Brothers and

their supporters are camped out at two ends of the city: northeast at the Rab3a junction on the road to the airport, and southwest in the piazza between Cairo University, the zoo, and the botanical gardens. They have been there for thirty-three days and they say they'll stay until Muhammad Morsi—deposed by the armed forces by popular demand on 3 July—is reinstated as president. A week ago, General Abd el-Fattah el-Sisi, Commander of the Armed Forces and minister of defense made a brief speech requesting the Egyptian people to "mandate" him to "deal with terror"— that is, to end the Brotherhood sit-ins and protests. People poured onto the streets to shout and sing the mandate he'd asked for; effectively a blank check. Fighter planes drew hearts in the sky.

Yesterday, the minister of the interior, General Muhammad Ibrahim, announced that the police and the army intend to break the sit-in in the coming four days. The police general is one of the remnants of Morsi's government in the new cabinet.

Morsi himself is being held at an unknown location—but was visited the day before yesterday by representatives of the European Union who found him to be well and defiant. Many of the Brotherhood leadership are in detention. Four, including the head of the Association of the Muslim Brotherhood (the AMB), Muhammad Badi3, are inside the Rab3a sit-in with warrants out for their arrest. AMB supporters are organizing marches throughout the country. Where they clash with citizens, people die. The country is awash with weaponry that's been flooding in through our western border since the fall of the Qaddafi regime in Libya: automatics, machine guns, RPJs. In Sinai, a low-intensity war is being fought. The AMB has said that Sinai will not quiet until Morsi is back as president.

The entire world is debating whether what happened in Egypt one month ago was a military coup or a political procedure, legitimate because it expressed the will of the majority of the people—

the millions who went out onto the streets on June 30 to demand early presidential elections.

The Brotherhood's failure to rule Egypt was spectacular; in the space of twelve months they lost everything they had worked toward for more than eighty years. They did this by demonstrating, again and again, that the only real project they had was their own empowerment. It started in November 2012 with Muhammad Morsi issuing a constitutional declaration giving himself absolute powers. He had to retract it a few days later, but by then he had pushed through the founding committee that would write the constitution and had appointed his public prosecutor. Then the country watched as the new elected president and his cabinet allied themselves with the enemies of the revolution. The Ministry of the Interior, the Dakhleyya, was courted and honored and got pay raises—as did the military. Morsi and his cabinet busied themselves with overtures to Mubarak's jailed or fugitive business elite, to the International Monetary Fund, to the Gulf countries, while ignoring the growing number of industrial and social protests sweeping the country. Soon, factory sit-ins were being broken up with police dogs, and young activists were vanishing from the streets and showing up at the morgue.

The president seemed to have no economic policy apart from soliciting loans from international lenders and donations from the Gulf; certainly nothing that might start moving the country toward the social justice that was one of the declared aims of the revolution. During the one year of his presidency the country saw more than seven thousand protests. His government paid no attention.

A group of young people came up with the "rebel" campaign: an A4 sheet of paper declaring "I, as a member of the AGM of the Egyptian People, withdraw confidence from the president and call for early presidential elections." People everywhere downloaded the statement, printed large numbers of it, and went out to solicit signatures. The campaign went viral.

At a mass rally, Morsi sat unmoving through hate speeches against Shia Muslims. Days later citizens murdered four Shia men in a village not forty minutes from downtown Cairo. Attacks against churches and Coptic citizens increased in provincial towns. For the first time in its history, the papal seat, the Cathedral in Abbaseyya, came under attack. And the president officially encouraged young men to go to "holy war" in Syria.

The purpose of democracy is to ensure that the people most affected by decisions get to make the decisions. The people saw the president steering the country to disaster. When, in the final days of his rule, Morsi appointed a round of county governors—all connected to the AMB—citizens prevented them from entering their offices. Armed AMB men confronted protests and people were killed in clashes on the street.

The MB insisted that when the Egyptian people elected Morsi president they entered into an unbreakable contract to keep him for four years. The protesters, on the other hand, said that Morsi had been elected on the basis of a stated commitment to the goals of the revolution and promises he'd made—and that he had honored neither.

But the constitution that the MB had pushed through did not describe a procedure to get rid of a president. So the people invented one: millions of endorsements to "rebel" and possibly twenty-five million people on the streets on 30 June.

On 30 June, across the whole country, Egypt staged gigantic protests. Once again we dominated the world's TV screens. How many millions? Was this the biggest mass action humanity had ever known? What about 1917? It's now said that the "rebels" were contacted quite early on by Egyptian intelligence and the military, that the path of their campaign was maybe smoothed, but there's no doubt that the campaign tapped into a deep and growing anger in the country.

That Sunday afternoon I sat on the curb at the Roxy intersection in Heliopolis watching the marches coming from every district of Cairo toward Morsi's seat at the Ettehadeyya Palace. People streamed by on both sides of the eight-lane road. Hour after hour they didn't stop. In the provinces the streets of one town after another filled up. Tahrir was fuller than it had ever been. Once again the Egyptian people had taken to the streets to drum a president out of office.

But there are differences between July 2013 and January/February 2011. The revolution, raising the banner of "Bread, Freedom, Social Justice," is against corruption, injustice, and brutality. In Revolution I, Mubarak's ruling National Democratic Party (NDP) was the known and declared enemy, as was the security establishment. The military was an unknown quantity that—in the optimism of our hearts—we might believe would protect the country in the process of transition.

The twenty-nine months between then and now have taught us a great deal. We've learned the extent to which our institutions are hollowed out. We've learned that large sections of our judiciary are crooked and partisan. We've seen the bankruptcy of the political elite that was considered the opposition to Mubarak. And the military, under the leadership of the SCAF, has demonstrated its devotion to its business interests and its murderous contempt for the people. These lessons have been learned the hard way, with young people losing friends and limbs and eyes. Getting rid of SCAF was Revolution II.

In June 2012, when we were in the terrible position of having to choose a president who was either an MB candidate or a military remnant of the Mubarak regime, I wrote: "The revolution will continue because neither the old regime nor the Islamist trend in its current form are going to deliver 'bread, freedom, social justice.' Neither of them are going to validate the sacrifices made by the 1,200 young people murdered by the regime, the 8,000 maimed, the 16,000 court-martialled" (*The Guardian,* 17 June). One week later, having listened to Morsi's promises, I allowed myself to hope: "Maybe, maybe, we have voted in a president whom we can support, or oppose with honor—without being shot" (*The Guardian,* 25 June).

Well, the shooting didn't stop when we got rid of SCAF, neither did the torture; Jeeka, Christie, el-Husseini Abu Deif, Muhammad el-Gindi, Muhammad el-Shaf3i are just a few of the young activists the country lost to the Morsi regime.

The economic situation worsened and Morsi outdid Mubarak in opacity and cronyism. And, on top of that, his regime was inefficient to a point of danger. A view of the situation in Sinai, our relations with Africa and with Syria, pointed to big disasters ahead. And so, one year into Morsi's presidency, we arrived, on 30 June, at Revolution III.

In Revolution III the whole country—the revolutionaries, the Dakhleyya, the "deep state," the "sofa brigade," and the remnants and supporters of the Mubarak regime—united against the Muslim Brotherhood. And so, on 30 June, revolutionaries who'd been steadfast for two years found themselves in bizarre company: the previous head of State Security led his own anti-Brotherhood march; there was a march of police in uniform; we saw protesting police officers chatting easily under the white banners of young men murdered by the police over the course of the preceding three years; a police band played on the stage in Tahrir. And although some voices were raised in an anticipatory reminder: "Down, down with military rule," the dominant chant was "The army, the people, one hand!" The people were calling on the army to step in—to be the executor of the people's will.

The people are, until now, insisting on treating the army as their own. People want to believe that the military has learned its lesson and doesn't want to rule. That it got what it wants in Morsi's 2012 constitution and, even if it's amended, no one will touch its interests. That Tantawi and the baddies are no longer in SCAF and that General Sisi will simply oversee another set of elections.

So, will the generals look after Revolution III better than they looked after Revolution I? General Sisi was, after all, part of SCAF and in charge of military intelligence.

Many of us now fear that Revolution III is in grave danger of being co-opted by the enemies of Revolution I. We point out that Revolution III is not against Morsi and the MB as such, but against the continuation of the policies that marked the Mubarak era. That we're in danger of the old regime slipping on yet another mask, slipping into power. But the sentiment of the people is: get rid of Morsi first and deal with the rest later.

Could we have waited for parliamentary elections and trusted that the dismal performance of the presidency over the preceding year would vote the MB out of the majority? The worry was that the government had been busy redrawing electoral districts to favor the MB, and that a large portion of the judiciary (who would have overseen elections) were MB supporters. And in the long tug of war between the presidency and the Constitutional Court over the election law, no one was sure when the elections would actually be allowed to happen.

When people protested on the streets, Morsi chose to fight back by shooting at them. As late as 29 June if he'd appointed a prime minister from outside the MB, people would have given him another chance and the Brotherhood would still have had a seat at the table. Now we were back to standing vigil at the morgue, clocking the murdered as they were carried in and fighting with the coroner to let parents check to see if their children were in his fridges. Graffiti on the Ettehadeyya wall says THE LEGITI-MACY OF YOUR BALLOT BOX IS CANCELED BY OUR MARTYRS' BOXES [COFFINS]. GO!

But today, 31 July, the MB in their thousands are marching through the streets of towns and villages to support the sit-ins and support the man they still count as their president. The rest of the country is determined to keep the MB out of power and out of office. The media are baying for blood. The armed forces and the Dakhleyya are weighing their options. No one knows how much room for maneuvering the one-month-old cabinet really has. No one knows how far General Sisi's ambitions extend.

There is a core, a resolute core, that does not lose sight of the aims of the revolution—bread, freedom, social justice—and what these bring of human dignity; that knows that what the people will finally demand is the administration that will put them on the road to achieving these aims. And that the people—even if they digress onto a side street—will return to insist on their original path and their essential aims.

But for the moment, we figure we can take three days off at the beach. We recuperate, cook, fly kites, and play with Khaled. Sun and sand and sea and wind. Soon, we'll be back on the streets, helping our revolution on its difficult path. And when you read these words, many months from now, maybe we'll be farther down the road toward its great, human aims.

Meanwhile, it does no harm to repeat, now and always:

Down, down with military rule.
Down, down with the rule of the Brotherhood.
As long as human blood is cheap / down, down with every
    president.
And glory to our martyrs forever.

A BRIEF AND NECESSARY HISTORY

1517

The sword-wielding Mameluke kings of Egypt were defeated by the Ottoman Turks' state-of-the-art cannon and gunpowder. Egypt was subsumed into the expanding Ottoman Empire and ruled from Istanbul.

1798

Ottoman decline and the growing British Empire in the East tempted Napoleon to invade Egypt, but his expedition did not last long. By 1801 a combination of British, Ottoman, and Egyptian forces had expelled the French. The Ottoman force was led by an Albanian/Macedonian soldier/adventurer, Muhammad Ali.

1805

The Ottoman Sultan, Selim III, under pressure from Egyptian notables, including Sheikh Omar Makram, appointed Muhammad Ali Pasha "Viceroy of Egypt," to rule it on behalf of Istanbul.

Muhammad Ali created a comfortable margin of autonomy for himself and embarked on a massive modernization program. He

retained French officers to help build a modern army, set up arms
and munitions factories, seized all agricultural land and made it
Crown Property, and instituted a centralized agricultural program
supported by massive public irrigation works. He put in place a
modern education system and in 1813 started sending hundreds of
young men to study in Europe. In 1821 he set up the Boulaq print-
ing press—which is still the state printer—and started an economic boom based on agriculture and industry. He forbade the
removal of antiquities from Egypt and created the Egyptian state
bureaucracy to run the country's administration. In the twenty
years of his reign, Egypt's population doubled and her society
became more diverse and mobile. On behalf of the sultan, he put
down rebellions in the Arabian Peninsula and Crete and expanded
into the Sudan. But Muhammad Ali saw Egypt's strategic depth
in Palestine and Syria and in 1832 he acted; the campaign of Ibrahim Pasha, Muhammad Ali's eldest son, swept through the cities
of Palestine, Lebanon, Syria, and Anatolia and paused at the gates
of Istanbul itself. The European powers, however, were unwilling to see a strong Egyptian state replace a weak Ottoman one.
Britain, Russia, Prussia, and Austria treated with the new young
sultan Abd el-Meguid I and in 1840 forced Muhammad Ali to
limit his ambitions to Egypt in return for a pledge that his rule
there would become hereditary.

1863

Ismail, Muhammad Ali's grandson, took up the next phase of
Egypt's modernization. He established elected local councils and
a house of representatives. He dug the Suez Canal (naming its
cities Port Said and Ismaileyya for his uncle, Said Pasha, and himself). He built Abdeen Palace and made it the seat of the ruler
instead of Salahudin's Citadel. He lit the streets and pumped water

into houses and, with his formidable minister of public works, Ali Pasha Mubarak, he laid out downtown Cairo—stretching from Midan el-Ataba, where he built the Opera House, to Midan el-Ismaileyya (now Midan el-Tahrir) and Qasr el-Nil Bridge. They dug canals and increased the area of agricultural land, built factories and energized trade, introduced state education for girls, and set up the National Library (1870) and the National Archives.

And along the way, Ismail incurred massive debts from European bankers. Books have been written about the issue of Egypt's debts, but in any case, in 1876 Ismail was forced to accept British and French supervision over Egyptian affairs to ensure repayment. In 1879 he was forced out of Egypt, and his son, the much weaker Tewfiq, was instituted as khedive of Egypt.

The issue of the debt and foreign dominance of Egyptian affairs was one of the triggering factors behind the revolt of the Egyptian army under the leadership of Orabi Pasha. But the revolt spread to demand a functioning parliament overseeing the cabinet, a strengthening of the army, and a review of the administration of the new Suez Canal by representatives of France and Britain.

1882

The Khedive Tewfiq asked his debtor friends for help. Britain invaded, declared Egypt a "protectorate," and exiled Orabi and his fellow rebels.

Now Egypt had two masters: the khedive, representing the Ottoman sultan, and the High Commissioner, representing Britain. When, in the First World War, Ottoman Turkey lost to the Allies and was stripped of her empire, the Egyptian national movement united against the British occupation and rose up in the celebrated but ultimately unsuccessful Sa3d Zaghloul revolt of 1919.

And since then the national movement in Egypt has developed

in two branches: the modernizing liberationist secular movement, which sees the future of Egypt as an independent nation-state; and the tradition-based movement, which does not see Egypt standing alone but envisions it as part of a powerful Muslim *ummah* (nation)—along the lines of the Ottoman or the Abbasid states—with a caliph at its head. This Islamist trend was articulated into the Association of the Muslim Brotherhood by Hasan al-Banna in 1928.

1952–1981

Nasser's 1952 revolution threw out both the king and the British. For some, it was a military takeover, hijacking and aborting decades of civil action that were just about to bear the fruits of liberation and democracy. But the revolution—even though it dealt harshly with the first strikes that confronted it, executing two young labor leaders, Khamees and Baqari in August 1952—was embraced by the bulk of the people; they felt that it was on their side. The revolution tried at first to work with the statesmen of the ancien regime, with the Americans and with the Islamists, but it soon found that it had to follow its own track. It quickly declared for the secular nation-state, for social justice and modernization, and for "positive nonalignment" in foreign policy. From 1954 onward, the Muslim Brotherhood was the state's internal enemy; its members were jailed, tortured, and driven into hiding or exile. Growing up in the sixties, I—and my generation, I think—were aware of the Brotherhood only as a "historic" reactionary faction.

The period from 1954 to 1967 is often likened to the Muhammad Ali period in its emphasis on modernity and development, centrally planned and orchestrated by a powerful state. Its progress was halted and its faults exposed by the Naksa, the defeat in the Six-Day War with Israel in 1967. Within weeks, though, we felt that the state had taken the terrible lesson to heart and was moving toward more serious openness and power sharing.

But in September 1970 Nasser died, and Anwar Sadat took over as president of Egypt. Sadat's overall project was to remove Egypt from the nonaligned camp and plant it firmly under the American umbrella, to adopt free market capitalism, and to make peace with Israel. To do all this, he needed to discredit the Nasser era and disempower the Left, the Nasserists, and the Progressives. The instrument he chose was the Muslim Brotherhood.

Sadat encouraged and nurtured religio-political groups, promoted religious discourse in public life, and clamped down on protest. Elections in student unions and in the professional syndicates were rigged to bring in Islamists. The Brotherhood, although never legalized, became a major social force, offering health and education services at a time when the state—cutting public spending—was allowing the running down of both. The MB set up businesses and started amassing wealth and running philanthropic projects.

Many in the Islamist current, however, did not agree with Sadat's policies—in particular his foreign policy and his closeness to the United States. Meanwhile his "open door" economic policy sent inflation soaring, introduced high-level corruption, and failed to bring in foreign investment in any area beneficial to ordinary citizens. Egypt started to borrow heavily from international financial institutions; the loans were twinned with "reforms" and restructurings that closed down industries and exacerbated the hardship already caused by inflation. Opposition to Sadat grew among both secular and Islamist circles. In January 1977 we saw bread riots—which the military refused to crush.

When Sadat signed the deeply unpopular Camp David Accords in 1979, Egypt—with that stroke of his pen—lost its standing in the Arab and the nonaligned worlds and became a pariah state. That same year the CIA and MI6 started running U.S. national security adviser Zbigniew Brzezinski's campaign to fund and arm radical Islamist forces. The campaign was designed to support volunteer fighters against the Soviets in Afghanistan (among whom were Osama Bin Laden and Ayman al-Zawahiri), but its effects spilled over into the entire region. The Muslim Brotherhood itself remained nonviolent, but various militant groups—known collectively as the Gamaʒat Islamiyyah (Islamist Groups) splintered off from it. It was one of these that assassinated Sadat in 1981.

While that assassination was not generally disapproved of, the wave of bombings that followed it and destabilized the country was deeply unpopular. So much so that in the mid-nineties the imprisoned leadership of the Gamaʒat issued a closely argued thesis from jail announcing an official, one-sided cease-fire in its battle against the state.

On Sadat's death, Hosni Mubarak became president, and it was during the first years of his presidency that the third of the Egyptian Islamist clusters came into being: the Salafis. Inflation and the drop in living standards experienced by the middle classes during Sadat's rule had sent many Egyptian professionals to look for work in booming Saudi Arabia. These expats, when they came home, brought with them not only petrodollars but Saudi Wahhabi puritanical ways of thought and behavior. Sadat's promotion of religious discourse in the political sphere had also allowed Saudi dollars to fund Egyptian preachers in Egyptian mosques. Wahhabi-influenced returnees came home to find Wahhabi-preaching mosques, and so the Salafi movement was born.

1981 TO 2011

Mubarak's policy was fire and iron against the Gamaʒat. Even though they had renounced violence, they remained in jail until the revolution of 25 January.

The Salafis' position was that they retreated from society, mixed only with Salafis, and tried to live an ethical life that followed the example of the earliest era of Islam, the time of the Prophet and his Righteous Successors, ending with the death of Imam Ali in 40AH/A.D. 661. They would not engage in politics, and they held that rising against "those who have been given dominion" was wrong. Nevertheless, Mubarak's police persecuted them and jailed them. Two of my sister-in-law Sohair's nephews are Salafis. They're French-educated, and they used to write pamphlets about Islam in French and hand them out free to tourists. For this they served five years each in administrative detention. Every time a court acquitted them, they would be detained again within days. The first time their mother went to visit them, she discovered thousands and thousands of young men held in Damanhour jail. The jail was under the control of the chief inmate, Abboud el-Zomor, one of the conspirators in the assassination of Sadat and the author of the cease-fire tract—and it was more or less a training camp for Islamist militants.

As for the Brotherhood, it continued to be banned as an organization, but its members and Mubarak enjoyed an ongoing flirtation. Sometimes he had them detained and imprisoned. Sometimes he allowed them to run for Parliament as independents, and they, in turn, agreed to contest only a limited proportion of seats. Meanwhile they built a formidable war chest and a remarkable organization on the ground with representatives in every town and village and cadres and foot soldiers, every one of whom took an oath to obey only his local leader.

The Mubarak strategy was to control the Islamists but keep them as the bogeyman with which to scare the West and the Gulf; they were the "mad bearded ones," the "militant suicide-bombing America-haters" who would take over Egypt if his regime did not get the support it needed to remain in power. Egypt would join the Iran-Hezbollah-Hamas gang—and where would that leave

Israel? The aid, the arms, the joint exercises, the loans kept flowing in, and the cash kept flowing out—to Swiss bank accounts, real estate in London, companies in Cyprus. And Egyptians got poorer and more desperate.

The non-religious opposition to the Mubarak regime acquired a visible presence in 2000 with the Palestinian Intifada. It gathered pace with protests against the war on Iraq (2003), then protests against the rigging of Egyptian elections (2004 and 2005). These were the first stirrings of what finally became the Revolution of 2011.

ACKNOWLEDGMENTS

I want to thank LuAnn Walther, my editor at Pantheon, first for making me write the 2012 part of this book and then for her patience while I struggled with it and with the circumstances surrounding it.

I thank Alexandra Pringle, my editor at Bloomsbury, who phoned me in Tahrir in February 2011 to tell me the moment for this book had come. Without her tenacious support and subtle judgment I don't think I'd have completed it.

Since 2000, the *Guardian* newspaper has been the British home for all my reportage and commentary on Egypt and the Arab world. That space has been of central importance to me at every level. I thank all the editors I've worked with there.

My Egyptian publisher, Ibrahim al-Moallem, and his editorial team at *Shorouk* newspaper bullied me into producing a weekly column. It's thanks to them that I've found my Arabic writing voice (hand?), a whole new audience, and the opportunity to serve the revolution.

I thank: always my agent, Andrew Wylie, and my friends at his London office; my dearest friend and guardian angel, Susan Glynn, for reading drafts—always with my best interests at heart; Ismail Richard Hamilton, my younger son, and my family and friends who had to put up with having overlong out-of-context bits anxiously read out to them at inappropriate times.

Finally, Omar Robert Hamilton, my older son. His critical acumen, forceful opinions, artistic sensibility, and thoroughness have been invaluable as I've struggled to produce my first sustained piece of work since the loss of my husband, Ian Hamilton; my mother, Fatma Moussa; and my friend and mentor, Edward Said. I am incredibly grateful to have him.

NOTES

1. "At 22:34 UTC (00:34 a.m. local time), Renesys observed the virtually simultaneous withdrawal of all routes to Egyptian networks in the Internet's global routing table. Approximately 3,500 individual BGP routes were withdrawn, leaving no valid paths by which the rest of the world could continue to exchange Internet traffic with Egypt's service providers. Virtually all of Egypt's Internet addresses . . . unreachable." http://gizmodo.com/5746121/how-egypt-turned-off-the-internet.

   All links given are live at time of publication, but if a video has been removed, just search YouTube with keywords; somebody will have posted a similar one.

2. http://www.youtube.com/watch?v=hWplnI-sWzs.

3. Throughout the nineteenth century, one of the many theaters to host the drama of British-French rivalry was archaeology—and the stealing of antiquities—in Egypt. Successive Egyptian governments of the period consistently favored the French. Three of the most important streets in the part of Cairo established by Khedive Ismail in the late nineteenth century are named after Frenchmen who made radical contributions to Egyptology. Jean-François Champollion (1790–1832) published his translation of the 7agar Rasheed (the Rosetta Stone) hieroglyphs in 1822. Auguste Mariette (1821–1881), for whom, in 1858, Khedive Ismail created the post of Director-General of Excavations and Antiquities, started the institutionalization of archaeology in Egypt. His sarcophagus rests in the garden of the Egyptian Museum. And Gaston Maspero (1846–1916) succeeded Mariette Pasha as Director-General of Excavations and Antiquities from 1880 to 1886 and 1899 to 1914. In 1902 he superintended the move of the Egyptian Museum collection from Giza to its new (and current) home. He is present in Shadi Abd el-Salam's 1969 film *Al-Moumya* (The Night of Counting the Years).

4. *Shabab* derives from the root *sh/b*, "to grow." I love the word; it carries the

same emotional load as *youth* with an extra dash of vigor, and it's both classical and colloquial in all Arabic dialects. It's unusual in that in its colloquial use it's plural without a gender marker. It also carries with it lots of words having to do with the progress of age: *shabba* ("he grew up"), *shaba* ("he grew old"; literally, "his hair grew white"), *shayb* ("white hair"), *shayeb* ("an old man with white hair"—generally used only if he's done something not befitting his age). Unpackaged, it carries the signification of "people, men and women, who are at the youthful stage of life with all its energy, hope, optimism, vigour, impulsiveness and love of life, and who are acting communally, together."

5. Diplomatic car runs over protestors 28 January 2011, http://www.youtube .com/watch?v=3luSbFP60a8.

6. Protestors comfort Central Security Soldiers 28 January 2011, http://www .youtube.com/watch?v=k8jrDxLs3lE&feature =related.

7. Muhammad Lazoghli, the man whose statue stands at the center of the *midan*, was a young soldier who came to Egypt with Muhammad Ali at the beginning of the nineteenth century, to re-establish Ottoman rule after the withdrawal of Napoleon. They say he was the brains behind the Citadel Massacre, which got rid of the remnant leaders of the old Mameluke era. His life's work was to set up a modern Egyptian state in the face of a for-the-moment-defeated French imperialism. He served as minister of defense, minister of finance, and first prime minister of Egypt from 1808 to 1823, and his statue—statesmanlike, bearded, robed—was sculpted many years after his death and posed for by an Egyptian water carrier who resembled him.

8. Ahdaf Soueif, "Egypt Tortures for US, So Why Not on its Account?," *Guardian,* 9 March 2006. "Over the past three decades, such arrests, detentions and kidnappings have become fairly common. People disappear. Friends hunt for them. Usually they are in the State Security Intelligence Bureau in Lazoghli Square in Cairo. They are generally held long enough to extract a confession. Their treatment ranges from insults, threats and beatings to fairly evolved methods of torture. Sometimes the person is not required to confess to anything; they are given a warning and let go. Sometimes the person dies. Mostly, they are sent to jail to await trial.

"Human rights cannot be regional. The rule of law cannot be selective. Guantánamo, Belmarsh, Lazoghli and Facility 1391 in Israel are part of the same configuration; they stand together or—one hopes—fall together."

9. Snipers on the roof of the Ministry of the Interior, Cairo, 29 January 2011, http://www.youtube.com/watch?v=V5kJholiV-8.

10. http://en.wikipedia.org/wiki/Hisham_Mubarak_Law_Center.

11. Aziz el-Shaf3i and Rami Gamal, Ana ba7ebbek ya bladi, http://www
.youtube.com/watch?v=btXZMh5tHDA.

12. Khaled Said was a young man killed by police in a cybercafé in Alexandria
on 6 June 2010. Because he was an "ordinary" young man—i.e., middle class,
and neither a criminal nor an activist—and because his brother managed to
get a photo of his face disfigured by his beating, he became a rallying point
for the opposition to police brutality in Egypt.

13. Protestors in Tahrir chant "Hosni etgannen" (Hosni's gone mad), http://
www.youtube.com/watch?v=U94PCrdHG4w.

14. *Millioneyya*: adding the suffix *eyya* to a noun makes an adjective. So *selm*
is "peace" and *selmeyya* is "peaceful"; *millioneyya,* in this case, is a million-
person event.

15. The story went that on 31 January, the day the F-16s buzzed Tahrir, Mubarak
had ordered the army to attack the protesters, the hundreds of thousands of
Egyptians in the streets and *midans* of the country. The story continued that
the army had already conducted a poll among the middle-ranking officers,
the men in the field who would have had to fire on the protesters, and learned
that if the order came to shoot, the officers would refuse. So when given the
order, Field Marshal Muhammad Hussein Tantawi had said, "I can't do it,
Mr President." Field Marshal Tantawi later (in October) testified that he had
never received such an instruction from Mubarak. This left open the question
why army spokespeople repeatedly boasted that the army had not attacked
the revolutionaries.

16. An officer in the Egyptian army joins protestors in Tahrir, http://www
.youtube.com/watch?v=bdaXYtbIEVg.

17. *Shaheed*—plural *shuhada*—means "martyr." The root *sh/h/d* is "to see" and
"to bear witness." A witness, for example in a court case, is a *shahed*. Being a
shahed is only part—a temporary part—of a person's identity or function. A
shaheed is someone who bears ultimate witness; someone whose sole function
now is to bear witness.

18. Quran, chapter 3, verse 169.

AN INTERRUPTION: EIGHT MONTHS LATER, OCTOBER 2011

1. One of the major protest groups, named after a massive strike by Mahallah
textile workers in 2008, where several people were killed by the police.

2. The first great quarrel among the "patriotic political forces" after the revolu-

tion had been run under the heading "The Constitution First." When SCAF announced the transitional program for the country, it was as follows:

1. Election of the two houses of Parliament
2. Parliament chooses a "founding committee" that writes the constitution
3. Election of the president

All the political forces rushed off to create parties; some activated existing parties that were in various conditions of decay or discreditation or division. One group saw the need to create a coalition of civilian forces to negotiate with or confront or in any case be the civilian voice of the revolution addressing SCAF and the world. They called the First Conference of Egypt on 7 May. It was attended by some five thousand people and was as close to broadly representative of Egypt as you could get—except that the Islamist currents were represented only by some of their shabab who were already moving away from their mainstream. On the economic front, the conference aligned itself with sustainable development and social justice and a more equitable distribution of wealth. It presented a strong paper on the constitution—almost a draft document. And it declared the formation of the National Council.

The first meeting of the National Council was convened on 7 June, and by then it was already defined by one main feature: it was calling for change of the SCAF schedule already agreed by the people in a referendum. Its position, put forward by some powerful lawmen and -women, was, How can we have elections without a constitution? The constitution is the foundation of everything. How can you start to build without a foundation?

But putting the constitution first would mean

1. Throwing out the results of the referendum, the first democratic exercise the country had engaged in, and whose results (agreeing to SCAF's schedule) represented "the will of the people."
2. Postponing elections, thereby giving the secular parties more time to organize and to try to catch up operationally with the Ikhwan (the Muslim Brotherhood), who had much more presence on the ground.
3. Removing the possibility that the constitution would ultimately be written by a founding committee chosen by a parliament with an Islamist majority.

Putting the constitution first would also mean keeping the country in limbo by maintaining the military in power for longer and postponing stability and an accountable government. The Constitution First campaign split the country into

1. Some powerful secular figures and new parties insisting on putting the constitution first.
2. Islamist figures and parties insisting on respecting "the will of the people," as expressed in the response to the referendum, and abiding by the SCAF schedule.
3. Figures (mostly non-Islamist) who said that in an ideal world it would make more sense to write the constitution first, but in our current circumstances, with the military seizing more power every day, the cabinet weak and paralyzed, and the revolution stalled, it would be best to move toward elections and an accountable government and write the constitution later. This group was also unwilling to discredit the first democratic exercise the country had gone through—the referendum.

Eventually, Group 1 came up with the idea of putting forward (a) proposals for the selection of the founding committee that would write the constitution—to ensure that it was representative of the country as a whole and not just of whoever happened to have a parliamentary majority at the time; and (b) a document listing a set of "constitutional principles" that everyone could agree would frame the constitution.

Many individuals and organizations started putting forward proposals and ideas. This activity took away from the support for Constitution First and so, eventually, Group 1—without officially renouncing its position—started putting forward its own proposals.

By then, however, their distrust of and dislike for the Islamist trend had become so obvious that the Islamists, Group 2, announced that even these ideas were an attempt to subvert "the will of the people" and that it was firmly against them and would not bind itself to any pre-constitutional documents or agreements whatsoever.

3. *Shaheed*: "martyr." See note 17 above.
4. *Mosireen*: "determined." A pun on *misriyyeen*, "Egyptian." A group of independent filmmakers who have set up a collective media center. See their website at http://mosireen.org.
5. Blog from Tahrir Cinema, http://www.cinerevolutionnow.com/2011/07/tahrir-cinema-needs-you.html.
6. http://literaryrevolutions.wordpress.com/2011/07/19/tweetnadwa-real-hope-for-egypts-future/.

7. Testimony of Mustafa Mursi, http://www.youtube.com/watch?v=ilyJAAw G74U.

8. Ahmad al-Musallami, "Al-Tabaa al-Oula," Dream TV, 17 September 2011.

9. http://en.nomiltrials.com/2011/10/egypt-end-military-trials-for-civilians.html.

THE EIGHTEEN DAYS RESUMED: 1 FEBRUARY–12 FEBRUARY 2011

1. Omar Robert Hamilton's film of Bloody Wednesday, http://www.youtube .com/watch?v=jx33QyWZo2s&feature=youtu.be.

2. Eyewitness report from the Nadeem Centre for the Rehabilitation of Victims of Violence, https://alnadeem.org/ar/node/346: "On the 3rd of February 2011 at about 2.30 p.m. an individual claiming to be the Azbakeyya investigation inspector broke into HMLC ordering everybody there to sit on the floor. He was followed by a Military Police lieutenant accompanied by two Military Police officers where the former stood on a chair and shouted: I have orders to shoot anybody who moves. A huge group of thugs then entered the centre accompanied by an intelligence officer. They searched the place, destroyed files and stole some of them, destroyed desks and took papers and CDs, searched personal bags of staff all the while throwing obscenities and accusations of destroying Egypt and conspiring with foreigners.

"After six hours of insults, verbal abuse, accusations of treason and tying the hands of staff members with leather strings the detainees were taken to the central administration of the Military Police in Khalifeh el Maamun in Heliopolis where their names were taken and photos and videos taken of them. They were then transported to some headquarters in Madinet Nasr, assumed to be one of the headquarters of Military Intelligence, where they were interrogated while blindfolded. They were released three days later.

"As for the centre, windows, doors, desks, drawers and file cabinets were destroyed. Two computers, a printer, fax machine, router and a scanner disappeared."

3. Barkha Dutt interviews Ahdaf Soueif, Shahira Amin, and Heba Fatma Morayef, http://www.3quarksdaily.com/3quarksdaily/2011/02/the-women-of -tahrir-square.html.

4. The abduction of Wael Ghoneim, http://www.youtube.com/watch?v=rgLlx Oqi1Hg.

5. Wael Ghoneim weeps over the shuhada, http://www.youtube.com/watch ?NR=1&feature=endscreen&v=crGZmVmULp4. These are the references

for the young shuhada shown in that program. "Lan-nansahom" means "we shall not forget them": https://www.facebook.com/AlShaheed.EslamBeker; http://www.lan-nansahom.org/#!martyr;698; http://www.lan-nansahom.org/ #!martyr;542; http://www.lan-nansahom.org/#!martyr;759; http://www.lan -nansahom.org/#!martyr;986.

6. Christiane Amanpour interviews Omar Suleiman, http://abcnews.go.com/ ThisWeek/video/omar-suleiman-crisis-12852023.

7. http://www.haaretz.com/news/diplomacy-defense/mubarak-slammed-u-s -in-phone-call-with-israeli-mk-before-resignation-1.342831.

EIGHTEEN DAYS WERE NEVER ENOUGH

1. http://www.nomiltrials.com/2011/03/diaries-of-citizens-under-rule-of.html.

2. Officer Muhammad Wadie singing on his birthday, http://www.youtube .com/watch?v=1qfKpLJdZow.

3. http://manalaa.net/node/88073.

4. Randa S., disabled in the revolution, observes elections from her wheelchair, http://www.youtube.com/watch?v=3qvKoomVfRA.

5. Ahdaf Soueif, "Ahdaf Soueif in Cairo: 'By early evening it was clear that this was Revolution II,'" Guardian, 23 November 2011.

6. Ahmad Surour's mother, http://www.youtube.com/watch?v=8pfcFGfErvI& feature=related.

7. Quran, chapter 33 (al-A7zab), verses 67 and 68.

8. *Shorouk,* 19 December 2011.

9. Abboudi's story, http://www.youtube.com/watch?v=Vop7OAKV660&feature =fvst.

10. The army above the people, http://www.youtube.com/watch?v=3a8akplbud Q&feature=fvst and http://www.youtube.com/watch?feature=endscreen& NR=1&v=bgG6ugMZkkg.

11. *Shorouk,* 21 December 2011.

12. It's later revealed that medical military personnel had orders to treat protes-tors without anaesthetic. The report of the Fact-Finding Commission on the Huhad and the Injured, as yet unpublished.

13. *Shorouk,* 9 December 2011.

14. Ultras in metro station on the way to Tahrir chanting against the military and police on 27 January 2012, http://www.youtube.com/watch?v=CatbTdWMzoo.

15. Ultras anthem, "The Sun of Freedom," http://www.youtube.com/watch?v =UmHHU4fQ7ps.

16. Ultras anthem, I was in my red Tshirt, http://www.youtube.com/watch?v=UD Vv2esX560.

17. Summing up of the Ultras' massacre, http://www.youtube.com/watch?v =YqPMuFwqPZw.

18. Mosireen film of Salma Said, http://www.youtube.com/watch?v=7JhA4jI v4bk.

19. Atef el-Gohari speaking in Tahrir, http://www.youtube.com/watch?v=MM Jn3FgJYLo.

20. Atef al-Gohari after his shooting, http://kenzo2010.blogspot.co.uk/2012/05/ blog-post_8224.html#.UbwpgPbACzs.

21. Egyptian solidarity convoy visits Gaza, http://www.youtube.com/watch?v =zPG474zBvko.

22. http://blogs.nature.com/houseofwisdom/2012/10/nile-university-students -discuss-their-dissertations-in-makeshift-tents.html.

23. Army versus Qorsaya, http://www.youtube.com/watch?v=g6PZcY6Qtu8.

24. Ultras White Coats hold a "funeral" for the Ministry of Health, http://www .youtube.com/watch?v=0CAuQshLEiA.

THE MAP OF LOVE

In 1901, Anna Winterbourne, recently widowed, leaves England for Egypt, an outpost of the empire roiling with nationalist sentiment. Far from the British colony, she finds herself enraptured by the real Egypt and in love with Sharif Pasha al-Baroudi. Nearly a hundred years later, Isabel Parkman, a divorced American journalist and descendant of Anna and Sharif, has fallen in love with Omar al-Ghamrawi, a gifted and difficult Egyptian-American conductor with his own passionate politics. In an attempt to understand her conflicting emotions and to discover the truth behind her heritage, Isabel, too, travels to Egypt, and enlists Omar's sister's help in unravelling the story of Anna and Sharif's love.

Fiction/Literature

IN THE EYE OF THE SUN

Set amidst the turmoil of contemporary Middle Eastern politics, this vivid and highly-acclaimed novel is an intimate look into the lives of Arab women today. Here, a woman grows up among the Egyptian elite, marries a Westernized husband, and, while pursuing graduate study, becomes embroiled in a love affair with an uncouth Englishman.

Fiction/Literature

I THINK OF YOU

Achingly lyrical, resonant, and richly woven, and with a spark of defiance, these stories explore areas of tension—where women and men are ensnared by cultural and social mores and prescribed notions of "love," where the place you are is not the place you want to be. Soueif draws her characters with infinite tenderness and compassion as they inhabit a world of lost opportunities, unfulfilled love, and remembrance of times past.

Fiction/Literature

The twenty-five years' worth of criticism and commentary collected here have earned Ahdaf Soueif a place among our most prominent Arab intellectuals. Clear-eyed and passionate, and syndicated throughout the world, they are the direct result of Soueif's own circumstances of being "like hundreds of thousands of others: people with an Arab or a Muslim background doing daily double-takes when faced with their reflection in a western mirror." Whether an account of visiting Palestine and entering the Noble Sanctuary for the first time, an interpretation of women who choose to wear the veil, or her post-September 11 reflections, Soueif's intelligent, fearless, deeply informed essays embody the modern search for identity and community.

Literary Criticism